P9-CJL-937

*William Faulkner, Letters and Fictions*

# William Faulkner

## Letters
## &
## Fictions

BY JAMES G. WATSON

University of Texas Press, Austin

First Edition, 1987

Requests for permission to reproduce material from this
work should be sent to Permissions, University of Texas
Press, Box 7819, Austin, Texas 78713-7819

The publication of this book was assisted by a grant from
the Andrew W. Mellon Foundation.

Library of Congress Cataloging-in-Publication Data

Watson, James G. (James Gray), 1939–
   William Faulkner, letters and fictions.

   Bibliography: p.
   Includes index.
   1. Faulkner, William, 1897–1962—Technique.
2. Faulkner, William, 1897–1962—Correspondence.
3. Imaginary letters—History and criticism.
4. Epistolary fiction, American—History and criticism.
5. Novelists, American—20th century—Correspondence.
6. American letters—History and criticism.
PS3511.A86Z98535   1987      813'.52      86-27274
ISBN 0-292-76503-7

*For Ann, Bill, and Rick*

# Contents

# Abbreviations Used

Works by Faulkner:

| | |
|---|---|
| AA | *Absalom, Absalom!* |
| AILD | *As I Lay Dying* |
| CSWF | *Collected Short Stories of William Faulkner* |
| E | *Elmer* |
| F | *A Fable* |
| Flags | *Flags in the Dust* |
| GB | *A Green Bough* |
| GDM | *Go Down, Moses* |
| HAC | *Helen: A Courtship* |
| H | *The Hamlet* |
| ID | *Intruder in the Dust* |
| KG | *Knight's Gambit* |
| LIA | *Light in August* |
| M | *Mayday* |
| Man. | *The Mansion* |
| Mar. | *The Marionettes* |
| Mos. | *Mosquitoes* |
| NOS | *New Orleans Sketches* |
| RN | *Requiem for a Nun* |
| SF | *The Sound and the Fury* |
| SO | *Sanctuary: The Original Text* |
| SP | *Soldiers' Pay* |
| SR | *Sanctuary* |
| T | *The Town* |
| U | *The Unvanquished* |
| USWF | *Uncollected Stories of William Faulkner* |
| WP | *The Wild Palms* |

Collections of Faulkner's Letters:

SL       *Selected Letters of William Faulkner*, ed. Joseph Blotner
LDB-II   *Faulkner: A Comprehensive Guide to the Brodsky Collection.*
         Vol. II, *The Letters*, ed. Louis Daniel Brodsky and Robert
         W. Hamblin
ESPL     *Essays, Speeches and Public Letters by William Faulkner*, ed.
         James B. Meriwether

# Preface

The publication of William Faulkner's personal correspondence has been an intermittent process since his death in 1962. The first self-contained collection to be published was Malcolm Cowley's *The Faulkner-Cowley File* in 1966, which describes the history of a friendship and the publication history of an important book, *The Portable Faulkner*, both told in "letters and memories." Less personal collections followed, most significantly Faulkner's correspondence with *Scribner's* magazine in 1973 and with the *Saturday Evening Post* in 1977, both edited by James B. Meriwether. The public letters, edited by Meriwether, were collected in 1965 in *Essays, Speeches and Public Letters by William Faulkner*. Joseph Blotner's *Faulkner: A Biography* in 1974 made available virtually for the first time a large number of personal letters and documents by and about Faulkner. These and additional letters were brought together in 1977 in Blotner's *Selected Letters of William Faulkner*; still more were added to the letter canon in Blotner's one-volume *Biography* published in 1984. Other biographical and personal accounts of Faulkner's life followed, many containing new letters. Meta Carpenter Wilde's story of her love affair with Faulkner quotes from his letters to her, and hers to him, and describes other letters and artifacts under seal until 2039 in the Berg Collection of the New York Public Library. Malcolm Franklin's memoir of his life with his stepfather at Rowan Oak contains several letters Faulkner wrote to him; Carvel Collins' several essays and introductions to Faulkner texts contain references to a trove of as yet unpublished letters in Collins' keeping. More significantly, Volume I of *Faulkner: A Comprehensive Guide to the Brodsky Collection* describes, and Volume II reprints, previously unpublished letters from Faulkner to correspondents as various as Oxford newspaper man Phil Mullen, Random House editor Saxe Commins, and actress Ruth Ford. There are unpublished letters at the Alderman Library and at others, including the Humanities Research Center at the University of Texas at Austin. More publication no doubt will follow, although many letters never will be offered to the public and some are lost forever.

Personal letters are fragments of autobiography in which the Self and the Word are designedly one. They deliver the letter writer figuratively into the hands of the reader, but because they do, the self written in private letters is vulnerable to intrusions. Joseph Blotner surely is right when he says, in the introduction to *Selected Letters*, that Faulkner's "personal letters were never remotely intended for publication" (SL, xiii). Faulkner himself wrote Saxe Commins in 1952 that "people who will open and read another's private and personal letters . . . deserve exactly what they get" (LDB-II, 94). Nonetheless, the letters have been the source of much that we know of his personal and his creative life. Faulkner learned to write by writing, in letters as well as in literature, and in the long unwinding of his career, little that he wrote was entirely abandoned. Even in the incomplete and often fragmented form that we have them, Faulkner's private and public letters show that he was acutely aware of epistolary strategies and conventions that give letters their uniqueness as written texts, and that this understanding was important to the creative work into which he almost immediately began inserting fictional letters.

Of the fictional letters there is a surprisingly large number. Eight letters are fully transcribed in Faulkner's first novel, *Soldiers' Pay;* seven are transcribed or quoted in *Flags in the Dust. The Sound and the Fury* integrates twenty-one separate letters and telegrams that are variously mailed, telegraphed and hand-delivered, read and unread, written and even unwritten. By the 1930s, inserted letters had become a standard narrative device in Faulkner's stories and novels. Better than half of the short stories he wrote between 1928 and 1932 employ written correspondence to portray character and move the plot: Miss Emily Grierson refuses to receive letters; Miss Zilphia Gant lives vicariously through them; Narcissa Benbow Sartoris arranges an assignation to retrieve them. A catalog of letter writers includes Joanna Burden, Charles Bon, and Aunt Louisa Hawk in the major fiction of the thirties; Buck and Buddy McCaslin in the forties; Temple Drake, David Levine, Gavin Stevens, and Flem Snopes in the fifties. The list of minor characters who write letters, and of major and minor characters who read them or whose significant scenes of letter writing and reading are described, is longer still. Indeed, even more than his own letters, Faulkner's lettered and letterly writing defines the contours of his writing life. Very early in his career he portrayed himself privately in handmade gift books that functioned in the manner of love letters; in the final decade and a half, in the guise of the public man of letters, he wrote lettered essays addressed to "The North" and to "The Negro Race."

*William Faulkner, Letters and Fictions* is an account of the epistolary conventions that govern Faulkner's own letters, private and public, and of the ways in which those "laws of letters" inform his lettered writing. If it is true, as James Olney has said, that "all writing that aspires to be literature is autobiography and nothing else,"[1] it seems equally true that much writing purporting to be the first-person record of a life—including letters—is self-consciously literary. In particular, letters bring with them powerful generic imperatives that place them midway between life and art. They span time and distance, but they also measure the personal distances between actual experience and imaginative re-creation, between the life of the man writing and his written self-image. Those distances vary with the kind of letter, but the man writing and his epistolary persona are never precisely the same. This is as true for the fictional letter writers, who write part of the stories and novels where their letters are transcribed, as it is for Faulkner himself.

Read primarily as a literary subgenre rather than as biographical documents, Faulkner's letters constitute a discrete canon created by the letter writer concurrently with the literary canon to which it lies in parallel and complementary relation. Inevitably, the proximity of two imaginatively charged bodies of writing produced crossings between them. These are both formal and substantive. Faulkner's fictional letter writers, because they are letter writers, draw upon the same generic laws and conventions that he does in his personal correspondence; because they are Faulkner's, they have access to the same strategies he employed, and the same content, and they sometimes assume to themselves epistolary personae similar to his own. At times Faulkner wrote himself into his fiction by the letter writers he created; and often enough he wrote himself out of it by the content and style of their miswritten letters. The juxtaposition of his literary and letterly writing is revealing of both canons. To follow the letter writer's images of himself from one letter to the next is to watch the unfolding of his conception of himself in a variety of contexts and to a variety of Receivers. In his own letters, Faulkner is by turns Aviator and Artist, Pater Familias and Lover, Provincial Farmer, and Mentor and Poet. Fictional letter writers reveal and conceal themselves in their correspondence in the same ways, and to follow them from one fictional text to another is to watch another kind of unfolding. The successive letters in the fiction permit us to trace formal and thematic relationships in and between books and to discover in the forms and content of fictional letters, and the strategies of letter writing and reading, the evolution of Faulkner's world from what he called his "postage stamp of native soil" into a "cosmos of my own."

Faulkner's letters, both personal and public, and the letterly and lettered texts of the literary canon, both private and published, are my point of reference and my subject in this book. I have used the published letters only: my primary interest is in Faulkner's writing practices rather than in William Faulkner the man—in epistolarity rather than biography—and the published letters supply me more than enough samples to illustrate the letter strategies and conventions that I call the "laws of letters." My texts for the fictional letters are the published poems, stories, and novels themselves.

# Acknowledgments

No such study would be possible without the archival and editorial work of the editors of Faulkner's letters—Joseph Blotner, Louis Daniel Brodsky and Robert W. Hamblin, Malcolm Cowley, and James B. Meriwether. I have built on work about letters and epistolarity by Janet Gurkin Altman, Peggy Kamuf, David Krause, Jacques Lacan, Ruth Perry, and Harold Toliver, and by my past and present colleagues at the University of Tulsa—Shari Benstock, Bernard Duyfhuizen, Joseph Kestner, and Thomas F. Staley, each of whom significantly contributed to my understanding of the relationship of letters and fiction. Every study of Faulkner's work is likewise indebted to the careful scholarship that has gone before it, and my debt to that body of work will be everywhere apparent.

The Board of Trustees of the University of Tulsa granted me a sabbatical leave during which much of this book was written. The Graduate School and the Office of Research supported my work by a Faculty Research Fellowship and two smaller grants. Professors Gordon O. Taylor and Donald E. Hayden arranged for me to have the time to write at the expense of their own time. Thomas F. Staley provided the means. Bernard Benstock, Shari Benstock, André Bleikasten, Norman Grabo, Joseph Kestner, Darcy O'Brien, Susan Resneck Parr, Gordon O. Taylor, and Winston Weathers read what I wrote and listened.

Portions of this book have appeared previously, in slightly or substantially different form, in *American Literature, Mosaic, New Directions in Faulkner Criticism,* and the *Southern Quarterly.*

JAMES G. WATSON
Tulsa, Oklahoma

*William Faulkner, Letters and Fictions*

# I. The Two Canons

"Man will keep writing on pieces of paper, on scraps, on stones, as long as he lives." —*Lion in the Garden*, 73

## [ i ]

The published record of Faulkner's correspondence opens early in the years when he began to travel away from Oxford, to Toronto and New Orleans and Europe, and extends with pronounced gaps but with notable strengths to the end of his life. The record is not complete, but incomplete though it is, and severely edited in many of its aspects, the canon of Faulkner's letters comprises a profoundly significant and revealing body of writing, a storehouse of his attitudes and opinions expressed over forty years to family and friends, lovers and writers, editors and agents, and occasional strangers.

To date, this correspondence has been used primarily for biographical purposes and as biographical evidence in support of literary analyses. Properly, the letters that date Faulkner's European travels, or document his earliest conception of a character or a plot, or explicate his artistic intentions have their first importance in that they are about William Faulkner and his work. A second, though hardly secondary, significance inheres in the proximity of this body of Faulkner's writing to the imaginative writing, published and unpublished, that he was concurrently producing. In their aggregate numbers and substance the letters constitute a second canon, separate from but complementing the literary canon to which it lies in parallel relation. Like the literary canon, this second, epistolary canon is defined by its own generic laws, in this case the forms and conventions of epistolary discourse; and those generic laws describe a form of writing as significant *as writing* as it is a source of names, places, and dates in Faulkner's life. Indeed, the self-consciously autobiographical characteristic of personal letters throws presumed factuality into doubt and brings biographical data into question. A first law of letters is that the letter writer is in the text, addressing himself or herself to the correspondent of the moment. But this is not to suggest that the letter writer so portrayed is always the same person. The self recorded in a letter is the contemplated invention of the Sender, a studied, epistolary image shaped from materials selected and formally arranged for the Receiver. Each letter is a fragment of autobiography and, in this sense, each is a fiction. Among others, this capacity of personal letters to be simultaneously fact and fiction, reality and invention, accounts for the seminal importance of letters to the history of the novel. And it locates an early point of conjunction and interrogation, a substantive one, between the letterly and the literary canons that Faulkner created.

Biography has clearly established Faulkner's life-long habit of role playing and his fondness for costumed disguises. Joseph Blotner says that for him "the line between reality and imagination was not as compelling . . . as it was for others" and that the disguises he assumed "confirmed a dream that he would make real in appearance, though it was not so in actuality."[1] At times such personae extended reality to a considerable degree. World War I came to an end before Faulkner had finished ground school in Toronto; he was discharged "in consequence of being Surplus to R.A.F. requirements," and his commission, when it came more than a year later, made him Honorary Second Lieutenant and authorized him to wear the Royal Air Force uniform only on special military occasions.[2] The Cofield photograph of him in December 1918, wearing a Royal Flying Corps lieutenant's uniform and leaning jauntily on a cane, is a striking contrast to the picture of him wearing the white-banded cap of the RAF cadet in Toronto in November.[3] It was the hero's image that caught his imagination, of course, and he adopted it as his own in Oxford and wrote it into "The Lilacs" in 1918, *Soldiers' Pay* in 1925, and the stories and novel of the Sartorises, where he based fictional characters and events on his family and his family legends.[4] Blotner speculates that much of Faulkner's early writing, in particular, "constituted an attempt to compensate, to construct a persona through the development of his gifts as an artist which would have the power and the attractiveness which he felt he lacked."[5] David Minter says of Faulkner's role as a British aviator that "there was expression as well as deception in the costume he wore and the limp he affected" and that such roles were "an imaginative rehearsal" for his art.[6] They were that and more. Faulkner's letters confirm that the connections between his acted and his written personae represent his literally writing himself into being: the letters document a process that the fictions imply. As if by trial and error, Faulkner's costumes changed from 1918 into the twenties from a military uniform to the tweeds and sleeve handkerchief of Count-No-Count to the ragged shirt and trousers of the Pascagoula beachcomber, and the self-expressive figures of his art changed with them, distanced however by the range of their imaginative invention and the increasingly literary character of their forms. The marble faun and Pierrot and the knight named Sir Galwyn of Arthgyl are among them, and they no doubt share with Faulkner some of the tensions attendant upon, and the imperatives that impelled, their making. This is particularly so of very personal writing, such as *Mayday* and Faulkner's several other handmade gift books. But letters, unlike literature, are texts that document the personal self by design: privately written, signed, and sealed, they represent the writer to the reader "sincerely" or "truly," and the personae created and inscribed there are not so easily altered. Or dismissed. Inconsistencies between fact and invention in his correspondence might, and occasionally did, cause Faulkner embarrassment, but though he edited his letterly self-images when the necessity arose he could not, or at least did not, disclaim them absolutely. It is precisely because they were written in letters that those personae clung to him as the same figures in his imaginative writing often did not: reaffirmed by their reappearance in analogous contexts, they testify to the depth at which in letters the Self and the Word are meant to be one. Faulkner's ambivalent recurrence to the British aviator in letters early and late exemplifies this condition and marks a subtle difference between the letterly and the literary canon.

By 1932, when he wrote the introduction for the Modern Library *Sanctuary*, Faulkner had begun, as he said there, "to think of myself again as a printed object" (ESPL, 177). The published writer was become a marginally public man, his own image imprinted with his printed texts. Pressed by his publishers for biographical information, he invented it in his letters to them, guardedly using his familiar disguises to protect his privacy as he had to express his private sense of himself. In a letter to the Four Seas Company in 1924, he had included in a bare list of his activities the statement "Served during the war in the British Royal Air Force" (SL, 7), the verb *served* conveying considerably more service than was strictly the case. An autobiographical letter to the editors of *Forum* in early 1930 expands the implication of war service into a fiction that effaces the writer from his text and supplants him with an ironic persona. The letter is without a signature and reads, in part: "War came. Liked British uniform. Got commission R.F.C., pilot. Crashed. Cost British gov't £2000. Was still pilot. Crashed. Cost British gov't £2000. Quit. Cost British gov't $84.30. King said, 'Well done.' Returned to Mississippi" (SL, 47). The little sketch is perfectly reflexive. The approximation of clipped upperclass British speech— adopted elsewhere in biographical pieces of this sort—and especially the admission "liked British uniform" describe Faulkner when he returned to Mississippi in the uniform of an RFC lieutenant twelve years earlier. The fictional persona invented in the letter to conceal the actual man is based on one the letter writer had invented in fact: it is literally an autobiographical fiction. Standing between life and art in the letter canon, and partaking of both, the aviator persona offers continuing evidence of Faulkner's practice of writing himself into his texts in guises of concealment. In the literary canon after *Flags in the Dust*, the aviator was largely supplanted by more complex, psychologically expressive figures he adopted in writing *The Sound and the Fury*, *Sanctuary*, and *As I Lay Dying*. There are random appearances of the aviator persona in the flying stories of the early 1930s, "Honor" and "Death Drag" and "Turnabout"; in the film scripts he made from them and in others, such as "War Birds"; and in *Pylon*. Faulkner was himself flying in the 1930s, at first with Capt. Vernon Omlie and then in his own plane with his brother Dean in airshows billed as "William Faulkner's (Famous Author) Air Circus." In his novels in the 1930s he was peopling Yoknapatawpha County with a rich variety of characters whose lives and legends were rooted in the American Civil War rather than the Great War and a fictional present no longer scarred by the disillusioning wounds like those the Great War inflicted on Bayard Sartoris and his fellows. With the advent of World War II, however, the RAF aviator reasserted itself as a prominent presence in Faulkner's letters—and in the unofficial biography of him that publishers and literary encyclopedists had been amassing from them.

Logically enough, Faulkner's correspondence during the 1940s is laced with references to his own war and his invented war service in 1918, and logically too he omits to mention that he *served* only as a cadet. For reasons of age and health, his going to this second war was probably never seriously at issue. But his imaginative ties to the RAF were still strong: he was a member, and wore the lapel pin, of the organization of WWI pilots called the Quiet Birdmen, and Jill Faulkner remembers his putting on his old uniform from time to time.[7] He wrote to Robert K. Haas in October 1940 that he was "trying to get a National Guard unit here, U.S. comm. for myself. I have received no call from RAF. I take it that ex-members who are aliens may volunteer for back-area service, but no call to be made upon them until things are worse than now" (SL, 136). A letter to Haas in March 1941 reported: "I am flying fairly steadily, still very restless. Civilian Pilot Training is not enough. If I had money to take care of my family and dependents, I would try for England under my old commission" (SL, 139). Under the pressure of very personal circumstances, the memories that sparked these references to a more heroic though imaginary time in his life found fuller expression. When his favorite nephew, Jimmy Faulkner, left for Naval preflight school in 1943, Faulkner wrote him a moving letter of advice in which the old fiction of himself as a combat aviator is presented as a standard of conduct for the flyer-to-be. He enclosed one of his RAF pips in the letter, as a "luck piece," he said. "I wore it on the shoulder-strap of my overcoat." Significantly that "luck piece" from his RAF uniform was an artifact of an invented self used now to authenticate the persona in the letter. In the absence of official documentation, fiction verified fiction: "I would have liked for you to have had my dog-tag, R.A.F., but I lost it in Europe, in Germany. I think the Gestapo has it; I am very likely on their records right now as a dead British flying officer-spy" (SL, 170). From what he called the "crack-up in '18" he had learned about "foolhardiness" and "fear" in the air, and he knew that Jimmy would "remember what good pilots have told you, so that when emergencies come, you will merely meet situations which you have already heard about." He concluded by advising his nephew, "Aeroplanes very seldom let you down; the trouble is inside cockpits" (SL, 171). It was just such "trouble inside cockpits" that he had invented to explain a fictional wound in 1918 when he returned to Oxford, where it was known that he had not been in combat abroad, and it was to the same kind of trouble that he resorted again when facts of his life threatened to conflict with his letterly fictions.

As late as 1945 it was publicly assumed, as Malcolm Cowley wrote in a draft of his introduction to *The Portable Faulkner*, that William Faulkner "had been trained as a flyer in Canada, had served at the front in the Royal Air Force, and, after his plane was damaged in combat, had crashed behind the British lines." Cowley concluded, "Now he was home again and not at home, or at least not able to accept the postwar world."[8] Cowley wanted a lost generation writer like those he describes in *Exile's Return* as the author of such stories as "Ad Astra" and "All the Dead Pilots." His version of that figure was very like the one Faulkner had invented for himself at Oxford and for his characters in those stories of his that Cowley was reprinting. It was precisely because he was not at home with himself as an uncommissioned cadet that he had worn the uniform and claimed the experience of an authentic airman. He had expanded on that persona imaginatively in his fiction and poetry and, more cautiously, he had written it into his personal correspondence where he presented it as a factual self-portrait. His letters to Cowley in 1945–1946, however, reveal a writer uncomfortable with his youthful invention. A letter in early January 1946 says of Cowley's introductory essay, "If you mention military experience at all (which is not necessary, as I could have invented a few failed RAF airmen as easily as I did Confeds) say 'belonged to RAF in 1918'" (SL, 215). Both the invented airmen and the verb *belonged* ironically are true. On January 21 Faulkner was back in the role of aviator, though equivocally so: he alluded obliquely to heroism and war experience, but he advised Cowley to omit them from the piece he was writing. "The only point a war reference or anecdote could serve would be to reveal me a hero, or (2) to account for the whereabouts of a male of my age on Nov. 11, 1918 in case this were a biography. If, because of some later reference back to it in the piece, you cant omit all European war reference, say only what Who's Who says and no more: Was a member of the RAF in 1918. . . . I'm really concerned about the war reference" (SL, 219). What concerned him was that his fictions of self would be published as fact. Whatever else was included in Cowley's essay, a crash at the front behind British lines was a confirmable untruth. When Cowley wrote that, although it was too late for extensive changes, he had excised the reference to the combat crash, Faulkner acceded to what he now said he recognized as a "'structurally' necessary" dimension of the *Portable* introduction (SL, 219).

Significantly, Faulkner made no such objection to the republication of his World War I flying stories, which Cowley believed to have been written from the same set of experiences he was editing out of the introduction. Moreover, the war record Cowley was deleting in 1946 is precisely what Faulkner himself had written as fact as recently as his 1943 letter to his nephew Jimmy. Whatever of himself he had projected on the Sartoris twins, and whatever the similarities between those fictional characters and his own epistolary guises, one image was a designedly public one and the other inviolably private. Absent for years from his life and his art, the commissioned British aviator was a persona to which he had recurrent application in his letters. By insisting that biography be no part of Cowley's essay, he was protecting that epistolary image from public exposure, as he had done also in letters where he listed his RAF service without comment or concealed it in ironic sketches. Perhaps also he was preserving it for his future use: a flexible vessel of possibility, loosely modeled on fact, through which he might express a fond conception of himself long held and still very dear. Assured that that was secure from publication, he now re-invented it for Cowley in his letter, revising in terms that would assure its continued secrecy and that Cowley, as his previous correspondent on the subject, would have reason to believe was true.

> I don't like the paragraph [of war experiences] because it makes me out more of a hero than I was, and I am going to be proud of your book. The mishap was caused not by combat but by (euphoneously) "cockpit trouble"; i.e., my own foolishness; the injury I suffered I still feel I got at bargain rates. A lot of that sort of thing happened in

those days, the culprit unravelling himself from the subsequent un-authorised crash incapable of any explanation as far as advancing the war went, and grasping at any frantic straw before someone in authority would want to know what became of the aeroplane, would hurry to the office and enter it in the squadron records as "practice flight." As compared with men I knew, friends I had and lost, I de-serve no more than the sentence I suggested before: "served in (or belonged to) RAF." (SL, 219–220)

This letter also is reflexive, consciously so. At the outset the letter writer contends that Cowley's heroic version of his life is a threat to his art. Because he is "going to be proud of [the] book," he rewrites the biography: combat becomes "cockpit trouble"; the aviator is reduced to cadet; his injury results from "foolishness" rather than heroism and is "got at bargain rates." Certainly no part of this confidential revela-tion could be published in Cowley's essay. Like the cadet he describes, Faulkner is "unravelling himself" in his letter from an "unauthorized crash" that literally had no bearing on "advancing the war," and like the cadet he does so by writing a fiction, an invention in a letter about an invented entry in a squadron record. At the end of the passage, the self-effacing writer gives up the mantle of heroism to the equally fic-titious "friends I had and lost," maintaining to himself only the con-notative "served in" in place of "belonged to."

Perhaps it is only in the security of such private writing privately conveyed that images of the self so patently fictional can stand as fact. Having invented an unpublishable secret in a letter that negated a public invention, Faulkner concluded by distinguishing between the two kinds of writing in which he and Cowley were engaged. "I see where *your* paragraph will be better for *your* purpose," he wrote, "and I am sorry it's not nearer *right*" (SL, 220; my italics). For him writing of every kind was a statement of self, and the self written into a letter, however at variance with fact, was uniquely, imaginatively true. He said as much in his last letter to Cowley before *The Portable Faulkner* was published. The un-edited introduction was "false":

Not factually, I dont care much for facts, am not much interested in them, you cant stand a fact up, you've got to prop it up, and when you move to one side a little and look at it from that angle, it's not thick enough to cast a shadow in that direction. But in truth, though maybe what I mean by truth is humility and maybe what I think is humility is really immitigable pride. I would have preferred nothing at all prior to the instant I began to write, as though Faulkner and Typewriter were concomitant, coadjutant and without past on the moment they first faced each other at the suitable (nameless) table. (SL, 222)

As sequel to the previous letter, this may be read as a gloss on it and a restatement of the significance it likewise accords to the letter writer's written image of himself as writing.

## [ ii ]

A second law of letters is that the letter is always about itself. The letter writer writes about writing. Letters deal with the circumstances of their creation and composition, describe themselves by reference to other letters the writer has written or received, depict the scene of their writing, and identify their office. This reflexivity is a function of the Narcissism of the letter, which also dictates that the writer will be in the text. Sourced in the same place, the writer who contemplates himself or herself and the writing that describes itself are the inherently complementary subject and form of the letterly text. At a basic level letters identify themselves as elements in a written discourse by citing other letters as the cause of their composition. When Faulkner answered letters promptly, he described them in proximity to himself: "Yours of 22 May at hand" (SL, 192) is characteristic. In less formal circumstances he might describe the epistolary convention he was observing. A letter to his mother-in-law, Mrs. Lemuel Oldham, personifies the letter as a messenger from the portrayed writer to the reader: "As the compleat letter-writer says, this leaves me well and hoping it finds you the same" (SL, 192). Often, the scene of writing is also portrayed with the writer and his text. At times the act of writing is implied in the description of the setting. A letter written at a lunch table in Pavia in 1925 lists everything except the pen and paper with which it is written: "And here I sit, with spaghetti, a bowl full of a salad of beans and pimento, tomatoes, lettuce, a bowl of peaches, apples, plums, black coffee and a bottle of wine, all for 50¢" (SL, 9). In another case, the contrast with a scene not conducive to writing makes the present writing implicit: "I was too busy and too mad all the time I was in California to write you. But now I am home again, eating watermelon on the back porch and watching it rain" (SL, 66). In still another, the act of writing is itself subject of the scene: "Hot as hell here; I have to work in front of a fan; I write with one hand and hold the paper down with the other" (SL, 84). In one letter from Europe, Faulkner's portrayal of himself writing on a regular schedule is offered as a substitute for letters he has written that were delayed in delivery:

"While I think of it: I have written every Sunday and Wednesday since Aug 4th. They may come in irregularly, but dont worry—just remember when Sunday and Wednesday come, that I am allright, feeling fine, and sitting down at the table writing you a letter" (SL, 15). In this letter, the writing about other writing done "while I think of it" exemplifies the momentary fusion of thought and action that a letter records. It is a reminder that *writing* fundamentally is what letters transmit.

Not all delays in correspondence are the fault of the postal system, but they all shape letters significantly. A long-delayed response to another's letter requires explanation and usually a fuller portrayal of the recalcitrant writer and the present writing. The scene of writing in Faulkner's first letter to Cowley, from Hollywood in May 1944, is described as a chaos of unsolicited and unanswered letters, ransacked but unread, from unwelcome correspondents. From this confusion Cowley's February letter proposing an essay on Faulkner's work was recovered in May "by idle chance." Faulkner asked to be excused in his personal correspondence for eccentricities that resemble in several details his misuse of others' mail when he was postmaster in the university post office at Oxford twenty years before.

> During the last several years my correspondence has assumed a tone a divination of which your letter implies. My mail consists of two sorts: from people who dont write, asking me for something, usually money, which being a serious writer trying to be an artist, I naturally dont have; and from people who do write telling me I cant. So, since I have already agreed to answer No to the first and All right to the second, I open the envelopes to get the return postage stamps (if any) and dump the letters into a desk drawer, to be read when (usually twice a year) the drawer overflows. (SL, 182)

A significant part of the scene of writing in this letter is its return address, mentioned in the third paragraph: "As you can see from above, I am at the salt mines again." In the "crowded" and "unpleasant" town of Hollywood, Faulkner told Cowley, he had a "cubbyhole" where he was welcome to stay if he came west. "Cubbyhole" may signify a *room* or a *letter box*. Both are *addresses*, unlike the "desk drawer," and so suitable for receiving letters. Some details of Faulkner's letter, such as the expense of travel to the West Coast, his uncertainty about "when I will come East," and his clear preference for "home" over Hollywood, suggest that if he was willing to share his "cubbyhole" with Cowley he preferred to do so by mail. As with literature, so with his letters at the beginning of this correspondence: Faulkner wished to be known by his writing, and he concluded his first letter to Cowley by asking that biography be no part of the essay Cowley had proposed.

The other letters in the canon declare their kind and function according to the same law as this belated one. Self-reference typifies letters of apology, public announcements, reports, contracts, letters of credit, and letters of love. Official letters draw attention to themselves as documents of record; letters of love and friendship declare their intimacy in the circumstances of their writing as they describe them. Affairs of any kind conducted by letter assume the quality of a constantly self-rehearsing narrative—a quality, not incidentally, adopted as a formal principle in the epistolary novel. In one of a series of letters to William Herndon in 1942, Faulkner carefully unravels their contractual relationship by citing five separate letters, four telegrams, and two communiqués that might have been letters or wires, to, by, and about the Hollywood agent—all of which was necessitated by breaks in the sequence of their correspondence (SL, 157–158). "I know nothing else about him but his letters," Faulkner told Harold Ober (SL, 160). Often his letters are so precisely what they say they are that Faulkner could ignore customary forms of identification: some letters are without salutation, the addressed envelope sufficing in place of a stated relationship to the recipient in the body of the letter text; others are unsigned. Still others conform exactly to conventional usage. A sympathy note that was self-consciously typed in a draft, revised, and recopied in pen opens with a denial of the office it serves: "Of course you dont want letters. They don't do any good" (SL, 175).

In the context of such varied methods of address in letters, some of Faulkner's experiments with fictional narrative suggest that he was searching for a similar union of content and form, put to similar effect, in his novels. The range of first-person narrators in his work, for example, and his own musing narrations of characters' musings, prompt the understanding that his books are frequently about themselves in the way that his letters are by nature about letters. Some books, of course, are explicitly about artists, some about theories of art. But many books and stories are about their own writing, about other of Faulkner's writing, or about one or another scenes or acts of writing, including, significantly, letter writing. Such reflexivity is essential to the ultimate sense he created of Yoknapatawpha County as a seamless, self-referential whole or "cosmos," but he had indicated the importance of reflexive form for him as early as *Soldiers' Pay*, much of which turns upon unsuccessfully written letters. In *Mosquitoes* he indulged an extreme of the self-critical impulse by incorporating unpublished poems of his own into his text to be discussed (and dismissed) by the shipwrecked company of artists and critics aboard the *Nausicaa*. A letter to Warren Beck in July 1941 states the problem he was trying to solve: "As yet I have found no happy balance between method and material," he wrote. "I doubt that it exists for me" (SL, 142). Probably it does not exist in *Soldiers' Pay* or the talky *Mosquitoes*. But the balance he speaks of breaks down in an unusual way even in the letter to Beck, though fortuitously so and in ways that are instructive of the parallels between the literary and the letterly canons.

In the letter to Beck we see behind the mask of the "old 8th grade man" to the self-aware, literate artist who has read Walter Pater and aspires to rewrite Shakespeare. Faulkner wrote very few letters to literary people other than his editors and publishers; in fewer still did he explain himself or his work. What he did say was not volunteered usually but was offered in response to others' opinions of him, and then characteristically he was circumspect, self-effacing, even on occasion deliberately naïve. In the spring of 1941, Beck had published three essays about his work—"Faulkner and the South," "Faulkner's Point of View," and "William Faulkner's Style." These were very early and very complimentary criticisms, the serious work of a serious academic, and when Beck sent copies to him Faulkner responded in kind with a compliment of his own. "I agree with them," he began. "You found implications which I had missed. I wish that I had consciously intended them; I will certainly believe I did it subconsciously and not by accident" (SL, 142). He had assumed a similar stance with other critics. In 1932 he wrote Maurice Coindreau, "I see now that I have a quite decided strain of puritanism (in its proper sense, of course; not our American one) regarding sex. I was not aware of it" (SL, 63–64); to Cowley, in 1946, he would express his genuine pleasure with *The Portable Faulkner* by saying, "By God, I didn't know myself what I had tried to do, and how much I had succeeded" (SL, 233). Later still he would speak of himself and his writing in humble country terms, saying that he was a "carpenter" and *The Sound and the Fury* a "chicken-house."[9] But in 1941 his defenses were down. His work was largely out of print and unread, and the circumstances of his life as they pressed against him were interfering with his writing. He had complained the previous year to Robert Haas of the "really quite alarming paradox" that debilitating financial burdens such as his should fall upon an artist such as himself, "a sincere one and of the first class" (SL, 122); the next month he began a lengthy investigation of how he might earn more by changing publishers (SL, 126–132). By 1941 he was planning to rewrite the stories that would be *Go Down, Moses,* but he told Haas, "I do not want to gamble the time and effort of getting this mss. in shape unless it will really benefit me" (SL, 140). At this time he engaged William Herndon to sell his work and his services to Hollywood, and when Herndon asked in June for *Soldiers' Pay*, Faulkner wrote Haas, "Can it be had? Could you send him a copy, unless it is a collector's item now" (SL, 141). A week later Beck's letter arrived with the three essays.

The unsettling conjunction of this letter with problems in his life and art shaped Faulkner's reply. In his answering letter the sincere artist he had described to Haas reappeared and momentarily supplanted his customary public persona. He sketched a bumpkin, who wrote "subconsciously," and he blamed his failures "on my refusal to accept formal schooling (I am an old 8th grade man), but mostly on the heat in which I wrote." But, in contradiction, he also told Beck that he had been "writing all the time about honor, truth, pity, consideration, the capacity to endure well grief and misfortune and injustice and then endure again." He had not been writing consciously about "liars and hypocrites and rogues"—some of whom presently were besetting him personally and one of whom, Herndon, would shortly reveal himself. And he was not writing for the masses or the general readers who had not bought his books. "But I believe there are some," he said, "not necessarily many, who do and will continue to read Faulkner and say, 'Yes. It's all right. I'd rather be Ratliff than Flem Snopes. And I'd still rather be Ratliff without any Snopes to measure by even.'" Beck was among such readers. He had praised Faulkner for his characters' capacity for pity, their refusal to surrender principle, and their idealization of honesty,[10] and Faulkner responded honestly, and here factually, when he wrote, "I had rather read Shakespeare, bad puns, bad history, taste and all, than Pater, and . . . I had a damn sight rather fail at trying to write Shakespeare than to write all of Pater over again so he couldn't have told it himself if you fired it point blank at him through an amplifier" (SL, 142).[11]

The interest of the passage is biographic and generic. Whether consciously or not, the letter writer's customary mask is down; in its place is the man and artist who not only has written about but also has endured in his own life as an artist the "grief and misfortune and injustice" he describes. Perhaps this was one of those occasions, as he had said to Haas, when "in spite of judgment and all else, I take these fits of sort of raging and impotent exasperation at [the] really quite alarming paradox which my life reveals" (SL, 122); certainly he was responding to a strong sympathetic strain in Beck's essays. In one of those Beck had said of Faulkner's style that "Faulkner himself probably would admit the relative inadequacy of instrument to purpose,"[12] and at the heart of his response Faulkner did admit he had "found no happy balance between method and material." The same criticism ap-

plies to his letter, which returns to itself and its own ostensible failures at the end. "Excuse all the I's," Faulkner wrote. "I'm still having
trouble reconciling method and material, you see" (SL, 143). Writing
about what he had just written, he used the failure of his letter to *conceal* the true artist as his means of validating the artist it *reveals*. Apolo-
gizing for the unconventional frankness of his letter in terms he drew
from Beck's essays, Faulkner affirmed Beck's frank assessment of his
art and made it his own.

## [ iii ]

Perhaps it is only because he did not know them well that Faulkner
automatically put on disguises in letters to casual correspondents and
strangers. He was, after all, a genuinely private man, and it is consistent with the social patterns of his life that he should guard his privacy
also in his letters. The Beck letter is an exception only because a private persona inhabits a first letter with a customary public one: it is
more Beck's essays that Faulkner the artist is addressing there than the
stranger who wrote them. But that letter is a reminder that some selec-
tively portrayed self, however much beyond calculation or conscious
design, stands between the letter writer and the Receiver in every letter. This is consistent with the laws of genre. The self-consciousness
of the letter writer and the text extends to include the person addressed: the Sender's consciousness of the Receiver of the letter deter-
mines why and what is written and the way in which he or she represents herself or himself. This is a third law of letters, that the Receiver
is with the Sender in the text they share. Reader-response criticism
holds that in order to succeed in writing at all the writer of a letter, like
the writer of a novel, must construct an imaginary audience receptive
to the message and mood.[13] In fact, letters are generally more radical
than this: the Receiver commonly is written into the text in a role that
complements the letter writer's own. As the Sender is first known by a
return address or postmark, the Receiver is identified by a name and
address on the envelope and is described in the salutation by a name
or a title that signifies the kind of relationship the Sender has imagined and desires. Faulkner's letter to Beck opens with conventional
formality, "Dear Mr Beck" (SL, 142); the sympathy note to Haas addresses his friend as a younger brother or son, "Bob, dear boy" (SL,
175). In a series of letters, changes in the salutation map the course of
development of the epistolary relationship. As Faulkner came to know
and trust Cowley during their four-year exchange of letters in the
mid-1940s, the salutations of his letters changed from "Dear Mr. Cowley" in the first (SL, 182) to "Dear Maitre" and then "Cher Maitre"

(SL, 184, 205) and, when the objectionable material had been excised from the *Portable* introduction, to "Dear Brother" (SL, 222). The "Dear Cowley" and "Dear Faulkner" of their working correspondence became "Dear Malcolm" and "Dear Bill" only after they met in 1948.[14] With William Faulkner, clearly, there were proprieties to be observed in letters as in life.

Just as clearly Faulkner was speaking about his books exclusively when he told Jean Stein in 1955, "I have no time to wonder who is reading me."[15] Failure to recognize and honor the Receiver in a letter threatens the exchange on which each expression in a letterly discourse depends. Even in an imperious letter to William Herndon in 1942, where he described himself as a gentleman of uncompromising principles, Faulkner was careful also to portray his Receiver in a way that Herndon could accept if he would. The opening paragraph reads:

> Your letter of July 14 received after I received your wire. I regret that I didn't get the letter first and I regret that you sent a wire like that at all. You accused me of deliberate underhand dealing, which is not true, and inferred that I could be forced by threats into doing what is right, which I will take from no man. I give you the benefit of the doubt to believe you were surprised at finding someone else trying for a job for me, and were worried over possible loss of a commission, and sent the wire before you had thought very clearly. (SL, 157)

As Faulkner describes them, Herndon's insults and his mistimed telegram disregard him as Receiver and violate proprieties of epistolary discourse that Faulkner as the present Sender was being very careful to observe. Herndon's authority as letter writer was an unwritten contract with Faulkner. Faulkner's letter attempts to regain authority over Herndon by imposing the transgressor's identity on him and insisting on a new set of rules for their continued communication. The alternative, as he says in his final sentence, is an end to discourse, silence: "If this is not satisfactory to you, then make good your threat [of legal action] and cause whatever trouble you wish" (SL, 158).

Expression must be shared, and nowhere more than in letters where the Sender-Receiver relationship is implicitly at stake in every communication. Faulkner's love affair with Joan Williams began by her mailing him stories to critique, and often in their letters love and fiction are mutually at issue. He tempered his criticism of her work with praise for her personally, writing in one letter that "you take Joan Williams seriously, but not the work" (SL, 351). In another he portrayed himself as a letter writer reluctant to cause so sensitive a reader pain: "I hate to send the letter," he wrote, "because I am afraid [of its] result on you: will discourage or depress you, because we dont agree on what you have done" (SL, 350). Mentor as well as lover, he rearranged the pages of that letter and instructed her on the order in which they should be read: "LATER. READ THIS ONE FIRST." Of course, not all letters contain such elaborate solicitude for the parties to the discourse. In an unsigned note written in 1957, well after Joan had married, the reference to an absent text is cruelly expressive of the Sender's state of mind. "I wrote you a letter about a month ago," Faulkner said, "then decided not to send it for a while, if at all maybe" (LDB-II, 285).

Some letters require less concern for Sender and Receiver than others. By far the largest part of Faulkner's correspondence was less personal, with agents and publishers, most of whom he seldom saw and knew primarily by their letters. To Bennett Cerf, at Random House, he wrote in 1948, "I would like to come up this fall, haven't seen anybody to talk to in 8 years now" (SL, 269). He said of his agent, Harold Ober, "I never see him, because we have nothing to talk about. We correspond, but that is all" (SL, 342). But even in presumably impersonal business letters about manuscripts and contracts Sender and Receiver are present, especially in Faulkner's letters in the 1940s, and especially then when the subject was money or reputation or both. When the *Partisan Review* rejected the "Notes on a Horsethief" excerpt from *A Fable* in 1947, Faulkner wrote Ober an accusatory letter demanding to know, "What is your opinion of this section in question? Dull? Too prolix? Diffuse?" (SL, 261). The letter leaves no doubt that the Receiver is significantly responsible for the woeful condition of the Sender. With his agent and "Bob cum Random House" Haas deceiving him, with no magazine in existence "which would have printed sections from Ulysses as in the 1920's," and with modern man generally "in a state of spiritual cowardice," he used a figure of apocalyptic abandonment to describe himself as "the man crouching in a Mississippi hole trying to shape into some form of art his summation and conception of the human heart and spirit in terms of the cerebral, the simple imagination." Three years later he would tell the Swedish Academy, "I decline to accept the end of man" and suggest that the poet's voice might be "one of the props, the pillars to help him endure and prevail" (ESPL, 120). But for the letter writer in 1947 such troubles were in the sole power of his Receiver to remedy. As usual in such letters, Faulkner asked Ober to reaffirm the value of his work. "What is your opinion of this stuff?" he asked again. "Will anybody read it in the next say 25 years? Are Random House by taking me on absolute faith as they have, wasting their money on it?" (SL, 261–262).

## [ iv ]

Letters say *I am,* but they require validation. In the context of generic laws and their corollaries that define the letter *as writing,* questions such as these Faulkner put to Ober press more for an answering letter than for answers. Ideally conceived, letter correspondence is a form of written discourse between parties who agree to follow the rules of writing and abide by mutually acceptable codes of conduct. A well-balanced epistolary relationship is circular: Sender and Receiver steadily trade roles, the Receiver becoming a Sender and the Sender a Receiver in an unbroken round of statement and response. They are *co-respondents,* each Sender and Receiver portrayed in terms of the prior letter being answered and the future one expected to be received, which likewise will portray the Receiver and its Sender in its turn. Succeeding texts are written in the context of the foregoing ones and become the foremost point in that accumulating body of writing that the next reciprocal letter addresses. In this way letters attempt to overcome the absence that generates them, for neither of the correspondents is entirely alone in the text and no text is alone in the immediate canon.[16] This model requires a degree of consistency from letter to letter, and of willingness on the parts of both parties to conform to the rules of the discourse, that is exhibited only in the most extended correspondences. In fact, mutual consistency is responsible for their extent. As Joseph Kestner has aptly said of the genre in his study of Jane Austen's *Letters,* "There is no other literary form which demands that the reader's response be the form itself, another letter. The irritation provoked by an unanswered letter reveals that the *émetteur* is incomplete and unfinished until he becomes a *récepteur* by obtaining a response to his enunciation. The one role demands the other to validate its existence."[17] Faulkner put the matter another way when he wrote to Joan Williams, "all I can answer is what you write to me" (SL, 304).

This is a dimension that the literary canon does not share, and it suggests a limitation of letters to which literature is not subject. If a Sender's letters acquire meaning from the letters written to him or her, then each Receiver, by his or her own writing, gives material shape and substance to that which he or she reads. The canon of their correspondence is double written and it resides in two places. For this reason a correspondence is seldom "complete." Fragmented by the usual lost and withheld letters and by editorial suppressions, Faulkner's letter canon is more acutely one-sided in that he apparently kept virtually none of the letters he received and made no copies of those he sent. In this situation biography infers relationships from the existing half of the correspondence and substitutes the actual persons addressed for their missing letters. In the isolated cases where Faulkner's correspondents kept his letters and copies of their own, the course of their written relationships can be more reliably traced: the Faulkner-Cowley letters and Faulkner's correspondence with the *Saturday Evening Post* are examples. But whatever its substance, the shape of the whole may inhere even in fragments, and in Faulkner's letters there are telling artifacts of epistolary discourse that record the presence of the Sender and Receiver in the letter text and confirm their relationship. For example, the Sender may portray himself as a prior Receiver. When Harold Raymond mailed him the Chatto and Windus edition of his Nobel Prize Address, Faulkner replied that "naturally a bloke is pleased and proud that his words should be considered worth printing, though *it was the letter from you which moved me most*" (SL, 327; my italics). Or the Sender may describe the scene of his prior or future reading, as Faulkner did in a letter from Hollywood to his daughter: "I go to the studio and walk into my office, and there on my desk is a letter from Mama and my Jill. That makes me feel just fine" (SL, 173). Or, as Receiver, he may distinguish between one Sender and another, as Faulkner did in a Hollywood letter where he praised the pictorial quality of the letter he was answering: he told his stepson, Malcolm Franklin, "I was glad to hear what Oxford is doing in Dec. 1942. I knew about what the picture would be, knew pretty well, but yours was the first black-and-white record I have had. So far, only Mamma and my mother and Jill have written me, and when a woman writes to her loved ones, the letter really never leaves whatever upstairs bedroom it was written in" (SL, 165). Here the different relationships between the Sender and those who write to him are implied by the different scenes of writing in which the Sender imagines his Receivers: the "upstairs bedroom" is more private than Malcolm's Oxford, and the letters from women to their "loved ones" more intimate than Malcolm's "black-and-white record." By reconstructing the scenes of writing from previous letters he has received, the Sender demonstrates the power those letters had to conduct him to those scenes. An example of the converse situation is a letter Faulkner wrote to his aunt, Mrs. Walter B. McLean, from Paris in 1925. He describes her waiting for his letter at the American Embassy where he mailed it rather than in Memphis where it was received: "I can imagine you with your charming grand-duchess air in the middle of these female cattle all saying at the same time: 'But there should be mail here for me: I know there should. I wish you'd look again.' And in one of those penetrat-

ing stage asides: 'It's disgusting. People wouldn't stand for such service in America'" (SL, 19). In this unusual case, where the Receiver is
asked to act the part of an American in Paris and speak in "stage
asides," Sender and Receiver are made to share the same address as
well as the same text, and the imagined scene of the letter's reception
is made to co-exist with the scene of its writing. The enabling impulse
for this imaginative leap across space and time is the prior letter from
Mrs. McLean that Faulkner was answering. "Thank you for the nice
letter," he said at the end. "You are a good letter writer—no, I mean a
good writer of letter. A stranger could even tell the color of your eyes
from your letters" (SL, 20).

Taken together a group of letters by one writer may cohere into a
single, rudimentary narrative, more episodic than one-sided, with the
missing letters in the discourse implied in the epistolary forms of the
extant ones. Such a grouping is constituted by Faulkner's first extended correspondence, the surviving seventeen letters and ten postcards that he wrote to his family in just over the first two months of his
four-month stay in Europe in the autumn of 1925. From the first postcard, postmarked Genoa/Rapallo, August 5, to the final letter, written
from Dieppe on October 15, these tell the story of Faulkner's walking
tour in Italy and Switzerland with Bill Spratling, his residence in Paris,
and his brief visit to England and return to France. None of the letters
written to him during that time survive, nor are there any from him to
correspondents outside his immediate family, although he did write
to others. A partial draft of a letter to Phil Stone, written probably in
September, is transcribed in the Blotner *Biography*,[18] and early that
month he would have mailed the last two of the sketches published in
the *New Orleans Times-Picayune* on September 20 and 27. In November
he mailed Stone a bogus letter, addressed to "Mr. H. Mencken, magazine orthur" and signed "Ernest V. Simms," to be forwarded by Stone
with the "Ode to the Louver" parody to Mencken at the *American Mercury*.[19] Blotner says that Faulkner wrote also to Stone about royalties
due him for *The Marble Faun*, and that he may have had letters from
his father about a debt still owed the Post Office Department.[20] In addition to Stone, he almost certainly would have written to others close
to him. He apparently mailed Estelle Oldham Franklin one of the
Odiorne photographs of himself;[21] whether or not he wrote to Helen
Baird from Europe, the evidence of several sonnets written there is
that she was much on his mind. In his letters to his family, of course,
he alludes to and sometimes describes the letters they wrote to him,
and before the European correspondence breaks off in mid-October
he says that he has received a letter from Bill Spratling and is expect-

ing one from Horace Liveright (SL, 27, 31). None of his other letters nor those of his correspondents are mentioned.

These are gaps to be lamented, but the twenty-seven fully transcribed pieces that remain nonetheless represent a discrete and self-contained body of writing, one which, if it is not consciously unified, is not entirely accidental in its form either. The subject matter often suggests the series of travelogues Faulkner said he was writing, modeled perhaps on the travel letters that his great-grandfather, W. C. Falkner, published in 1884 as *Rapid Ramblings in Europe*. But Faulkner's letters were not written for publication as those were, and the devices and strategies he adopted in them were at once personal to him and more letterly than the Old Colonel's essaylike ones. As a body, the letters reveal that in 1925 he was already an enthusiastic and accomplished letter writer, as skilled in the creation of epistolary as of poetic personae, and sensitive in his personal letters as he was also in his most personal poems to the interests and feelings of his readers. In effect, it was a single audience that he addressed from Europe. Although twenty-three of the letters and cards are to his mother, they must have been written with the understanding, even the intention, that his father and brothers would read them too. He mentioned them to Maud by name when he urged her, "Tell me about everyone—Pop and Jack and Whiz [Dean], and Jimmy specially" (SL, 17). And he spoke indirectly to them: he said of an English tweed jacket, "Whiz will curl up and die when he sees it" (SL, 31).Without exception his letters to Maud Falkner address her literary and artistic interests. He wrote her about the Castle of Chillon and Joseph Conrad's Kent, about the Louvre and Rodin's museum and the work of Cézanne, Matisse, and Picasso, and about the music in the Luxembourg Gardens, a Rimsky-Korsakov ballet at Moulin Rouge, and a piece by the Scandinavian composer Sibelius. He spoke of the considerable amount of writing he was doing, as well, described his writing schedule, and sent word counts on the novel *Elmer*. He was busy with his art, and he said so in his regular letters. "I am working steadily on my novel," he wrote in his second week in Paris, "besides a book of poems for children I am writing, and a few articles on the side, you might say. So much writing that I feel fairly 'wrote out'" (SL, 16–17). When he temporarily did stop writing poems and fiction, he kept up his letters. He traveled to the battlefields at Amiens and to Chantilly in September, where he wrote five postcards, and to England in October, where he wrote twice to his mother. Then, as in Paris when he was working, he was abstemious. "I'm so busy writing I dont smoke much," he said in August (SL, 15); knowing his mother's dislike of alcohol, he said only that he took wine with his meals in the French fashion, and brandy once at Rennes for a cold and to keep him warm. Whiskey he left to the English. To whatever extent they were shared at home, his long, detailed letters to his mother are in contrast to the one piece of mail he addressed to his father: a postcard showing a mounted hunt at Chantilly. Here the Sender addressed himself to a different Receiver who, as he knew, would be interested in red-coated hunters, "the best-looking horses you ever saw," and barrooms "full of bow-legged cockney grooms and jockeys" (SL, 26). A second postcard picturing Chantilly, sent to eighteen-year-old Dean, describes the hunt but omits the bars (SL, 27).

Faulkner's imaginative writing held so little attraction for his father that it is hardly surprising he chose not to directly address him in his letters. Murry Falkner would claim that he never read his son's work,[22] and in 1925 he was far from being reconciled to his son's artistic aspirations and pretensions. Much of what Maud encouraged, Murry deplored: if he saw him that autumn less as an emerging artist than as an unemployed twenty-eight-year-old American tramp abroad, it was not without some justification. Conversely, if Faulkner did not write to his father it was perhaps because he suspected Murry would not answer him. Yet he clearly needed his father as a Receiver, even if an implied one, for the epistolary image he was constructing of a responsible man and serious writer. In this regard, to know that his father *read* him was enough, and he implicitly appealed to him for his reading in his letters to Maud. For Murry's sake as well as for hers, Faulkner modulated his adventures with his traveling companion Bill Spratling and the "gang of Chicago art students" (SL, 22) he fell in with in Paris, emphasizing in his letters home the stable virtues of a southern aristocrat of simple tastes. It was for both parents, too, that he kept track of his expenses, detailing the cost of his rooms, his dinner, his pipe tobacco, his coat, a bus tour, and a museum ticket. His letters are filled with references to austerity. In Paris in mid-August he was eating at "a restaurant where cabmen and janitors eat" (SL, 12). "Country folks are my sort, anyway," he wrote. "So I am going to move next week. I think that I can live cheaper than $1.50 per day" (SL, 12). When he shortly did move, however—to 26 rue Servandoni in Montparnasse—it was not country folks that attracted him but the proximity of the Luxembourg Gardens. If these letters included his father implicitly, a letter from Pavia that begins "Italian locomotive look like this" (SL, 8) was more directly addressed to Murry's interests. The accompanying illustration and the paragraph describing the eccentricities of Italian railroad men clearly were designed for the former engineer, conductor, and then treasurer of the Gulf & Chicago Rail Road in Mississippi.

Faulkner's personal and compositional problem in these letters was the same: he was attempting to validate a literal and a literary identity that was still very much in transition in the autumn of 1925. Whether the spurt of letters from Europe was generated by his sense of himself as artist or only by his absence from home, Faulkner's first extended correspondence fortuitously coincides with the turmoil in the parallel canon attendant on his turn from poetry to prose. Europe and the European letters are on the cusp of that change. In December 1924 he had claimed in a wire to the Four Seas Company that their delay in sending him copies of *The Marble Faun* was "HOLDING UP MY SAILING EVERY DAY" (SL, 7); when he actually embarked for Europe aboard the *West Ivis* seven months later he had just mailed Boni & Liveright the manuscript of his first novel. *The Marble Faun*, when it arrived in Oxford at Christmas 1924, attested to his identity as a poet; *Soldiers' Pay*, published in February 1926, would confirm him a novelist. In the interim, in Europe, he continued to write poetry and fiction, much of it personal and autobiographical. In his letters he justifiably laid claim to the title of artist. As his imaginative writing coincided for the first time with extended letter writing, however, the line between literature and letters blurred. He described his novel *Elmer* in his letters, but in the novel he attributed his own reading of Clive Bell and Elie Faure to his fictional hero (E, 344). From a sketch of himself as a New Orleans artist, written the previous spring, he borrowed a phrase for a letter where he said that Cézanne "dipped his brush in light" (SL, 24; NOS, 46). At home in America during the winter and spring of 1925, he had written eight letters into *Soldiers' Pay* and quoted from or described several more; now in Pavia and Paris and Tunbridge Wells, Kent, he was writing letters himself, and the uses to which he had put the fictional ones in his novel verified for him the range of invention real ones might permit. Whether fictional or actual, the laws of letters applied to both the same.

Faulkner's letters from Europe are self-consciously inventive in themselves, aware of their own imaginative language and artistic effects as they are also of the poems and fictions on which they report. As a body of writing, they constitute a fictional as much as a biographical narrative, one that can be read in the manner of imaginative autobiographical sequences, such as the private poems of *Vision in Spring* or even the eclogues of *The Marble Faun*. The letters are fragments of art as well as documents of a life: the fictional devices and the letterly conventions the letter writer draws upon as he writes give his ongoing narrative accretive retrospective form. Paired letters show him shaping events that he reshapes after the fact, sometimes for reasons of a specific Receiver but as often for aesthetic effect. In his first letter from Paris, August 13, Faulkner told his mother he had spent two days the week before cutting hay in a village above Lake Maggiore. He described himself as a type of Tolstoy's Konstantin Levin going humbly to the harvest fields with his peasants. "The day I left," he said, "the whole village told me goodbye" (SL, 10). In the next paragraph, invention outstrips possibility: "We climbed an Alp and called on a Russian princess, daughter-in-law to a member of the Czar's family, and herself a daughter of the last Doge of Venice" (SL, 11). The last Doge of Venice abdicated in 1797. An account of the same experience in a letter to Mrs. McLean dated September 10 omits the Russian princess, names the village Sommarive, and recasts the communal farewell at dawn as an evening meal, "outdoors at a wooden table worn smooth by generations of elbows." For this Receiver the letter writer adds the significant additional detail that he had been "mildly drunk" talking with "those kind quiet happy people by signs" (SL, 19). Such *rewriting* of places and experiences is produced in another way on a postcard, a more occasional and public form of letter less demanding of a response because it represents a place more than it does the person writing. Picture postcards are inherently reflexive. The text of a card Faulkner mailed to his mother imaginatively redescribes the picture on the other side, which the printed legend identifies as "MILANO—Piazza del Duomo": "This Cathedral! Can you imagine stone lace? or frozen music? All covered with gargoyles like dogs, and mitred cardinals and mailed knights and saints pierced with arrows and beautiful naked Greek figures that have no religious significance whatever" (SL, 9). A letter from Paris on August 16 to the same Receiver adjusts the same language to Notre Dame. In the narrative comprised by these letters, it constitutes a rewriting of the previous text and a second rewriting of the picture on the card. In the expanded space a letter affords, the letter writer expands upon both. "The cathedral of Notre Dame is grand. Like the cathedral at Milan it is all covered with cardinals mitred like Assyrian kings, and knights leaning on long swords, and saints and angels, and beautiful naked Greek figures that have no religious significance what ever, and gargoyles—creatures with heads of goats and dogs, and claws and wings on men's bodies, all staring down in a jeering sardonic mirth" (SL, 12). Granted that the cathedrals are similar, Faulkner was borrowing from letters for letters here as it was his life-long custom to borrow from writing of all kinds, including letters, for all kinds of writing.

Three other letters, in a group of five that remark on the progress of his beard, contain pen-and-ink self-portraits, which complement the epistolary persona developed in the text. "My beard is coming along fine," Faulkner wrote on September 6, in the letter with his first drawing. "Makes me look sort of distinguished, like someone you'd care to know" (SL, 18). The drawing in the third one, on September 22, shows him in the upper-left-hand corner of the page, pen in hand, drawing himself into the letter he is writing. The drawing and the letter are done on the verso of a discarded page from the novel *Elmer*. "I did this from a mirror my landlady loaned me. Didn't notice until later that I was drawing on a used sheet. This [is] part of 'Elmer.' I have him a half done, and I have put him away temporarily to begin a new one. Elmer is quite a boy. He is tall and almost handsome and he wants to paint pictures. He gets everything a man could want—money, a European title, marries the girl he wants—and she gives away his paint box. So Elmer never gets to paint at all" (SL, 25). *Elmer* is heavily, if ironically, autobiographical: Elmer Hodge gets everything Faulkner does not except the opportunity to paint, which Faulkner demonstrates by his pen-and-ink self-portrait. The letter and the manuscript fragment form a palimpsest, the frustrated fictional artist on one side of the page balanced against and read through the letter writer–illustrator on the other. The link between the author and his character is reinforced by that between Elmer Hodge as Faulkner describes him and the persona of Faulkner the letter writer: the bearded figure in the letter is literally the "other side" of the fictional person in the novel. But both sides are the work of William Faulkner, and both prove him an artist: the fragment of fiction a novelist, the drawing an illustrator. His beard, conversely, was a disguise that failed him. Although he thought that it made him look distinguished, and said in his letter, "My beard is getting along quite well," he said too that when his great-aunt Vannye saw him in Paris she "laughed at it, because she could see right through it to the little boy I used to be" (SL, 25). The written self in the letter was the reality, here supplemented by a drawing, and if the fictional character he described as tall, wealthy, and married was as yet but "a half done," the artist he portrayed on the reverse of that sheet in late 1925 was approaching completion.[23]

In this pattern of telling and retelling, the successive letters and cards "respond" to one another, and the gathering pool of material supplied Faulkner by his European experience takes significant narrative form. In some letters, details of the written experience are overtly fiction, as with the daughter of the Doge of Venice. Others echo fictions or exaggerate facts: the letter from Dieppe, for example, describes work aboard a Breton fishing boat in a way that recalls Faulkner's apocryphal stories of bootlegging. He had eaten shark with the Bretons, he told his mother, and "it was cold, cold! Hands raw all the time" (SL, 31). Two other letters cast scenes in dramatic dialogue, with the letter writer's French translated for the Receiver to comic effect (SL, 16, 25). But fiction or fact, the pervasive theme of the narrative that unwinds from these letters is Faulkner's complete immersion in Europe, particularly in France. From the first postcard, at Genoa, where he calls his knapsack "le sport baggage" (SL, 8), to the last letter from England where he says, "I am tramping again—en promenade, as us french fellers says" (SL, 30), half-mocking allusions to a European identity cover intense allegiances developing below the surface. By the time Vannye laughed at his beard late in September, the assimilation was nearly complete. He had been in Paris since August 13, and he could describe himself now as one with those people of all classes who gathered in the Luxembourg Gardens, where "the bands play Massenet and Chopin and Berlioz and Wagner, and the kids are quiet, listening, and taxi-drivers stop their cars to hear it, and even day laborers are there rubbing elbows with members of the Senate and tourists and beggars and murderers and descendants of the house of Orleans" (SL, 23). In Jackson Square, ten months before, he had felt the same easy absorption into what he later would call "our Quarter, the Vieux Carre" (ESPL, 173). His letters from Europe record a transformative experience not unlike the earlier one in New Orleans that produced his first novel. Now as then he had reliable guides. In addition to the paintings of Cézanne and Picasso he saw in the Paris galleries, he had a friend in the photographer William C. Odiorne, who likewise had ties to the Vieux Carré. To his mother he spoke of "a man here who admires me very much, who kind of looks after me" (SL, 27), and an unnamed painter—"a real one," he said—whose painting was modeled on life, not art. "He wont go to the exhibitions at all," he told Maud Falkner early in August, in the third of twelve letters from Paris. "He says its all right to paint the damn things, but as far as looking at them, he'd rather go to the Luxembourg gardens and watch the children sail their boats. And I agree with him" (SL, 13). Whatever the influence of such guides, the impact of the Luxembourg was immediate and profound. Soon after arriving in Paris he moved there himself, to "a nice room just around the corner from the Luxembourg gardens, where I can sit and write and watch the children" (SL, 13). Here was his focal point in Paris, associated over and over in his letters with his recreation and his writing. And it was the subject and scene of his best work in Europe, a short story that in his own best judgment was "perfect—a jewel" (SL, 17).

His story climaxed his imaginative writing in Europe, and it is one of the incidental ironies of the European letter narrative that his description of that climax should fall precisely at the midpoint in the twenty-seven extant letters—in the thirteenth, to his mother, and the fourteenth, to Mrs. McLean. In the first of those Faulkner wrote, on September 6, "I have come to think of the Luxembourg as my garden now. I sit and write there, and walk around to watch the children" (SL, 17). He concluded with his first drawing of the beard that he said made him look distinguished. The Luxembourg and personal distinction are both elements of his description of his story.

> I have just written such a beautiful thing that I am about to bust— 2000 words about the Luxembourg gardens and death. It has a thin thread of plot, about a young woman, and it is poetry though written in prose form. I have worked on it for two whole days and every word is perfect. I havent slept hardly for two nights, thinking about it, comparing words, accepting and rejecting them, then changing again. But now it is perfect—a jewel. I am going to put it away for a week, then show it to someone for an opinion. So tomorrow I will wake up feeling rotten, I expect. Reaction. But its worth it, to have done a thing like this. (SL, 17)

Almost certainly this is the piece that became the concluding scene of *Sanctuary*, where the "old old man" from the Luxembourg Gardens mentioned twice in the Paris letters (SL, 12, 15) sails toy boats in the pool while "from beyond the circle with its spurious Greek balustrade, clotted with movement, filled with a gray light of the same color and texture as the water which the fountain played into the pool, came a steady crash of music" (SR, 308).

The second letter, written September 10 to Mrs. McLean, includes in its description of the Luxembourg Gardens the old man from the short story, whom Faulkner told his aunt "sails a toy boat on the pool, with the most beautiful rapt face you ever saw" (SL, 19). And, like the letter to his mother, it contains a drawing of the beard, although the annotation is less expressive: "I have a beard. Like this" (SL, 20). However, instead of describing the story as the earlier letter does, this focuses on the letter writer's sense of his dissociation from it, in particular on the distinction between the beautiful story and his own bearded face. "I have just finished the most beautiful short story in the world. So beautiful that when I finished it I went to look at myself in a mirror. And I thought, Did that ugly ratty-looking face, that mixture of childishness and unreliability and sublime vanity, imagine that? But I did. And the hand doesn't hold blood to improve on it"

(SL, 20). Years later, in a letter to Joan Williams, he would draw the same sort of distinction between "the work and the country man whom you know as Bill Faulkner—what little connection there seems to be between them" (SL, 348). Now perhaps, less than a week after writing this story, the reaction he predicted to his mother had set in. If so, it prompted the passage of self-examination just quoted, and perhaps a second one describing a moment of dissociation recalled from years before. Mrs. McLean had written to say that his great-aunt Vance Carter Witt was coming to Paris with her daughter, and her name, in connection with what he had called in his letter his "childishness and unreliability and sublime vanity," evoked a suppressed memory of childhood fear.

> I will be awfully glad to see Vannye again. The last time I remember seeing her was when I was 3, I suppose. I had gone to spend the night with Aunt Willie (in Ripley) and I was suddenly taken with one of those spells of loneliness and nameless sorrow that children suffer, for what or because of what they do not know. And Vannye and Natalie [her sister] brought me home, with a kerosene lamp. I remember how Vannye's hair looked in the light—like honey. Vannye was impersonal; quite aloof: she was holding the lamp. Natalie was quick and dark. She was touching me. She must have carried me. (SL, 20)

Writing on the same day to Maud Falkner, he said nothing of this except to state tersely, "I had a letter from Aunt Bama today. Vannye is to be in Paris this week, so I'll see her" (SL, 21). The differences between the letters to his mother and his aunt are not entirely a matter of Faulkner's habit of rewriting experience, or of his concern always to address his Receivers as individuals. In the letter to Mrs. McLean, he associated the aunt who had saved him from childhood loneliness with the favorite aunt he addressed who had announced Vannye's coming to Paris, and the following day he rewrote his memory of Vannye in a note to her. He said there, "The last time I saw you that I remember, I was 3 years old and crying: you and Natalie had brought me home from Aunt Willie's in Ripley, where I had gone to spend the night, and I lost my nerve. You held a kerosene lamp, and your hair looked like honey" (LDB-II, 5). So powerful was his association of her with his childhood that he signed his note "William C. Falkner," reclaiming there the spelling of his surname, changed in 1918 to Faulkner. In his last letter about Vannye, on September 22, he told his mother she had seen through his beard "to the little boy I used to be."

Vannye's arrival in Paris temporarily unmasked the vulnerable boy behind the man and artist Faulkner had portrayed in his letters.[24] When he wrote the story about the Luxembourg Gardens and death in the first week of September, he had been abroad for one month and away from home for two. The day he wrote to his mother about it, he had put Bill Spratling on the morning boat train for New York. The loneliness and sorrow occasioned by that parting, and stimulated by his story, he described to Mrs. McLean in the form of his childhood memory and recalled in his note to Vannye. Something of the same, in fiction, would trouble the child, Elmer Hodge, in the novel he was then writing; and it would trouble Horace Benbow, who "dreamed that he was a boy again and waked himself crying in paroxysm of homesickness like that of a child away from home at night, alone in a strange room" (SO, 60) in the original *Sanctuary*, where the Luxembourg Gardens story lodged in 1929. The story was the climax of his achievement in Europe, as he said it was, but it also marked the beginning of the end of his imaginative writing there. To this signal point in the European letters, midway in the narrative of his stay, Faulkner had spoken of his writing repeatedly, almost obsessively. Thereafter, the remaining letters report, he wrote less and less, and he wrote less in his letters about writing. On September 10, the day he wrote to Mrs. McLean, he told his mother that "the novel is going elegantly well— about 27,500 words now. Perhaps more" (SL, 20); but he said too that his writing schedule was breaking down. "Used to be I'd run out and have coffee and a piece of bread, buy my bread and cheese and wine for lunch, and go to work by 9:30. Now I never seem to get back before noon. But it's so nice to dawdle around in the gardens, helping the lads sail their boats, etc." (SL, 21). By September 13 he had put *Elmer* away and started "a sort of fairy tale . . . the book of my youth, I am going to take 2 years on it" (SL, 22). But a week later he left for Rouen on a walking tour, and by October 3, when he had been back in Paris only four days, he was ready to leave again. He said, "I have got sort of restless in France, in Paris, that is," and for the first time in his European letters he balked at descriptive writing. "I saw so much on my trip that I shall [not] try to write it," he told his mother. "I'll save it to tell when I get home" (SL, 27). Only one story is mentioned after September 13, "a queer short story, about a case of reincarnation" (SL, 31) that he described in his final letter, October 15, from Dieppe.

Arguably, the letters themselves are as important to his efforts at self-composition as the imaginative work in Europe that they document and describe. At a time in his life when every piece of writing contributed to his developing sense of himself as an artist, his residence in Europe supplied him an audience for letters that he only was beginning to develop for his fiction and poems. If his father be excepted, that audience was favorably predisposed toward reading him. The letters he wrote to his family afforded inherent opportunities for self-invention, and the laws of letterly discourse assured him confirming responses. He was writing into existence in his letters a self that fit in the real world, and as he wrote and rewrote, giving it significant form, the laws of letters conspired to give him back life in return.

# II. Crossings

"The mail was in and the window had opened and even those who expected no mail, who had received no mail in months must needs answer
one of the most enduring compulsions of the American nation."
—*Soldiers' Pay*, 111

[ i ]

When William Faulkner chose to incorporate transcribed letters into
his first novel, he was working in a distinct social tradition and a literary one, both of which he knew well. His was a letter-writing society.
As university postmaster from late 1921 to 1924, he had observed, if
he had not always served, the American compulsion for mail, and it is
significant to the realistic surface of his novels that his characters
should receive and send letters. Later, letters of his own would generate fictional ones and serve as their models. Writing letters into fictions is as old as the novel itself, of course, and Faulkner was conscious of historical antecedents as he also was aware of contemporary
manifestations. The classics of English epistolary fiction were standard books in family libraries in the South. He told Marshall Smith in
1931 that he had not yet written a "real novel" but intended to—"Perhaps write a *Tom Jones* or a *Clarissa Harlowe*," he said.[1] In his foreword
to *The Faulkner Reader* in 1954, he said he had received his early education in his grandfather's library from Scott and Dumas and from books
chosen by his grandmother in the late 1800s "when women did most
of the book-buying and the reading too, naming their children Byron
and Clarissa and St. Elmo and Lothair after the romantic and tragic
heroes and heroines and the even more romantic creators of them"
(ESPL, 179). In "Knight's Gambit" (1949) *Clarissa* is in Gavin Stevens'
library. In *Soldiers' Pay* Gilligan reads to Mahon from Rousseau's *Con-
fessions*, and it is tempting to speculate that if Faulkner knew that book
well enough to name it in his novel he also may have known Rousseau's letter-novel, *Julie ou la Nouvelle Héloïse*. If he needed contemporary models, several were immediately at hand. Joseph Hergesheim-
er's *Linda Condon*, which he had reviewed in 1922 for the *Mississippian*,
contains three transcribed letters. Joyce's *Ulysses*, on which he was
modeling parts of *Soldiers' Pay* in 1925, contains a number of inset

letters, with recurrent references to them and to their writing and reading.[2]

In the epistolary novel letters *are* the text and offer themselves for analysis and interpretation according to the laws of the letter genre. The transcribed letters of *Soldiers' Pay* are documents woven into the fabric of the text, but like their antecedents in the epistolary novel they constitute fictional narratives that convey character and establish and resolve relationships. They tell a story. Cadet Lowe's courtship of Margaret Powers in letters is an example. His letters from San Francisco also record the passage of time in the novel in April and May of 1919, and their substance helps to sustain the several love affairs in counterpoint to one another. Lowe is present in his letters as Sender and, therefore, present to the novel in spite of his absence from the company of characters surrounding Donald Mahon. In the enriching context of the world depicted in the book, these and other letters in *Soldiers' Pay* define and productively draw upon such corollary issues about themselves as the question of ownership of personal letters, the power of letters over Sender and Receiver, and the characteristic outcomes of certain kinds of correspondence.

Ruth Perry is surely right when she says in this regard that fictional letters "must be more than vehicles for wit or information. . . . The novel-reader must be able to feel that the letters serve some more complicated function, such as release or clarification, for the fictional letter writer. They cannot be uniformly glib but must convey the sense that the writing is part of a complex interpersonal process that is not easy to set down accurately. Successful novels grew out of those fictional letters which took pains to delineate character (exemplary or otherwise) and sketched in a relationship between two or more people."[3] Perry is speaking broadly of the foundations of the epistolary novel in the eighteenth century, but much of what she says here is also true for lettered books like *Soldiers' Pay*, where inserted letters, though not the whole of the fictional text, are integral and not incidental devices. Uniquely realistic, they share their inherently fictional aspect with the fiction of which they are a part and bring to it genre conventions of their own that serve as internal standards of reference. In complement to physical relationships between characters, and their spoken words to one another, letters between characters span time and space by the written word and document relationships in written records. A character in the novel writes part of the text that a reader in the novel reads. In *Soldiers' Pay* those writings and readings are subtext in a pattern of tellings and retellings that Faulkner would shape to more sophisticated ends, and often by letters, in novels to come.[4]

Nonetheless, the letters of *Soldiers' Pay* are firmly grounded in the

themes and the accordant structures of Faulkner's postwar "wasteland" novel. Generated by and expressive of the lost ways, diversions
from planned paths, and actual separations of characters—past, present, and to come in the book—the letters document the difficulty of
interpersonal communication in the frenetic world of the war's ending, where identity is no longer defined by tradition, nor yet by offi-
cialdom, but by the constantly changing partnerships and shifting al-
liances of what Joe Gilligan calls a world "turned upside down" (SP,
41). The book opens with directionless travel—only Donald Mahon is
headed home—and with undelivered and purloined letters. In Chapter I, Margaret Powers remembers that her last letter to her husband at
the Front was answered "casually and impersonally" by a government
notice of his death (SP, 36). Homeward bound with his debilitating
wound, Donald Mahon carries with him a letter from Cecily Saunders
filled with "all the old bunk about knights of the air and the romance
of battle" (SP, 41). When Mahon is delivered to Charlestown and Cecily,
she breaks the engagement her previous letter confirmed. Cadet Lowe
parts company with the travelers on April Fool's Day in a flurry of
letters and wires in which Margaret offers to send a note home to
his mother, and Lowe extracts her promise to write him. His six letters and one postcard to her commence on the train from St. Louis
on April 2 and are transcribed in Chapters III, IV, V, VII, and VIII;
Margaret's letters to him are alluded to in his third and seventh letters. Her last one is returned unopened to Rector Mahon. Other correspondences and letter relations complement these: Margaret and
Dick's letter courtship and their brief marital correspondence (SP, 162–
164), Emmy's "laboriously worded letters" to Mahon in France (SP,
120), and Cecily's two letters to George Farr to arrange assignations
(SP, 146, 213). In a novel where Faulkner described waiting for mail
as "one of the most enduring compulsions of the American nation,"
virtually all of the characters write or receive "a stamped personal
communication of some kind, of any kind" (SP, 111, 112). Even Joe
Gilligan, in the aftermath of Mahon's death and Margaret's departure,
finds a foreboding message for himself in the unreadable writing of
"dark trees like spilled ink upon the pale clear page of the sky" and
the "pen strokes of iron pickets . . . upon the dark soft grass" (SP, 312,
315). At the end of the novel, the Negroes sing "Feed Thy Sheep, O
Jesus," and the music in which Gilligan finds "all the longing of mankind for a Oneness with Something, somewhere" (SP, 319) recalls
again the need to communicate implied in the American compulsion
for mail. But Gilligan has already heard other voices singing of silence
and separation and an end to writing: "Yet ah, that Spring should vanish with the Rose! That Youth's sweet-scented Manuscript should close!

The Nightingale that in the Branches sang, Ah, whence, and whither flown again, who knows!" (SP, 314–315). Echoing this, in the following Section 7 of Chapter IX, Margaret's last letter to Lowe is returned stamped with the legend "Removed. Present address unknown" (SP, 315).

The majority of these letters, as this listing indicates, are love letters, and it is highly significant that their intimacy is immediately and repeatedly violated in the novel by readers other than the intended Receiver. Thematically, this bears on Faulkner's long-time concern with lost privacy; structurally, it brings into juxtaposition diverse characters whose personal expressions of self are at threat. Margaret recalls that Dick Powers' letters "addressed to his dear little wife" prompted her to write him every day in return, but she admits to Gilligan that she shortly tired of the masquerade and "found that writing bored me, that I no longer looked forward to getting one of those dreadful flimsy envelopes, that had already been opened by a censor" (SP, 164). Letters in their "flimsy envelopes" are vulnerable to intrusion, and military censorship officially sanctions intruders. Uninvited access of this kind to another's writing exposes the private selves lodged in the letter and steals the force from the writer's words. Thus Margaret loses interest in reading Dick's censored letters. Yet when Gilligan appropriates and reads Mahon's letter from Cecily, he defends himself on the grounds of service to a superior officer. "Suppose I did do something that ain't exactly according to holy Hoyle," he says, "you know damn well that I can help him—if I don't let a whole lot of don'ts stop me" (SP, 40). On this shifting ethical ground where disservice is service, Margaret will share Lowe's first love letter with Gilligan in her turn. The letter is hers to share as the addressee, but it belongs at least equally to Lowe who wrote it and signed it "With love / JULIAN" (SP, 103). When the Sender is compromised by the infidelity of the Receiver, the intruder gains secret authority over him. Gilligan never is jealous of Lowe in his own futile courtship of Margaret, for example, and for the same reason he is able to predict that Cecily will jilt Mahon. "Don't you kid yourself," he tells Margaret. "I've seen her picture. And the last letter he had from her" (SP, 40). The only intentionally open letter in the book has no force or impact at all. Lowe's postcard at the end of the novel lacks even a salutation to suggest ownership and give the message focus, and Faulkner emphasizes its lack of value as a letter when he writes, "You buy them for a penny, stamp and all. The post office furnishes writing material free" (SP, 285).

Conversely, private letters privately kept are documents of potentially great power. George Farr succeeds in seducing Cecily when he receives a letter from her, whereas Januarius Jones fails when he attempts "blackmail" (SP, 220) on the basis of an overheard conversation. Cecily's first letter to George is a surreptitious note written "on a scrap of wrapping paper" and inviting him to "come to-night after they have gone to bed" (SP, 146). The crude stationery emphasizes the impropriety of the message, and George values the letter as an erotic object in itself, reading and rereading "her spidery, nervous script until the words themselves ceased to mean anything to his mind" (SP, 146). The source of such power is suggested by a passage Faulkner added in typescript to his description of Cecily's second letter to George: "When he took the square white paper from the post office, when he saw her nervous spidery script sprawled thinly across it, he felt something like a shocking silent concussion at the base of his brain" (SP, 213).[5] Literally, in this untranscribed letter, the medium is the message. Cecily is in her letter as a dangerously alluring presence in absence—a *spider* palpable in her own handwriting, a thin girl "sprawled thinly" on the page for her lover. Dick Powers' *power* is likewise in his letters, which seduce Margaret into marriage when verbal proposals cannot, and then sustain their relationship when he leaves for France. Except for the three days spent together before Dick leaves for the war, their married life is lived exclusively in letters, and when their writing ends so does their love. Dick writes a last letter saying "he didn't know when he'd be able to write again," and Margaret calls off their marriage in an answering letter that arrives after Dick's death, "wishing him luck and asking him to wish me the same" (SP, 164).

These outcomes conform to three possibilities for closure in the epistolary love novel: sexual union, the ostensible object of love letters; the death of one or the other of the correspondents; and renunciation of love by one or both of the lovers.[6] All three stop writing. *Soldiers' Pay* is not *Clarissa*, but each alternative is realized in the lettered subtext of the novel: in Margaret's marriage to Powers, in his death, and in her rejection of him as husband and correspondent. The first two outcomes complement a recurrent theme in the novel, which is explicitly expressed at the head of the final chapter: "Sex and death: the front door and the back door of the world. How indissolubly they are associated in us! In youth they lift us out of the flesh, in old age they reduce us again to the flesh; one to fatten us, the other to flay us, for the worm" (SP, 295). Structurally, the conjunction of sex and death is made explicit in Chapter IX where, on the day of Mahon's funeral, scenes of Emmy's submitting to Januarius Jones alternate with those of the burial. In the letters it impels and explains Margaret Powers' behavior. She conceives of her husband as two men, the lover and the letter writer. Married to Dick through the power of his letters, Margaret is widowed before she can divorce him. In her view, the fact that Dick never read her last letter is an "infidelity: having him die still believing in her, bored though they both probably were" (SP, 36). Subsequently, the man she took as lover and the letter-writing husband her letter betrayed merge accusingly in her dreams, in broken phrases from their love and letters: "(Dick, my love, that I did not love, Dick, your ugly body breaking into mine like a burglar, my body flowing away, washing away all trace of yours . . . Kiss and forget me: remember me only to wish me luck, dear, ugly, dead Dick. . . .)" (SP, 184). Such tensions require, and receive, resolution. Margaret's correspondence with Lowe after the war rewrites her broken correspondence with Powers, her marriage to Mahon just before his death re-creates her marriage to Powers, and the letters and marriage together erase the tormenting "infidelity." By the time the post office returns Margaret's last letter to Lowe "telling him of her marriage and of her husband's death" (SP, 315), she is gone from Charlestown, "removed," as the stamped legend says, beyond the call and the emotional entanglements of all letters, her own "present address unknown."

## [ ii ]

Whether in the winter and spring of 1925 Faulkner knew or cared enough about letters *as letters* to utilize all of their forms in his book is probably suspect. Like all of his writing, letters included, he learned by doing. It is almost enough to say that the letters of *Soldiers' Pay* for the most part do follow generally understood conventions of ownership and outcome and do support themes and motifs in the book. Cadet Lowe's letters are a curious exception in that by breaking some laws of letters and following others they suggest a more conscious art and a more conscious artist at work.

Lowe is at once the most autobiographical and the most artificial character in the book, a figure Faulkner introduces in Chapter I as a foil for Donald Mahon and then separates from the company of travelers, apparently to enable him to write letters.[7] Why Lowe writes is unclear: he is never a credible suitor to Margaret, nor a friend to Gilligan, nor does he have a serious interest in Mahon. What he writes is only peripherally and ironically to the point of events taking place in Charlestown, where even his name is not recognized at first. In order to write at all, indeed, Lowe must overcome obstacles put in the path of no other letter writer in *Soldiers' Pay*, and his letters are full of these difficulties. In the first one, April 2, he says, "This dam train rocks so I cannot write any way" (SP, 103). Letter writing requires solitude, but Lowe has none at home. His second letter, April 5, opens, "As soon as I got away from mother I am sitting down to write to you," but after one short paragraph he concludes, "Well mother is dragging me out to tea I had rather I had be shot than go except she insists" (SP, 153). His social life in San Francisco postpones letters and intrudes in them to reveal other lovers than the Receiver he addresses. Nine days after his second letter, Lowe ingenuously writes, "I got your letter and I intended to answering it sooner but I have been busy running around. Yes she was not a bad kid she has shown me a good time no she is not so good looking but she takes a good photo she wants to go in the movies" (SP, 186); he closes, "I have got to go out on a party now or I would write more" (SP, 187). Uncertainly focused to begin with, Lowe's epistolary relationship with Margaret changes dramatically in mid-correspondence. On April 14 she is "Dear Margaret" and he "Your sincere friend / JULIAN LOWE" (SP, 186, 187). Jilted by the would-be film star ten days later, he writes on April 24, "Girls are not like you they are so young and dumb you cant trust them" (SP, 246): Margaret has become "Margaret dearest" and he "J" (SP, 246, 247). Alone now, he has both the solitude and the time to write, but his problems as writer continue to plague him. He tells "Darling Margaret" on April 25: "How can I tell you how much I love you you are so different from them. Loving you has already made me a serious man realizing responsabilities. They are all so silly compared with you talking of jazz and going some place where all the time I have been invited on parties but I refuse because I rather sit in my room thinking of you putting my thoughts down on paper let them have their silly fun" (SP, 278). Whatever the nature of Emmy's "laboriously worded" letters to Donald Mahon, they hardly can be more ironically involuted than Lowe's tortured phrasings. His main obstacle to writing is his own inability to write; his insistence on writing is a function of his inability to be in life what he tries to be in letters—a soldier home from the war, the aviator and the lover. In effect his letters are self-designed narcissistic mirrors: he writes himself to himself. The letters, as letters, let him externalize his fantasies in writing, and Margaret, who knows he is none of those things, confirms them by answering, for her own reasons, with letters of her own, which Faulkner does not transcribe. When Lowe tells her, "I have done a little flying but mostly dancing and running around" (SP, 187), he *is* "the ace" Gilligan jokingly calls him (SP, 104); but when Margaret writes that she will marry the dying aviator Lowe longs to be, he withdraws that epistolary persona. The postcard he substitutes for a letter contains no image of him but his name, "JULIAN L."; his promise, "will write later," implicitly denies that the present postcard contains writing at all (SP, 285).

For all of his sometimes spurious silliness, Cadet Lowe represents an experiment with narrative that cannot lightly be dismissed. No doubt Lowe's letters are overdone, but they are the most extended, fully transcribed body of correspondence in a canon of stories and novels that is thoroughly, if irregularly, lettered. His felt presence in letters prefigures Caddy Compson and Charles Bon, to name but two major characters from succeeding novels who, though absent, are present in their writing. What he writes to Margaret, and the way he writes it, looks forward to Byron Snopes in *Flags in the Dust* and to David Levine in *A Fable*. Lowe's letter narrative documents his return from home RAF ground school in Toronto and his life with his mother after the war—including various philanderings conducted in the role of aviator, a plan to enter the university, losing his girl, and going to work in a bank. These are details so patently indebted to events in Faulkner's own life at various times after the war as to suggest that Lowe's letters mirror their author's author. It is true that much of *Soldiers' Pay* is "autobiography minimally transferred," as Michael Millgate has it,[8] and that Lowe is a character who parodies positions and attitudes that were Faulkner's own. Nonetheless, it is curious in the context of Faulkner's efforts at personal privacy, in his 1945–1946 letters to Cowley especially, to find Lowe in a parody of guises Faulkner himself had assumed writing of things Faulkner took very seriously about himself. "I see fellows my age that did not serve specially flying which is an education in itself," he writes to Margaret in his last, most intimate letter, "and they seem like kids to me because at last I have found the woman I want and my kid days are over" (SP, 277).

Biographically considered, here are bitter ironies indeed. But perhaps Faulkner's publication of this private persona in his novel is the point of Cadet Lowe. Millgate, and with him David Minter, finds in the plethora of details Faulkner borrowed for the novel from his own life and his writing evidence that he was at pains to enroll himself "among the wastelanders"—both as a member of the disillusioned generation that had fought the war and of the group of American writers of that generation who were recording their experiences and disillusionments in novels and poems.[9] Granting that, it remains to be said that the means he chose to portray Cadet Lowe in his novel specifically dissociates him from his character. Imbedded in the often self-consciously artistic prose of the book, the ungrammatical letters create a measurable distance between the novel writer and letter writer as well as between the letter writer and his epistolary persona. It seems clear in this context that Lowe was included in *Soldiers' Pay* as a writer, to write letters, and to write them in just the ways that he does. As Faulkner worked on the novel in New Orleans, he had traded with Sherwood Anderson the short series of comic tall tales called "The Al Jackson Letters." The calculated comedy of Lowe's self-conscious letters differs from those in that it derives from his exaggerated bad writing rather than the adventures he writes about. Manuscript drafts of the letters in *Soldiers' Pay* show that this was Faulkner's aim from the outset.[10] In the typescript he carefully revised for suggestive inaccuracies, changing "of course" to "of coarse," for example, and the phrase "love you always" to "love you all ways."[11] The resulting letters complement Cecily's "occasional coarseness" (SP, 214) and contribute to the several sexual puns in the book. But as bad writing, Lowe's letters do more: they emphasize his lowliness as a writer fumbling to remake the world in his image, and his abbreviated narrative casts into perspective the achievement of Faulkner's first extended one.

The distinction speaks to Faulkner's conception of prose narrative in 1925, and especially to the relationship of writer and reader with which letters are so crucially concerned. In a first novel that is as conventionally artistic in its style as it is conventional in its postwar subjects and themes, Julian Lowe's miswritten letters are all the more unconventionally unreadable. Letter reader and novel reader alike reconstruct him from the ill-fitting disguises of his garbled texts, and it is very much to the point that the reconstruction is often an ironic antithesis of what the letter writer intends. Margaret forgets the name of her "child" correspondent in the letter signed "JULIAN"; Gilligan identifies him ironically as "the ace" (SP, 104). This is a function not only of bad writing but also of bad letter writing, which ignores the laws of the genre. In Lowe's correspondence, the circular structure of letter discourse is abandoned. His self-consciousness seldom includes his Receiver as a person sharing his text, and he makes scant provision for himself as a future Receiver. Because of this, and likewise because they serve a private need of her own, Margaret's replies are not transcribed in the novel. Lowe is not writing love letters but first-person narratives about love, and badly written ones, transparently autobiographical, that reveal in their immature writing and clumsy strategies of concealment a significant distance between the real and the written writer. Margaret and Gilligan, and the novel reader, *read* Lowe in his letters in the clear and sustained antithesis between the self he imagines and the too intrusive actual one: the man and the "child," aviator and cadet, suitor and mother's son. He is to this extent less an autobiographical figure than a narrative device by which the apprentice novelist tested for himself the authority of his own authorship.

Structurally, too, the distinction between Lowe's writing and Faulkner's provides an analogue for the productive juxtaposition after Chapter I of Lowe's San Francisco and Mahon's Charlestown. Lowe's home with his mother exists in *Soldiers' Pay* exclusively in the letters he writes there. No scene of the novel is set in San Francisco, but the scenes of writing he describes to Margaret portray a milieu of postwar parties and casual affairs similar to Charlestown. In a number of particulars, however, they serve the novel as the reverse image of Mahon's home with his father, where the letters are received and read. The dates on the letters and the chronology of their reading fix common points for comparison and contrast.[12] Without exception in these circumstances, Lowe is undone. Sometimes the letter writing takes place simultaneously with events in Charlestown that contradict his propositions. On April 5, for example, he writes, "It's boreing all these girls how they go on over a flying man if you ever experienced it isn't it" (SP, 153): on that day in Charlestown, Cecily Saunders refuses to have more to do with her aviator fiancé, writes a letter of seduction to the civilian, George Farr, and that night becomes his lover. More often the contradictory events coincide with reading the letters. On April 24 Lowe writes, "I sit in my room and I think you are the only woman for me" (SP, 246): on the day she reads the letter, Margaret tells Rector Mahon, "I'm going to marry [Donald] myself. I intended to all the time" (SP, 277). In his most passionate letter, dated April 25, Lowe promises that "it will not be long till I see you and take you in my arms at last and always" (SP, 278); but on May Day, when Margaret receives it, she marries Donald Mahon. These contrasts and ironic conjunctions make Lowe foolish, but they also assert the futility of romantic love and romantic writing. In what amounts to his erasure from the text, the recurrent denial of his authority as letter writer finally permits Lowe so little expressive space in the novel that he stops writing altogether. His last and briefest letter is his cryptic postcard, and when Margaret's answering letter is returned to Charlestown unread it brings the subtext and the book to a close. The train that brings that letter back brings Cecily unhappily home with George and takes Margaret away widowed again.

Whatever of his own experience there is in Cadet Lowe's abbreviated military service and his envy of Mahon, Faulkner also was writing about writing and reading when he wrote Lowe into *Soldiers' Pay*: about the necessity of writing from personal experience and the inherent dangers of self-exposure that involved. Two essays about his own reading and writing at this period complement and extend his management of the theme in his novel and suggest again that these are not at all unimportant concerns for the first novelist. "Verse Old and Nascent: A Pilgrimage" was written in October 1924 and published slightly revised in the *New Orleans Double Dealer* in April the following year while Faulkner was working on *Soldiers' Pay*. What he said there about reading verse, and the uses to which he put it, is largely true of

Lowe's aim in writing letters: "I was not interested in verse for verse's sake then. I read and employed verse, firstly, for the purpose of furthering various philanderings in which I was engaged, secondly, to complete a youthful gesture I was then making, of being 'different' in a small town. Later, my concupiscence waning, I turned inevitably to verse, finding therein an emotional counterpart far more satisfactory for two reasons: (1) No partner was required (2) It was so much simpler just to close a book, and take a walk." [13] To a remarkable degree Lowe's letters appear to serve him as verse did Faulkner at the same age. Though hardly poetic, the letters Lowe writes to Margaret Powers are part of his own youthful gesture as a man and lover, and in his self-involved use of them they provide him a successful counterpart for lovemaking with Margaret and a substitute for courtship of the girl who jilts him. Faulkner may have had Lowe's writing directly in mind in a second essay, a draft of his 1933 introduction to *The Sound and the Fury*, where he compared language and women and spoke again of writing in terms of seduction: "I had learned a little about writing from Soldiers' Pay—how to approach language, words: not with seriousness so much, as an essayist does, but with a kind of alert respect, as you approach dynamite; even with joy, as you approach women: perhaps with the same secretly unscrupoulous intentions." [14] Lowe never learns from his letter writing what Faulkner learned from Lowe, and so he lapses into silence. Writing, Faulkner knew, was an end in itself, like reading in "Verse Old and Nascent," that fulfills the writer-reader in the way that seductions do lovers. In their distance from that, Lowe's childish letters, by contrast, are only auto-erotic. Their language palls and in the end they seduce no one, not even Julian Lowe.

### [ iii ]

Given Faulkner's experiments with epistolary forms in *Soldiers' Pay*, and the provocative body of his European correspondence in the months after finishing the novel, it is not surprising that other crossings between letters and literature should occur almost simultaneously. His residence in New Orleans in the winter and spring of 1925 was his first extended absence from home since 1918, when he spent April, May, and June with Phil Stone in New Haven and July through November in Toronto. Living in New Orleans generated personal letters as well as fictional ones. As he worked, he reported his progress on the novel to Stone in Oxford, and Carvel Collins hints at other correspondence that spring with women in Arkansas, Tennessee, Oklahoma, and Mississippi. [15] There was no need to write to his then current love, however, for Helen Baird was there with him in the city. Later, in an undated letter signed "Bill," he would say, "I remember a sullen-jawed yellow-eyed belligerent humorless gal in a linen dress and sunburned bare legs sitting on Spratling's balcony and not thinking even a hell of a little bit of me that afternoon, maybe already decided not to. But damn letters anyway." [16] In late June, with his novel in its next-to-final draft, Faulkner followed Helen to Pascagoula, where he continued his courtship. He proposed marriage, was rejected, and on July 7 sailed with Bill Spratling for Europe. That long absence generated the European letters, and some love poems, and perhaps a small book for Helen. He returned before Helen herself left for Europe, in time to give her the gift book *Mayday*, a forty-seven-page fictional romance, handlettered and -bound, and illustrated with pen-and-ink drawings in the endpapers and three small watercolor paintings. *Mayday* is dated "Oxford, Mississippi, 27 January, 1926." Helen left for Europe in February, and her absence inspired a second handmade book, dated from Oxford in June: the sonnet sequence *Helen: A Courtship*. A draft of a letter written to her that August of 1926 reads in part, "I have made you another book. It's sonnets I made you, all bound. . . . you must come back." [17] When Helen did come back, it was to marry Guy C. Lyman, and this book may have been given her as a wedding present. [18] In the meantime there was Estelle Franklin, whom he had lost in 1918 yet still loved. She had returned with her children from Shanghai in mid-March, but she too was away from Oxford in the summer of 1926, at Monteagle, Tennessee. By mid-September she was gone again, although she would return permanently in January 1927 and dissolve her marriage to Cornell Franklin fifteen months later. [19] In October, after her departure, Faulkner made her a special gift book also, one of several he gave her in the course of their long, interrupted courtship. *Royal Street: New Orleans* is a handmade reproduction of the vignettes published in the *New Orleans Double Dealer* in January–February 1925, now slightly revised and with the final piece replaced with the vignette "Hong Li." Like the love letters they surely were intended to be, these gift books were generated by the separations they attempt to overcome. This and other letterly characteristics distinguish them, to a degree, from similar literary gifts and from other imaginative work that employs similar language and investigates similar themes.

Faulkner had been making and giving such gifts as long as he had been writing seriously, and their forms are as various as are these three. Of five others composed and constructed between 1920 and 1927, *The Lilacs* (1920), *Vision in Spring* (1921), and *Mississippi Poems* (1924) are sequences of poems; *The Marionettes* (1920) is a verse play, handprinted and illustrated with pen-and-ink drawings, made in several copies; and *The Wishing Tree* is a fictional romance, which again was reproduced by hand in several editions.[20] Recipients ranged from close friends, such as Phil Stone and Myrtle Ramey, to Estelle's daughter, Cho-Cho; copies of *The Marionettes* were sold. Physically the books are no less diverse. By contrast to *The Marionettes* and *Mayday*, for example, *Mississippi Poems* consists of a typed cover sheet bearing the holograph legend, "Autographed for Myrtle Ramey / 30 day of December, 1924 / William Faulkner," and twelve carbon typescript sheets of poems, each signed by Faulkner and formally inscribed by his self-appointed literary agent, "Publication rights reserved. Not to be published without the written consent of the author or that of Phil Stone."[21] By their artfulness in different genres and different mediums, such gifts proclaimed Faulkner an artist, and he made and gave them for that purpose even after he had published books to give. *Mississippi Poems*, in fact, was accompanied by a copy of *The Marble Faun* (1924), likewise signed for Myrtle Ramey. Whether he portrayed himself as the boy magician Maurice, or as the commedia dell-arte clown Pierrot, Faulkner customarily wrote himself into the gift books in personae divided between the demands of life and art. That was the point of giving them: to say *I am* and to validate that self-proclaimed self in writing. It was part and parcel with his other ways of declaring his differences to a small town and a way of revealing himself psychologically to special friends, behind the concealing mask, as a writer all too conscious of trying to be both a man and a man writing.

Perhaps because of the special relationship between lover and beloved, letters of love depict the letter writer with special intensity and complexity. In love letters, and in the gifts of love Faulkner made for Helen and Estelle in 1926, writing attempts to substitute for the act of love, written intercourse for sexual union. Although this convention is qualified somewhat in the special circumstances represented by the gift books, each, letterlike, is intimately and revealingly addressed to a named Receiver. The most complex such salutation is the figurative one in the front endpapers of *Mayday*, where Faulkner's drawing, together with his inscription, illustrate his purpose in making the book. The drawing shows a bearded satyr piping for a naked woman who faces away toward the images conjured by his music. These include the spectres from the story, Hunger and Pain, and in the upper-left corner a second satyr pursuing two female figures who dance away ahead of him. The satyr, or faun, is remarkably like the bearded self-portraits in Faulkner's European letters to his mother and aunt, September 6 and 10, 1925, and it is a figure clearly appropriate to a book celebrating the rites of spring proposed by the title *Mayday*. Allegorically, the woman is Helen, the music is the narrative, and the goatish piper is the artist himself, divided between his love and his art, piping the music of sexual pursuit. The whole is a multiple, reflexive self-portrait, introducing the book and complementary to it, in which Faulkner the illustrator depicts Faulkner the piper depicting Faulkner the man pursuing Helen through the several mediums of his art. The inscription addresses the complex little book to Helen Baird: "to thee / O wise and lovely / this: / a fumbling in darkness" (M, 45). *Helen: A Courtship* opens with a poem rather than a drawing, distinguished from the other poems as the only nonsonnet in the book: "To Helen, Swimming" casts Helen architecturally in the "hewn changing battle-ments" of sea waves that conceal and reveal "her boy's breast and the plain flanks of a boy" (HAC, 111). *Royal Street* is inscribed, "To Estelle, a / Lady, with / Respectful Admiration: / This,"[22] and the front end-paper is decorated with a Beardsley-like pen-and-ink drawing that suggests the relationship of *Royal Street* to others of the gift books. The drawing picks up the swirling motif of the *Mayday* illustrations, even including the figures of Pain and Hunger from that book; in a formal garden borrowed from *The Marionettes,* a woman wearing a formal tiara feeds a peacock and a naked infant holds a tall formal candlestick topped with a single flame.[23]

The texts that follow the ornate opening pages of these little books recall that neither Helen nor Estelle was physically, or perhaps even emotionally, accessible to Faulkner as a lover in 1926 when he wrote them. Helen had refused his proposal the previous summer, and Estelle still was married to Cornell Franklin. Thus, Sir Galwyn of Arthgyl in *Mayday* dies for a visionary woman; the poet "Bill" in *Helen: A Courtship* substitutes poetry for his absent mistress; and the Oriental philosopher Hong Li, in *Royal Street,* turns with bitter logic to rationalized arguments against lust. As there were no possible letters of response to these texts, so there are no unions in them except loveless couplings or imaginary love making. Two of the books, in fact, were not delivered to the woman they address until well after they were written. What is required in them all is that the letter writer accommodate his art to his life and his life to his art. Casting his personal experience, letterlike, into private writing privately conveyed, Faulkner recorded that struggle, substituting for the man anguished by lost love and the writer driven by his ideal of love a third figure expressive of both—the fictionalized Man-as-Writing, who exists only in the text, at a safely objectified distance from the other two.

To this end the letterly form of the books was particularly suited. All three are handlettered and -bound, placing the writer's *hand* directly into the hands of his readers. The isolation of the Sender, the presumed privacy of his text, and the intimacy of his subject accord his written words the power that spans physical distance. In love letters, especially, fantasies about the beloved often outstrip fact. *Mayday* is cast as a quest for the ideal woman Faulkner pictured naked in the first watercolor painting and described with "a face all young and red and white, and with long shining hair like a column of fair sunny water" (M, 50). Neither this image nor the fulsomely endowed figure in the painting is anything like the actual Helen, who was dark complexioned and boyish. In the course of his quest, Sir Galwyn encounters mythic women—Yseult, Elys, and Aelia—who satisfy lust but not love: the union for which he and, presumably, Faulkner both long is perhaps romantically depicted in the third watercolor, where the knight and his lady stand arm in arm in the moonlight. But there is no such union in the text. It is death, the ultimate separator, that governs the end of *Mayday*. Led by "good Saint Francis," Sir Galwyn finds the face of his vision in the hurrying stream of Time and there gives himself into the arms of "Little sister Death" (M, 87). In the final drawing, on the back endpaper, he broods with Hunger and Pain above his own gravestone: "hic jacet / Galwyn / ap / Arthgyl / Knyghte" (M, 89). What this context reminds is that *Mayday* was a letter of melancholy farewell. The symbolic separation forecast by the death of the hero occurred almost immediately in the actual relationship in February, as Faulkner knew it would, when Helen left for Europe.

With this conclusion confirmed, he turned from elaborate love letters to work begun in Paris the previous autumn, the novel *Mosquitoes*. Although she was absent, however, Helen stayed in his mind and she infused his work. In *Mosquitoes* she is the model for Pat Robyn, and for the sculpted bust of what Gordon calls his "feminine ideal: a virgin with no legs to leave me, no arms to hold me, no head to talk to me" (Mos, 26). That bust, or an armless and legless one very like it, is pictured in the first watercolor in *Mayday* as the inspiration of Sir Galwyn's vision. The letterly gift book ends with the knight's gesture of eternal fidelity, which the novel reverses when Gordon takes a real woman in the final pages of *Mosquitoes*. Sir Galwyn joins his eternal woman in oblivion, but in his lust Gordon sets aside his ideal. The alternate endings of death in the gift book and sex in the novel perhaps suggest the limited extent to which any living woman ever could embody such visions of ideality, even in art. As Gordon holds his whore against the sky, "*voices and sounds, shadows and echoes change form swirling, becoming the headless, armless, legless torso of a girl, motionless and virginal and passionately eternal before the shadows and echoes whirl away*" (Mos, 339).

In June, with Helen still abroad, Faulkner paused long enough from his work on *Mosquitoes* to make her a second book, this an anniversary gift based on their courtship at Pascagoula the previous June and his memories of her during his subsequent absence in Europe that autumn. *Helen: A Courtship* consists of the introductory poem, "To Helen, Swimming," and fifteen sonnets: the first eight poems bear the subscript "Pascagoula—June—1925," the final eight have place names in Europe and dates in July, August, and September of that year. The book is not a collection of intimate occasional poems written under the impulse of immediate feeling, however. Rather, it is an arranged sequence: fully half of the sixteen poems were written at places or times other than those indicated in the text, and as many as four of that group were composed in some form before Faulkner met Helen Baird. According to Carvel Collins' evidence, Poems II, IV, V, and perhaps XIII were written prior to 1925. In addition to these, there is evidence that Poems III, VII, VIII, and XV were not composed at the precise place or time Faulkner indicates. Those that apparently were composed where and when indicated are "To Helen, Swimming," and Poems I, VI, IX, XII, and XIV.[24] Of this final group, it is worth noting that four were written in the first two weeks of Faulkner's stay in Europe, between his arrival in Genoa August 2 and his first letter from Paris August 13. Counting Poem VIII, written aboard the *S.S. West Ivis*—not at Majorca as the text indicates[25]—five of the eight European sonnets (Poems VIII through XII) were written in the painful six-week period immediately following Faulkner's leaving Helen in late June.

In light of this evidence, the dates and places that purport to describe the course of the "courtship" instead appear to be a device of the poet's retrospective fictionalizing, a subtext dated and arranged in a structure that delineates the dilemma of unrequited love at Pascagoula in June, the separation of the lovers, and the poet's attempts to accommodate himself to lost love at Genoa, Pavia, Lago Maggiore, and Paris. In his letters from Europe, Faulkner mentions writing only "a book of poems for children" (SL, 16) and "a poem so modern that I dont know myself what it means" (SL, 17). Yet five of the *Helen* poems apparently were written as figurative love letters from Europe. Unlike the Pascagoula poems that open the book, Poems VIII through XII were composed when Faulkner and Helen actually were apart, in the first stages of their separation, and they acquire particular characteristics of letters from the circumstances of their composition. Several of the five, for example, represent the writer's urgent attempts to overcome absence by substituting a fantasy woman for the actual one. A year later, in June of 1926, Faulkner could be detached enough about Helen to borrow for his celebration of their courtship from work quite unrelated to her: Poems II, IV, and V predate the courtship at Pascagoula and serve the interests of art rather than life. But the European poems of 1925 have more immediacy, and the crossings between the genres of poetry and letters in Faulkner's private writing create a telling context for reading the gift book.

Letterlike, the European poems create personae for the poet-Sender and his beloved. In Poem IX of *Helen*, dated "Genoa—August—1925," the real woman addressed and the written one are conceived of as "two sisters," the absent virgin and the "froward" lover present in the poet's imagination. The sometimes frustrating fulfillments of that division are explicit in the opening lines:

> Goodbye, goodnight: goodnight were more than fair
> Since happed I in the losing one, found two,
> Gaining in this high and hungry air
> Too thin for one, two sisters I must woo. (HAC, 120)

Faulkner's work is filled with similar dilemmas, of course: *Mayday* is an immediate example, and *Mosquitoes*, and Mr. Compson uses some of the same language of "high and hungry air" when he describes Quentin in *The Sound and the Fury*, "contemplating an apotheosis in which a temporary state of mind will become symmetrical above the flesh and aware both of itself and of the flesh it will not quite discard" (SF, 220). But in *Helen*, as in *Mayday*, the fantasy woman supplants the actual one whose absence inspired the poem: Poem X, from "Pavia—August—1925," concludes that the night woman will succumb to seductions the day woman resists.

> But look how does white spring the whole day through
> Sing golden-twinned, self-sistered, 'til unfaced
> By sun she finds to whom that song was raised,
> And there's a marriage made 'tween dusk and dew.
> So you no virgin are, my sweet unchaste:
> Why, I've lain lonely nights and nights with you. (HAC, 121)

Essentially, the poet *writes* a Helen, as he writes himself also, by writing to her. In Poem XI, from Pavia, the written woman surpasses even the mythic "deathless golden Helens" of "lonely paradise." To that image, housed in his dreams and poems, the poet alone in Europe clings.

> Let that sleep have no end, which brings me waking
> My blanched pillow's womb untwinned, to see
> No more this myriad night for whose vain slaking
> Night's self is loath, frame this still face to me.

What would I in their lonely paradise
Though deathless golden Helens harp their hair,
Remembering a mouth that sings and sighs
By its own shape in sleep, which is not there?

Let me only wake when long forgot
These thin sweet shoulders bearing yet unbent
The world's whole beauty, leaching, slow assuaged
By this hair's simple twilight, what is not
To all the white that is, though it were blent;
These grave small breasts like sleeping birds uncaged. (HAC, 122)

These are not letters in form, but they are in their function and in the function of the book of which they are a part. The irony could hardly have escaped Faulkner when he made the book in June of 1926 that he and Helen had exchanged places in the year since he had written the poems, but without exchanging the poems themselves, which still were unmailed.

In the eighteen months before he bound these poems for Helen Baird, the scope of Faulkner's writing had dramatically broadened. He published poems, essays, a series of prose vignettes, story-sketches, and a novel. He wrote travelogues, stories, poems, a fairy tale romance, part of a novel about an artist, and letters about them all. By the time he revised and bound *Royal Street: New Orleans* for Estelle in October, he had finished another novel, about writers and critics and a sculptor and their theories of art, in which he named himself as a man no one remembers. He entered that book in another way by inserting a poem of his own called "Hermaphroditus," and exited it, perhaps, by a letter from one of his autobiographical characters. "Dear Mr. Fairchild," David West writes when Pat Robyn rejects his proposals of love, "I am leaveing the boat to day I have got a better job I have got 2 days comeing to me I will not claim it I am leaveing the boat be fore the trip is over tell Mrs. More I have got a better job ask her she will pay you $5 dollars of it you loned me truly" (Mos, 236). It is not in the least beside the point that Faulkner himself owed Sherwood Anderson a debt for helping with his writing career, or that he unkindly repaid it by portraying Anderson as Fairchild in *Mosquitoes* and parodying his style the next year in the foreword to *Sherwood Anderson and Other Famous Creoles*. In this potpourri, where events of his life and the several mediums of his art mixed in his writing, he freely appropriated the language of his poetry for prose fiction; he used narrative strategies to shape collections of poems and prose-poems; and he accommodated letters to published novels, and private books to the conventions of letters. He was learning to use words. In his 1923 review of Joyce's *Ulysses*, T. S. Eliot had written that "one can be classical in tendency by doing the best one can with the material at hand. . . . And in this material I include the emotions and feelings of the writer himself, which, for that writer, are simply material which he must accept—not virtues to be enlarged or vices to be diminished." [26] Faulkner was "classical" in this way, and he was finding, as Eliot would say in *East Coker* that he had found, that "every attempt / Is a wholly new start, and a different kind of failure."

The letterly aspects of private writing, such as *Royal Street*, can be traced to these crossings within the literary canon and between letters and literature, as well as to the generative impulse of absence. Separated from Estelle yet again in the autumn of 1926, wishing to speak to and about her, Faulkner made her the intricately crafted book to serve as a letter would, and to it he appended the particularly personal postscript he titled "Hong Li." One of the last of such gifts, it proclaims like the earliest of them that the writer is both lover and artist. The vignettes published in 1925 and reproduced here confront that uneasy division of self less dispassionately, however, than the books made for Helen Baird, or even earlier gifts for Estelle, such as *Vision in Spring*.[27] In Poem I of *Helen: A Courtship*, titled "Bill" and dated "Pascagoula—June—1925," the raging poet ominously is silenced by his discovery of love, "and he's quiet, being with her" (HAC, 112). At the end of *Helen* art supplants life and words again fill the silence: in Poem XV, from "Paris—September—1925," the poet consigns himself to his poem. He has known love and loss, and when he dies his spoken words will die with him, like leaves stripped from a branch. But his written words, he insists, will live to move other lovers to the same passions they record. Years later he would say that writing was the artist's way of "saying No to death for himself by means of the hearts which he has hoped to uplift, or even by means of the mere base glands which he has disturbed to that extent where they can say No to death on their own account by knowing, realizing, having been told and believing it: *At least we are not vegetables because the hearts and glands capable of partaking in this excitement are not those of vegetables, and will, must, endure*" (ESPL, 181–182). At the conclusion of *Helen* he expressed the same ideal in the classically literary metaphor he chose to describe his self-consciously literary poems. The final sonnet concludes:

> Though warm in dark between the breasts of Death,
> That other breast forgot where I did lie,
> And from the stalk are stripped the leaves of breath,
> There's yet one stubborn leaf that will not die

But restless in the wild and bitter earth,
Gains with each dawn a death, with dusk a birth. (HAC, 126)

No matter the outcome of love for the man writing, he was declaring to the woman he had idealized in his book, the apocryphal poet he had created still would speak and still inspire love from the poem's page, that "stubborn leaf" where the man is the writing and the Self and the Word are one.

Virtually none of this high idealism is evident in the vignettes of *Royal Street*, where all of the speakers in the darkness are irreparably broken by internal divisions, including especially the Artist possessed by "a dream and a fire which I cannot control" and the widowered Cobbler whose only wife is a "bush of golden roses. . . . twisted and gnarled with age." [28]

The second of the vignettes, "The Priest," extends the theme of forced celibacy that Faulkner customarily lodged with the faun in such poems as "L'Apres-Midi d'une Faune," *The Marble Faun*, and *Helen* III and IV. The disjunction in the Priest between spirit and flesh both gratifies and appalls: it erotically doubles every prayer of his and frustrates expression. In the twilight, evening is both a "nun" and "a girl slipping along the wall to meet her lover." [29] Mary becomes Magdalen, and the Mystical Rose of the Litany of the Holy Virgin is confused with the woman in Swinburne's poem "In the Orchard," who offers her lover "my flower, my first in June / My rose, so like a tender mouth it is." The frustrating collision of ideals with actualities, past dreams with present imperatives, and aspirations with their broken ends suggests that New Orleans as Faulkner conceived it in 1925 was not so much a place as a condition. The Tourist in the last of the *Double Dealer* pieces describes the city as a seductress, "And those who are not of the elect must stand forever without her portals" (NOS, 14). [30] By replacing "The Tourist" with the Oriental vignette "Hong Li" when he made *Royal Street*, Faulkner apparently was trying to make all of this relevant to his frustrated love for Estelle, who was then at Shanghai with her husband. But the bitter misogyny of the speaker at the end of the gift book only darkens an already dark world. [31]

Perhaps the completion of *Mosquitoes* in September brought on a period of depression like that Faulkner predicted he would suffer when he finished his story about the Luxembourg Gardens and death the previous year (SL, 17). Probably he knew in late October that Estelle was leaving Cornell Franklin and would come home expecting him to act on the love he had so long declared for her. Whatever the case, unlike the *Double Dealer* "New Orleans," the privately made version, with the Oriental postscript relating specifically to Estelle, is inherently reflexive, and the formality of the opening inscription, "To Estelle, a / Lady, with / Respectful Admiration," belies as it contrastingly intensifies the sexual fear and disgust of the closing piece. It is to images in Faulkner's own writing rather than to Wordsworth and Swinburne that Hong Li alludes when he says, "It is written that a man's senses are as bees which, while hiving the indiscriminate honey of his days, cement unawares the imperishable edifice of his soul." [32] The language most immediately recalls Faulkner's metaphor in praise of his lover's body in *Helen* V, "Proposal," where "the cloying cloudy bees / . . . hive her honeyed hips like little moons" (HAC, 116). *Helen* V predates Faulkner's courtship of Helen Baird by two years (HAC, 58): conceivably, it was written, in 1923, for Estelle. Five years later, in *The Sound and the Fury*, Faulkner drew on the poem again for two of Quentin Compson's most agonized sexual reveries. One of these is forecast in the *Royal Street* vignette when Hong Li argues that sensuality grows stale: "What matter if at times the honey seem oversweet to him, or seem to his inferior clay, bitter even? The honey's sweetness is but comparative: soon sweet becomes pallid and without taste; oversweet, but sweet; and at last bitterness strikes no responding chord and man is as a gorged reptile supine before the croaching rumor of worms." In this context, where Hong Li also describes the sullied soul as "a battened pig grunting and jaded in its own filth" and woman as "a little parcel of scented flesh, an articulation of minute worms," the same language that looks back in altered form to the celebrative 1923 poem seems also to look forward to Mr. Compson's description of women that haunts Quentin: "Because women so delicate so mysterious Father said. Delicate equilibrium of periodical filth between two moons balanced. Moons he said full and yellow as harvest moons her hips thighs. Outside outside of them always but. Yellow. Feet soles with walking like. Then to know that some man that all those mysterious and imperious concealed. With all that inside of them shapes an outward suavity waiting for a touch to. Liquid putrification like drowned things floating like pale rubber flabbily filled getting the odour of honeysuckle all mixed up" (SF, 159).[33] Hong Li's veneer of rationality covers attitudes all the more striking in a book and a vignette addressed personally to the woman Faulkner had loved and courted for years. The artistic detachment fostered in the novel by the subjective self-portrayals of the speakers is hardly possible in the private writing of the letterlike book, where the personal is so little distanced that the Receiver could not fail to see the Sender and herself intimately portrayed.

Much of the very personal material that is in *Royal Street,* and the mode and manner Faulkner chose to express it, might have been prompted by passages in *Mosquitoes* where Fairchild and the Semitic man link sex and death, art and excrement, in a series of perverse metaphors. In that book Faulkner ascribed his own poem, suitably titled "Hermaphroditus," to the poet Eva Wiseman and had Fairchild describe it as "a kind of dark perversion. Like a fire that don't need any fuel, that lives on its own heat" (Mos, 252). Faulkner's Oriental philosopher possesses the "voraciousness" that Fairchild says "makes an artist stand beside himself with a notebook in his hand always" (Mos, 320), but Hong Li lacks the emotional detachment of the poet in the concluding poem of *Helen*, for whom art supplants life. Hong Li's lost love shapes his contention that "happiness is as the orchid that rots the trunk to which it clings" and that bereavement is "a thing for unlettered beasts to lift yowling inarticulate faces to the remote contemplation of Cosmos." The enduring comforts of the written word are not for Hong Li. Were he pure reason, distanced from feeling and desire, he might say what Quentin imagines himself saying of sexual longing had he been born unmanned: "O That That's Chinese I dont know Chinese" (SF, 143). Accidental or not, the example is instructive. Hong Li *is* "Chinese," and he is troubled by the same frustrated longing that troubles Quentin and that troubled William Faulkner in the autumn of 1926 when he made Hong Li his epistolary persona in *Royal Street: New Orleans*. What Faulkner reveals of himself in that private text, he was working out also in the novel he began writing eighteen months later, of which he said, "When I began it I had no plan at all. I wasn't even writing a book." [34] In another version of this introduction to *The Sound and the Fury*, he included himself when he said of the southern writer that he "unconsciously writes into every line and phrase his violent despairs and rages and frustrations or his violent prophesies of still more violent hopes." [35]

The self-critical impulse enacted here is proposed by another of the theories put forth in *Mosquitoes*, this by the Semitic man, when he tells Fairchild, "A book is the writer's secret life, the dark twin of a man: you can't reconcile them" (Mos, 251). That also is true of all private autobiographical writing, including letters, and it applies particularly to the gift books, which are rooted in the letter as well as the literary canon, partaking of aspects of both. Neither *Helen: A Courtship* nor *Royal Street: New Orleans* was delivered promptly to the women it addresses with such urgency. Unmailed letters, rather than opening or continuing discourse, encapsulate images that mirror the letter writer to himself. Like diaries, in this sense, they are exercises in recording instead of transmitting thought and feeling, written less for self-expression than for self-contemplation. This produced different results in the two unmailed gift books because of the writer's different relationship to the women involved. Faulkner must have known in June of 1926 that Helen Baird was beyond his serious appeal, and he comforted himself by withdrawing into his art. But Estelle was on the verge of a divorce, and he addressed her in "Hong Li" in terms he had used in other gifts and gift books to describe the conflicting and irre-solvable demands on the artist of the ideal and the real woman. Noel Polk points out that Faulkner at one time intended to include in *The Marble Faun* a fragment from *The Marionettes* designed to introduce into the faun's garden a figure like Shade of Pierrot in the play, "a sen-sual human 'lover' to stand in direct complement to the rife fecundity of the nature around him, and therefore in direct contrast to the statue's own lifelessness. He was apparently to represent to the faun the same thing that the 'Shade' represents to the sleeping Pierrot, his own ideal of sexual vigor."[36] An earlier draft of the same material was written into the endpapers of Faulkner's copy of Ralph Hodgson's *Poems* sometime between 1917 and 1920. According to Judith Sensibar, it may have been written there for Estelle, and that book inscribed to her as Faulkner's copy of Swinburne was also intimately inscribed at about this time.[37] The lines in the Hodgson book read, in part:

> Your little feet have crossed my heart,
>     Love
> Your little white feet
> And I am a garden sprung beneath your footsteps
> And the world is throbbing for us
>     Love
> Beneath your little slender feet[38]

In 1920, Faulkner incorporated these lines, slightly abbreviated, into the seduction song of the Shade, and he inscribed a copy of the play for Estelle's infant daughter, addressing the mother through the child with a phrase used by the Shade to describe sexual union: "To 'CHO-CHO,' / A TINY FLOWER OF THE FLAME, THE / ETERNAL GES-TURE CHRYSTALLIZED; / THIS, A SHADOWY FUMBLING IN / WINDY DARKNESS, IS MOST RESPECTFULLY TENDERED" (Mar, 89).[39]

Six years later, in another book made for Estelle, Hong Li is troubled, and repelled, by insistent sexual images that draw on the same lan-guage. He says at the end of the sketch, "I root out and destroy the tares which her dead and delicate feet sowed across my heart, that my soul may be as a garden beyond the rumors of the world for the con-templation of the evening of my life. For it is written that sorrow is as the fire in which the sword is tempered, but that despair is an attribute of beasts. But Ehee, Ehee, her little feet." Whatever the comforts of art elsewhere in the canon of fiction and poems written at the time, neither art nor reasoned argument can compensate Hong Li for his lost love or permit him to put her aside. That failure, perhaps, is one source of the bitterness of the piece. Faulkner was addressing himself as artist to his disappointments as a man, and he found that he lacked the detachment either to accept his sorrow or to substitute for it an artifact of his own crafting. When he married Estelle two and a half years later, he expressed some of the same bitter ambivalence in a letter he wrote to Hal Smith, where he said, "I am going to be married. Both want to and have to. THIS PART IS CONFIDENTIAL, UTTERLY. For my honor and the sanity—I believe life—of a woman. . . . It's a situation which I engendered and permitted to ripen which has become unbearable, and I am tired of running from devilment I bring about. This sounds a little insane, but I'm not in any shape to write letters now." [40]

## [ iv ]

This conjunction of books and letters brings together in very private writing autobiographical material that Faulkner intended only for his Receivers, if in fact he *intended* it even for them. But biography is not its only interest. Both independently and together as a sequence, the gift books and associated writing show Faulkner in his fiction and poetry commenting on his fiction and poetry. In his work, as in that of his modernist contemporaries—Eliot and Joyce and Pound chief among them—self-portrayal and self-analysis of this kind take the form of literary self-criticism and may serve as a gauge of the writer's sense of his own development. His judgment of his work is implicit in the way he tells and revises and retells, the way he shapes and reshapes experiences and returns to what has been most valuable to him. It is implied in what he omits as well as includes, what he deletes as well as appends. In Faulkner's work such self-criticism is one aspect of the accretive process by which Yoknapatawpha County itself took significant form. To this self-conscious process, letters and letterlike private writing are particularly relevant. Faulkner wrote about his writing in letters to agents and publishers, he wrote forewords and introductions to books where he addressed himself personally to his reader, and of course he used letters in novels as modes of serious, sometimes parodic, self-judgment. The means by which letter writers portray themselves and their text in letters, their salutations and signatures, scenes of writing and reading, and the calculated selection and arrangement of details in a series of letters, where what is left out is as important as what is put in—all of this is inherently self-analytic. In letter discourse, even the time a letter writer permits to elapse after receiving mail is a significant commentary on the answering text. Falling as they do into the space between the two canons, the gift books of 1926 address artistic as well as personal matters, often in ways adopted from work either written for publication originally or amended for it later. In this literary sense of self-criticism, each successive version of an image, a character, or a situation is potentially a comment on and a criticism of each preceding one. Such patterns exist, of course, in the various manuscript drafts of a given text, and in the language and events of individual books, and they can be traced in the entire corpus of a writer's work. Regardless of the scope of the pattern, repetition confirms lines of development that revision redirects.

In the mid-1920s especially, Faulkner's concern with aesthetic form and his own authority as author found expression in private writing and published work employing the same language and infused with the same self-imagery. The pattern formed by the textual antecedents to *Royal Street: New Orleans,* and especially to "Hong Li," is instructive. Work originated as poetry was transformed in subject matter, in language, and even in genre as it first was prepared for publication then appropriated for a letterly text. In the process, the distance between the personal self of the writer and the portrayed self altered according to the form and intended function of the writing. The pattern begins with the manuscript sonnet "New Orleans," signed "William Faulkner / Oxford / 30 October 1924." The subject of the poem is the city of the title. The force of its attraction is sexual.

> The moon of summer wanes, and she is old.
> The poppy's breath is hers, the poppy's red
> Her subtle mouth kissed oft and close. Her head
> Her ravened weary wings of hair enfold.

> The virgin's hair is neither brown nor gold.
> Neither, blanching, has her life-blood sped
> To be kissed back: no lover's lying dead
> Within her breast that's white and steep and cold.

> Within this garden, Life, with breath for wall,
> Who has not served his day, since day began?
> Where breathes he who has not found that all

Who break her spell to seek youth for a span
Return to her, importunate for thrall,
When she smiles across her languid fan?[41]

The existence of this poem, and possibly one other called "Mary Magdalen," confirms the speculation that Faulkner brought with him to
the city at least part of the impressive amount of writing that he had
almost immediately available for publication in New Orleans in January 1925.[42] He drew on some details of the "Mary Magdalen" poem for
the tenth of the *Double Dealer* vignettes, "Magdalen"; the "New Orleans" poem he recast in its entirety into prose for the tailpiece of the
sequence, "The Tourist." The city he describes there, like the city in
the sonnet, is "a courtesan, not old and yet no longer young" who
dwells in twilight (NOS, 13), and her power over the imagination of
the Tourist is expressed in the language of the sonnet. His monologue
ends, "New Orleans . . . a courtesan whose hold is strong upon the
mature, to whose charm the young must respond. And all who leave
her, seeking the virgin's unbrown, ungold hair and her blanched and
icy breast where no lover has died, return to her when she smiles
across her languid fan. . . . New Orleans" (NOS, 14). In October 1926,
when he revised and copied the sequence of vignettes for Estelle,
Faulkner replaced "The Tourist" with "Hong Li," retaining the prose
monologue form of the first piece but looking to other sources for language that more closely accorded with his more personal subject matter. As Hong Li perversely reveals, the real woman holds the same attraction for him that the city does for the Tourist. Darkly transformed
by imagery of sexual disgust, the conflict between reason and desire
inspired by Estelle still is analogous to the conflicting attractions for
the Tourist of the virgin and Mary Magdalen.

Put another way, the 1924 sonnet and the "New Orleans" vignette
published in the *Double Dealer* describe a city as a sensual woman;
*Mayday* and *Helen: A Courtship* idealize an absent woman as an inaccessible vision and a dream; and *Royal Street: New Orleans* reclaims the
context of the darkened city in the published sequence for a meditation on a second absent woman, Estelle, still compellingly and disturbingly present to the imagination. To this progression of letterlike
books, Faulkner's work on *Mosquitoes* in the winter, spring, and early
summer of 1926 was central, for the novel comments critically on
strategies of personal accommodation to art and life that he was employing there and in his private writing. Like *Mayday*, *Mosquitoes* is
dedicated to Helen Baird, and the Semitic man implicitly is speaking
both of Sir Galwyn's drowning himself and of Faulkner's writing *Mayday* and the novel when he says, "you don't commit suicide when you

are disappointed in love. You write a book" (Mos, 228). In *Helen* it is that conclusion, rather than the one Sir Galwyn chooses, that occurs when the poet "Bill" translates his grief into poetry; but in *Royal Street* neither death nor a curative art suffices for Hong Li, and his bitter misogyny constitutes a nasty corrective to the sequence of writing, private and published, that goes before it in this pattern.

How essential Faulkner found such private writing, with its autobiographical representations and letterly intensities, is apparent in the use to which it was put at a succeeding stage in his developing art. In January 1927, Estelle returned permanently to Oxford with her children and instituted divorce proceedings against Cornell Franklin. The period following, Faulkner told his French translator Maurice Coindreau, was a time of "intimate difficulties" [43]—with his writing, when *Flags in the Dust* was rejected by Horace Liveright, and apparently also in his personal life, in his ambiguous relationship with Estelle. In 1928, when he began work on the novel he at first called "Twilight," Faulkner recombined elements from *Royal Street* and the *Helen* poems for his more profoundly imagined portrait of Quentin's relationship with Caddy, which Quentin resolves in the way that Sir Galwyn does his with "Little sister Death" in *Mayday*. By extension, this too is self-critical: realigned for the novel, personal images from the letter books are retained for their generative power and force of expression in the portrayal of another fictional persona. Faulkner once asked Joan Williams to address her letters to him to Quentin Compson, General Delivery, Oxford:[44] he told Jean Stein, "Ishmael is the witness in *Moby-Dick* as I am Quentin in *The Sound and the Fury*."[45] The point is not that Faulkner *is* Quentin Compson, but that he found in the most intimate aspects of his own life and art the way to conceive and portray Quentin.[46] In a favorite phrase of his, Faulkner had spoken of *Mayday*, in his inscription to Helen Baird, as "a fumbling in darkness" (M, 45), and a "fumbling" the little book decidedly is: a fumbling for detachment with a personal love experience, a fumbling too with an allegorical form that would not quite fit his need. In 1928 as he worked on *The Sound and the Fury* he was working to resolve some of the same kinds of problems. In the transforming contexts of that first masterwork, his difficulties of 1926 and the gift books where he had tried to express them came also under his self-critical eye, taking expressive shape in Quentin's sufferings, "antic and perverse mocking without relevance inherent themselves with the denial of the significance they should have affirmed" (SF, 211).

Faulkner quotes *Mayday* and *Helen* and *Royal Street* in *The Sound and the Fury*. And his earliest attempts at shaping that material to his need are recalled, if not directly assessed, by the pervasive motif in the novel of interlocking frustrations with language and sex. None of the three Compson brothers can speak or perform an act of love. Benjy's "trying to say" to the Burgess girl, for example, is motivated by a heightened memory of Caddy and punished by castration (SF, 64). Quentin associates Caddy with sex and sex with Negroes: he asks, "*Why must you do like nigger women do in the pasture the ditches the dark woods hot hidden furious in the dark woods*" (SF, 113–114). He thinks of Negroes as "a sort of obverse reflection of . . . white people" (SF, 106), yet his own speaking voice mocks him with repressed images of his secret and frustrated longing: in Massachusetts he is said to speak, himself, "like they do in minstrel shows. . . . he talks like a coloured man" (SF, 148). Jason's neurotic insistence on "what I say" (SF, 223ff.) is confounded by his failure to say anything in answer to Lorraine's love letter: he imagines himself impotent at the end of the novel (SF, 383), and he links impotence to literary expression when he borrows a cliché about the American novel to describe Benjy as "the Great American Gelding" (SF, 328). It is one of the achievements of *The Sound and the Fury* that it in fact affirms its vitality by repetitions and modifications such as these. Recurring in each section to the problem of self-expression, Faulkner made each section of the novel a commentary on each of the other sections—including the final one, which reasserts authorial authority, and even the "Appendix: Compson," which he added fifteen years later. Like the title of the novel, with its paradoxical appeal to Shakespearean symmetries, Faulkner's historical "Appendix" and his retrospective judgments of the book in the 1933 introductions are stages in a progressive structure of self-criticisms that comment on the achieved splendors and splendid failures of the novel and its antecedents.

Of course Faulkner was drawing on more than his gifts of love when he wrote those, with other work, into "June Second 1910." *Elmer*, *Flags in the Dust*, and assorted stories and sketches are among his resources. To several of the self-images in these he returned as Yoknapatawpha County evolved from book to book into a fictional cosmos, revising and expanding early personae in terms of present imperatives, inventing new ones, and dismissing those no longer suited to his need. A sketch called "Afternoon of a Cow" in 1937 parodied the youthful romanticism of his 1919 poem "L'Apres-Midi d'une Faune" as well as the faun persona adopted then and held to through the mid-1920s in his letters and in *Mayday* and *Helen*. He purged himself of his other *Mayday* persona in the mid-1930s also, in a long story crafted from his Paris novel and called "A Portrait of Elmer." [47] In some respects the story is as much autobiography as the drawing of the faun and the painting of the knight in *Mayday* are self-portraits: it brings forward unchanged from the unfinished novel events from Faulkner's European trip, including his visit to the Forest of Meudon described to Maud Falkner in a letter on August 30, 1925. In the story, but not in the novel, Elmer Hodge drives to a "blue hill" at Meudon and there paints "a picture of three trees and an inferior piece of an inferior river" (USWF, 638, 632). In 1926, within a month of his return from Paris, Faulkner had painted nearly the same picture for Helen's book. The third watercolor in *Mayday* shows a knight and his lady arm-in-arm in an enchanted forest: it is a night scene, with a blue hill, three trees, and a piece of a river. Elmer's fictional picture parodies the romantic picture in Faulkner's fiction. About to be reunited with his own lady in the story, Elmer is beset not with a sexual nor even an artistic frenzy but with an intestinal flux; he uses his painting neither to court Myrtle Monson nor to gain himself fame but to wipe his bottom. The excrement on his canvas puts Elmer into his picture also, but not as a knight: the ironic self-portrait, produced by his own hand, is the only pictorial "portrait of Elmer" in the story of that title, a comic retrospective on the picture in *Mayday*, the persona pictured there, and the romantic idealism that had inspired them in 1926. Faulkner had said in sketches and letters in 1925 that Cézanne "dipped his brush in light" (NOS, 46; SL, 24), and he had emulated Cézanne in his letter book, even to painting there the Forest of Meudon where Cézanne lived and painted. Now he dismissed those self-images, dipping his figurative brush elsewhere than in light in an act of literary self-criticism that scourged idealized love and love affairs and blotted an intimate persona of the artist from his work.

# III. Integrated Letters

"I must pore out on paper must talk"—Byron Snopes, *Flags in the Dust*, 244

## [i]

In February of 1927 Faulkner was engaged in writing the fifth novel he had begun, and the third he would finish, since he began work on *Soldiers' Pay* in the winter of 1925.[1] By the time that novel was delivered to his new publisher, Harcourt, Brace and Company, in late 1928, he had finished another. "Well, I'm going to be published by white folks now," he wrote Mrs. McLean from New York in October 1928. "Harcourt Brace & Co bought me from Liveright. Much, much nicer there. Book will be out in Feb. Also another one, the damndest book I ever read. I dont believe anyone will publish it for 10 years. Harcourt swear they will, but I dont believe it" (SL, 41). *Sartoris* was published January 31, 1929, heavily cut and revised from the typescript of *Flags in the Dust*, and *The Sound and the Fury* appeared the following October from his third publisher, Cape and Smith. An edition of *Flags* was issued by Random House in 1973. Whether as *Sartoris* or *Flags in the Dust*, the novel rightly is considered a turning point in Faulkner's career, the end product of his apprenticeship in the novel and the beginning book of the Yoknapatawpha County cycle. Looking back thirty years later he would say of *Sartoris* that it had "the germ of my apocrypha in it."[2] It was the point, he told Jean Stein in the famous *Paris Review* interview in 1955, where he discovered "that my own little postage stamp of native soil was worth writing about and that I would never live long enough to exhaust it, and by sublimating the actual into apocryphal I would have complete liberty to use whatever talent I might have to its absolute top. It opened up a gold mine of other peoples, so I created a cosmos of my own. I can move these people around like God, not only in space but in time too."[3] Yet *Flags in the Dust* signifies no break with the large canon of writing that went before it. As so often is the case with Faulkner's writing, one has the sense that every surge forward involved his circling into the canons of his published and unpublished writing, in all of the genres in which he had worked, including even his letters. If it is true that Sherwood Anderson advised him, "You have to have somewhere to start from: then you begin to learn" (ESPL, 8), it is certain that he took that to mean more than a geographical place to start from. In the months that he worked on *Flags in the Dust* he was looking back in a number of ways that drove the book forward: back to the generative legends of his family and region, of course, but back also to the book he had begun in late 1926 and called *Father Abraham*, where he invented the Snopeses; back to *Elmer* and *Mosquitoes* for the relationship between brothers and sisters, among other things; and farther back still to forms he had experimented with and motifs he had used in *Soldiers' Pay*, and to the language of sketches and poems and fragments of writing he had used and re-used before that.

As he worked, his enthusiasm for the new project and his growing confidence in himself spilled into his letters, where he likewise looked back to familiar epistolary personae as well as forward to new ones. It was Faulkner the provincial country poet who thanked Liveright for his gift of the books that "give me a good start on the library I hope to own some day. (I possess no books at all, you see)" (SL, 34). Writing in the next month to William Stanley Braithwaite about a royalty due him for *The Marble Faun*, he assumed the same guise to appeal for fair play to that representative of the eastern literary establishment. "It never occurred to me," he told the famous poet-anthologist, "that anyone would rob a poet. It's like robbing a whore or a child" (SL, 35). The "child" was then nearly thirty years of age. But it was Faulkner the southern aristocrat who told Liveright that February, "I envy you England. England is 'ome to me, in a way" (SL, 34). In that letter he agreed to editorial deletions in *Mosquitoes* and announced, "I am working now on two things at once: a novel, and a collection of short stories of my townspeople" (SL, 34). When he sent Liveright the novel in October, he called it "the damdest best book you'll look at this year, and any other publisher." But even that valuation was couched in the context of the novels he had published before. "At last and certainly," he proclaimed, "as El Orens' sheik said, I have written THE book, of which those other things were but foals" (SL, 38). T. E. Lawrence's sheik says that of a Hadley-Page bomber parked among smaller fighter planes in Lawrence's *Revolt in the Desert*,[4] and the allusion suggests Faulkner's estimation of the size of his accomplishment. *Flags in the Dust* was mature work, and a sign of his own maturity and his growth as a novelist from *Soldiers' Pay* and *Mosquitoes*. That sense of himself and all of the writing that had gone into it were put at risk when Liveright rejected the manuscript. Where Faulkner saw progress and growth, Liveright saw a falling away from achievements of the recent past. What was particularly damaging about his valuation was that he too looked back.

> Soldiers' Pay was a very fine book and should have done better. Then Mosquitoes wasn't quite as good, showed little development in your spiritual growth and I think none in your art of writing. Now comes Flags in the Dust and we're frankly very much disappointed by it. It is diffuse and non-integral with neither very much plot development nor character development. We think it lacks plot, dimension and projection. The story really doesn't get anywhere and has a thousand loose ends. If the book had plot and structure, we might suggest shortening and revisions but it is so diffuse that I don't think this would be any use. My chief objection is that you don't seem to have any story to tell and I contend that a novel should tell a story and tell it well.[5]

There followed a desultory correspondence about money, and rights to the manuscript, with Faulkner insisting, "I still believe it is the book which will make my name for me as a writer" (SL, 39). Other publishers followed Liveright in rejecting the book, and early in 1928 Faulkner began extensive revisions. But by March he had started on *The Sound and the Fury*, which he was calling "Twilight." The turn homeward to his "little postage stamp of native soil" was accompanied now by a dramatic turn inward, and he used another significantly epistolary reference to describe that change when he wrote in 1933 that "one day it suddenly seemed as if a door had clapped silently and forever to between me and all publishers' addresses and booklists and I said to myself, Now I can write. Now I can just write."[6]

The *Flags* correspondence deserves careful attention, for elements of it and of the persona Faulkner assumed in his letters to Liveright found their way into *The Sound and the Fury*. But it first must be said that Faulkner was engaged in an enterprise with *Flags in the Dust* considerably different than what he had attempted in earlier work. This was nothing less than a search for a form in which to cast a world of his own. Inserted letters and analogous oral narratives subjectively founded offered one means of verifying the multiplicitous cosmos reflexively, from within.

In an introduction to *Sartoris* drafted about two years after its publication, Faulkner wrote that he had tried "by main strength to recreate between the covers of a book the world . . . I was already preparing to lose and regret," that he had refused to have anything to do with its editing when told "that the book lacked any form whatever,"[7]

and that he understood how well he had accomplished his first purpose only when he saw the cut version:

> I realised for the first time that I had done better than I knew and
> the long work I had had to create opened before me and I felt myself
> surrounded by the limbo in which the shady visions, the host which
> stretched half formed, waiting each with its portion of that veri-
> similitude which is to bind into a whole the world which for some
> reason I believe should not pass utterly out of the memory of man,
> and I contemplated those shady but ingenious shapes by reason of
> whose labor I might reaffirm the impulses of my own ego in this
> actual world without stability, with a lot of humbleness, and I specu-
> lated on time and death and wondered if I had invented the world to
> which I should give life or if it had invented me, giving me an illu-
> sion of greatness[.] [8]

By the time Faulkner drafted this introduction, three other Yoknapatawpha County novels and the stories in *These 13* already had extended the scope of the "long work" posited in *Flags*. If this permitted
him to write with some confidence of making a world, he had imagined still more of it that as yet was unwritten. Phil Stone remembered
in 1957 that "the core of the Snopes legend was an idea I gave Bill
back in the 20's, after *Mosquitoes* was written and before *Sartoris* was
written" (LDB-II, 207): that dating corresponds precisely to the composition of *Father Abraham* in late 1926, which itself was the germinal
book of the Snopes trilogy. "I thought of the whole story at once,"
Faulkner said of the trilogy at the University of Virginia, "like a bolt of
lightning lights up a landscape and you see everything but it takes
time to write it." [9] It was not only *Flags in the Dust*, then, but the fictional world of which *Flags* was to be a part that confronted Faulkner
as the novel began to take shape. That world took a great deal of time
to write indeed, and it underwent a number of transformations as
Faulkner's art developed and evolved. In the *Sartoris* introduction he
recalled Ben Wasson's telling him when he edited the book, "you had
about 6 books in here. You were trying to write them all at once." [10] One
way and another those books and others were sorted out, and he came
to understand, as he told Jean Stein, that "not only each book had to
have a design but the whole output or sum of an artist's work had
to have a design." [11] *Flags* was a beginning. [12]

Yet *Flags in the Dust* initiated a search for expressive form that never
was finished. Hugh Kenner undoubtedly is right when he says,

"Faulkner's root need was not to symbolize (a condensing device) but to expand, expand: to commence with the merest glimpse and by way of wringing out its significance arrange voices and viewpoints, interpolate past chronicles, account for just this passion in just this ancillary passion, and tie the persons together, for the sake of intimacy, intensity, plausibility, with ties of blood and community and heritage."[13] The problem, Faulkner told a questioner at Virginia, "is to make imagination and the pattern conform, meet, be amicable, we'll say. And when one has to give, I believe it's always the pattern that has to give."[14] It was pattern, or patternlessness, that troubled Horace Liveright when he called *Flags* "diffuse and non-integral." But it is clear even in the edition of *Flags in the Dust* edited in 1973 from Faulkner's heavily revised typescript that he was working initially toward some of the methods of organization and expansion that Kenner describes. He was experimenting with fictional form, unsuccessfully in the editorial judgment of Horace Liveright—of whom Faulkner reportedly said, he "should have probably been a stockbroker or something,—anything rather than a purveyor of creative literature."[15] What is clear is that it was the method more than the material of *Flags* that differed so dramatically from the previous books of his that Liveright had published. After all, Horace Liveright could hardly have known in the autumn of 1927 that Jefferson, in Yoknapatawpha County, Mississippi, in the end would be any more significant as a place to tell a story than Donald Mahon's Charlestown, Georgia. It was lack of story he objected to, not lack of differentiated place, although the place would prove crucial to the stories set there. God, we remember, created Eden before he made Adam and Eve.

What is apparent now is that Yoknapatawpha County was not only a place but also a way to tell stories.[16] No doubt the South gave Faulkner a pattern to work from, but for all of its many connectives in his Mississippi, Faulkner's Yoknapatawpha County was shaped from novel to novel and story to story to accommodate specific imaginative imperatives of his own. He was speaking of his attempts to reconcile meaning and form when he told Jean Stein in 1955, "Life is motion" and "the aim of every artist is to arrest motion, which is life, by artificial means and hold it fixed so that 100 years later when a stranger looks at it, it moves again since it is life." Form, he was saying, is both the means by which the motion of life is artificially arrested and the vehicle by which the fictional approximation of that motion is conveyed. Insofar as it is a region of the imagination created in fiction, Yoknapatawpha County itself is just such a form, and Faulkner typically spoke of it in formal terms, calling it a "design" and describing it as a "keystone in the Universe." [17] It is at once *the* form in which the fictions are set and *a* form created within each work. It embodies and projects from within the apocryphal standards of time and place that impact on the characters who create them. In *Flags in the Dust*, the stories told by old man Will Falls, Miss Jenny Du Pre, and Simon Strother take their shapes not from actual history, nor even from southern versions of actual history, but from the apocryphal history of the fictional world as Faulkner imagined and made it. As narrators of that history, such characters become the fictional makers of Yoknapatawpha itself. As believers in that history, they render it legend. As reenactors of their own legends, they affirm themselves the creatures of what they create. In Miss Jenny's story of Carolina Bayard's and Jeb Stuart's raid on Pope's supplies, for example, Faulkner himself tells us that her interpretation is a romantic fabrication: what had been "a hair-brained prank of two heedless and reckless boys" becomes, in her telling, the tragic and gallant story of "two angels valiantly and glamorously fallen and strayed" (Flags, 12). But Faulkner also validates her interpretation when he adopts her metaphor and describes Stuart and Bayard as "two flaming stars garlanded with Fame's burgeoning laurel and the myrtle and roses of Death, incalculable and sudden as meteors" (Flags, 13); and her auditors affirm its validity when, from their point of view, "Bayard Sartoris' brief career [sweeps] like a shooting star across the dark plain of their mutual remembering and suffering, lighting it with a transient glare like a soundless thunder-clap, leaving a sort of radiance when it died" (Flags, 19). Belied by actual fact, the reality of the apocryphal tale is asserted in the same imagery by the author, his character, and her listeners: when young Bayard wakens from dreams of Johnny's death in a flaming plane to stare in despair at the "black and savage stars" (Flags, 240), he too is shown to be under the spell of the Sartoris legends, and that is confirmed by the manner of his own death in a fall from the sky. Unlike Donald Mahon, Bayard Sartoris is not wounded by the war but by surviving it, and his death is a propitiatory gesture to the legends by which he lives.

More even than similarities to actual Mississippi scenes and situations, it is reflexive forms such as these that have tended to give Yoknapatawpha County a life of its own. Within the fiction, the county is self-defining and self-sustaining. It can be mapped, as Faulkner himself mapped it, and even satisfactorily superimposed on the map of Lafayette County, but it is an aesthetic not a geographical construct. It takes as many forms as the characters who create it endow it with and assumes as many functions in their lives as the ways in which they choose to employ it. Any one of those characters might ask with

Faulkner himself whether he had invented his world or it him, but none with more reason than those few who write the world with him from within in notes and letters.

## [ ii ]

Chief among these characters in *Flags in the Dust* is Byron Snopes. Four of his six amatory letters to Narcissa Benbow are fully transcribed there, and his secret writing bears directly on Faulkner and his fiction. Byron is parodically literary to begin with, one perhaps with the children Faulkner said were named in the late 1800s after the heroes and heroines of romantic literature "and the even more romantic creators of them" (ESPL, 179). As frustrated writer and lover named for the poet of *Don Juan*, he employs a boy named Virgil to copy the letters he sends to the sister of Horace, and bride of Bayard, herself named out of Ovid. He is a "book-keeper" (Flags, 71). His compulsion to "pore out on paper" his love for Narcissa (Flags, 244) is very like Julian Lowe's need to sit in his barren room "putting my thoughts down on paper" (SP, 278) for Margaret Powers. Indeed, *Flags* recurs to a number of significant character types and situations of that first book: wounded aviators returning to small southern towns in the spring of 1919, disrupted marriage plans, disappointed seductions, and doomed heroes.[18] And letters. Byron's ungrammatical letters to an inaccessible woman essentially rewrite Cadet Lowe's: his early letters, like Lowe's, are shared with a second party, and his correspondence ceases abruptly when Narcissa, like Margaret Powers, marries a doomed RAF veteran. Both letter writers have another girl who refuses to submit to them, and both work in banks. Biographically, the bank where Byron keeps books and writes letters is modeled on the First National Bank of Oxford where Faulkner clerked for his grandfather in 1916 and no doubt wrote his poems on the bank's time. Byron's coded letters are addressed to an agent who bears Maud Falkner's maiden name, Butler (Flags, 99). Like Snopes himself, Snopes' letters mark an advance in letter writing and its function in the novel over Julian Lowe and his letters to Margaret. Narcissa is intimately depicted in his letters as an object of desire: "Your big eyes your black hair how white your black hair will make you look. And how you walk I am watching you and a smell you give off like a flowr. Your eyes shine with mystry and how you walk makes me sick like a fever all night thinking how you walk" (Flags, 243). Snopes himself is an immediately felt presence in his letters: "I can tell you something you will be surprised I know more than watch you walk down the street with cloths. I will some day you will not be surprised then. You pass me you do not know it I know it. You will know it some day. Be cause I will tell you" (Flags, 100). The letters themselves signify reciprocated desire: "You kept my letter but you do not anser. That is a good sign you do . . . not forget me you would not keep it" (Flags, 99). And even when response is impossible, the Receiver's failure to write in return is portrayed as a broken obligation: "You do not answer. I know you got it I saw one in your hand. You better answer soon I am a desprate man eat up with fever I can not sleep for. I will not hurt you but I am desprate. Do not forget I will not hurt you but I am a desprate man" (Flags, 244).

Readers in Oxford might find ironic traces of Faulkner in Snopes—more, perhaps, than in Lowe—but he and his letter writing are less patently self-portraying than was the case in *Soldiers' Pay*. Faulkner had grown as a writer by writing, whatever Horace Liveright might think, and he had come to know letters as a genre as he had come to know novels. Snopes' letters, and Horace Benbow's and the several others in *Flags*, may be, as in *Soldiers' Pay*, a means of testing and affirming authorial authority. But they are more fully and successfully integrated in *Flags in the Dust*. Faulkner gave close attention there to transcribing, describing, and detailing the impact of his characters' writing, and he gave them some of the epistolary understanding he had acquired and was practicing himself. Horace Benbow knows, with Belle Mitchell, "that letters are only good to bridge intervals between actions" (Flags, 157), and he writes letters accordingly; but Faulkner uses his and others' letters as a fully developed dimension for counterpoint in a novel so thoroughly counterpointed that nearly every interval and action are doubled. He not only was experimenting with fictional devices in *Flags*, as he had in *Soldiers' Pay*, but was actively testing the limits of narrative itself. As his conception of the human heart in conflict drew him increasingly beyond the limits of a single story set at a single time and place, the demands on his craftsmanship increased proportionately. The more multifaceted his vision of a story, the more he sought for devices and techniques by which to express it within the confines of a single pattern. The explosion of imagination that took place in 1926–27 is indicative of the scope of his problem as artist, and Yoknapatawpha County provided him his long-term solution. The several stories in the story of *Flags in the Dust* were an early way of creating the sense of simultaneity he sought for his fictional world and a start at the job of controlling it. Multiple narration soon would follow, and both techniques were carried forward into the canon. But from *Soldiers' Pay* onward he worked with writers in his fiction, as well, and letter writers and their letters continued to serve him.

Writing about writing in *Flags*, Faulkner used letters to define poles of inarticulacy. Snopes disguises "the flowing Spencerian hand he had been taught in a Memphis business college" (Flags, 94) with Virgil Beard's "neat, copy-book hand" (Flags, 99); his miswritten letters say things unclearly that Narcissa will not admit she clearly understands. Horace Benbow's florid letters are incomprehensible in their meaning and form: Narcissa "had always found Horace's writing difficult, and parts that she could decipher meant nothing" (Flags, 351). The forms and the formal conventions of letter writing are tested in the novel as well. Bayard abandons all private expression when he abandons his family, sending postcards rather than sealed letters, and a wire for money from Mexico City "that was the last intimation he gave that he contemplated being at any stated place long enough for a communication to reach him" (Flags, 347). Horace uses a wire as a letter with no better success in communicating with Narcissa. She says of his telegram "over fifty words long" that "it was such an incoherent message . . . Horace never could say anything clearly from a distance" (Flags, 27, 28). Extremes of adherence to letter conventions are no less expressive than departures from them. When Jeb Stuart raids General Pope's supplies, for example, he leaves a letter as a formal caller might. "Scribbled hastily upon a scrap of paper," the medium of the message belies the convention just as the circumstance of the writing does the sentiment expressed: "General Stuart's compliments to General Pope," Stuart writes, "and he is sorry to have missed him again. He will call again tomorrow" (Flags, 17). Similarly, Snopes demands answers to anonymous letters that bear no return address, and they ironically trouble Narcissa most intimately because they are unsigned. In the related Sartoris story "There Was a Queen," she proposes an illicit sexual liaison to retrieve not letters she wrote but the anonymous ones she received.

That Faulkner used letters in these ways is clear evidence he was coming to understand and appreciate the inherent potential of the letter as form. As he refined his epistolary sense writing *Flags*, his personal correspondence shaped and was shaped by his fiction. In an indecipherable letter to his sister, whom he apostrophizes with his "one almost perfect vase of clear amber . . . as Thou still unravished bride of quietude" (Flags, 162), Horace says of her that "I seem to be unified and projected upon one single and very definite object, which is something to be said for me, after all" (Flags, 339). His ideal of Narcissa helps him survive the emotional torments of spring. Writing to Mrs. McLean in the spring of 1928, the second spring since he had begun *Flags*, Faulkner told his aunt that the manuscript was "almost incoherent" and that he was a "little weary of it." He looked forward to seeing her, however. "I have something—someone, I mean—to show you," he said. "Of course it's a woman. I would like to see you taken with her utter charm, and intrigued by her utter shallowness. Like a lovely vase. It isn't even empty, but is filled with something—well, a yeast cake in water is the nearest simile that occurs to me. She gets the days passed for me, though. Thank God I've got no money, or I'd marry her. So you see, even Poverty looks after its own" (LDB-II, 8). The language of his letter is close enough to the letter in the novel to suggest a relationship between the two, whichever came first. If the analogy of "a yeast cake in water" is unclear with relation to Estelle, the ostensible subject of Faulkner's letter to Mrs. McLean, it does describe Narcissa, who is pregnant when Horace writes to her. Conceivably, Faulkner also had his own letter and his incoherent manuscript in mind when he wrote that "Horace's pen ceased and he gazed at the sheet scrawled over with his practically illegible script, while the words he had just written echoed yet in his mind with a little gallant and whimsical sadness" (Flags, 339). Words echo in just this way from novel to novel, of course, and as writing—particularly as contemporaneous writing—letters are as receptive to fictional language as they are suggestive of it and of internal fictional forms. Whatever the crossings between the two—and there are a number of them—it was integrated form Faulkner was seeking, and to a considerable degree succeeded in finding, as he worked with the letters of *Flags*.

The placement, the content, and the description of Horace's letter to Narcissa that opens Chapter Five of *Flags* all suggest that Faulkner was trying to use it to bring that aspect of his multiple narrative to closure. Thematically, the letters Horace writes every other day bridge an extended interval between actions forbidden a brother and sister: the incest represented in Chapter Three, 9, when Horace visits Narcissa in her bedroom and announces he will marry Belle Mitchell. His caresses there are unreturned, but his marriage and departure from Jefferson make possible an epistolary relationship that grants him access to a forbidden woman through writing in the way that his letters to a married woman did during the war. His letter is a surrogate for sexual intimacy with Narcissa, and Horace thinks of it in those terms when he puts it on the mail train: "He looked back and saw the cars slide past, gaining speed, carrying his letter away and the quiet, the intimacy the writing and the touching of it, had brought him" (Flags, 344). Horace is married to Belle, but their "rented frame house" (Flags, 346) is like a house of assignation; Narcissa is his Platonic lover, but she is so tangibly present in his letters that writing itself is described as an illicit act: Horace conceives of the words he has written as "washing one woman's linen in the house of another" (Flags, 340). In this circumstance his letter acquires a life of its own: the letter *becomes* Narcissa and he, the letter writer, her postcoital lover, resting after his exertions. "A thin breeze blew suddenly into the room; there was locust upon it, faintly sweet, and beneath it the paper stirred upon the desk, rousing him; and suddenly, as a man waking, he looked at his watch and replaced it and wrote rapidly" (Flags, 340). What he writes to his sister now is news of his new home with his wife and her daughter, but like a man returning home from an illicit love affair, he dissembles. He realizes that "though one can lie about others with ready and extemporaneous promptitude, to lie about oneself requires deliberation and a careful choice of expression," and he therefore scratches out the unfinished lie, "I believe that Harry" and concludes with an easy lie about Belle: "Belle sends love, O Serene" (Flags, 341). That lie echoes accusingly in his mind as he bears his letter to the train and returns home with Belle's shrimp: "Belle sends love Belle sends Ah, well, we all respond to strings. And She would understand, it and the necessity for it, the dreadful need; She in her serene aloofness partaking of gods Belle sends" (Flags, 344). His interior monologue owes a formal debt to Leopold Bloom and *Ulysses*, but Faulkner characteristically turned his source back on itself, doubling the irony of the allusion. Like Bloom, Horace returns home to an adulteress with "ghosts in her bed" (Flags, 347), but it is he who as the adulterer and she who claims he "lied lied took me away from my husband" (Flags, 346–347). He thinks of his marriage to Belle as "obscene"—"giving him nothing, taking nothing away from him" (Flags, 347)—but he thinks of it also as a violation of his Platonic love for his sister: just as he betrays Belle now by writing letters to Narcissa, it was his relation to Narcissa that he betrayed with Belle. Faulkner chose an appropriately epistolary image to suggest that, one fully commensurate with Horace's sense of Narcissa and with the nature of his letters to her: "to Narcissa," he realizes, "in her home where her serenity lingered grave and constant and steadfast as a diffused and sourceless light, [his marriage] was an adolescent scribbling on the walls of a temple" (Flags, 347). The desecrated temple recalls Narcissa as well as the institution of marriage, and the "adolescent scribbling" indicts the self-serving letters Horace writes in a nearly unreadable scrawl. Placed as it is at the end of the novel, the letter and the scene of self-contemplation it prompts bring Horace's part in *Flags in the Dust* to a close, although typically nothing is resolved. The division into man and man-writing is a familiar motif in Faulkner's personal and fictional letters, but the man-as-writing whom Horace creates as his personae is lodged in an unreadable text.

*Flags* is constituted of similar ironic divisions, and the several love stories in particular interlock through letters like this one. The division in the letter writer that paralyzes expression complements the juxtaposition of words of love with concomitant acts—of letters with lovers. The pattern is pervasive; its recurrence in scene after scene of the book suggests Faulkner's attempts to achieve balanced form as his story expanded and expanded. Thus Horace finds a love letter from Belle in his pocket on the night when he alienates Narcissa: both he and the letter smell of Belle's perfume, both Belle and the letter are "dirty" and dirty him (Flags, 190). On the day Belle's sister Joan leaves his bed, Horace receives a second letter from Belle that he leaves unopened (Flags, 299). It is a letter from Snopes that Horace comes to Narcissa's room to deliver when he tells her he is marrying Belle (Flags, 243), and Byron's last letter to Narcissa is generated by her engagement to Bayard (Flags, 248–253). In his own letter to Narcissa, Horace alludes to "Byron's ladies' mouths" (Flags, 339) in *Don Juan*, unwittingly recalling the letter from Byron Snopes that he delivered, where Snopes writes of "your lips like cupids bow when the day comes when I will press them to mine like I dreamed like a fever from heaven to hell" (Flags, 244). With Snopes, and with Horace in their linked circumstance, bad letter writing is rendered morally bad, and the sense that writing is potentially corruptive extends to Narcissa's letter reading. Miss Jenny says of the anonymous letter Narcissa shares with her, "You want to keep it . . . Just like a young fool of a woman, to be flattered over a thing like this" (Flags, 59).[19]

Narcissa *is* flattered, and more: as all of the letters in the novel suggest, writing love letters and reading them are not only self-conscious activities but also autoerotic ones. Miss Jenny suggests as much about readers when she tells Narcissa, "We all are convinced that men feel that way about us, and we cant help but admire one that's got the courage to tell us about it, no matter who he is" (Flags, 59); Horace confirms it of writers when he writes, "I daresay you cannot read this as usual, or reading it, it will not mean anything to you. But you will have served your purpose anyway, thou still unravished bride of quietude" (Flags, 340). Narcissa's name suggests her inclination to self-love, and the symmetry of the Snopes and the Horace letters measures the equal attraction for her of their mirroring surfaces, where she is alternately whore and "unravished bride."

The Snopes letters she keeps provide her an erotic self-image that requires no physical partner for fulfillment. By hiding Byron's letters among her underwear, she takes her anonymous lover figuratively into her body with his words. Byron withdraws those amatory letters on the night he breaks into her room, replacing them with a letter written in his own hand "in which he poured out his lust and his hatred and his jealousy, and the language was the obscenity which his jealousy and desire had hoarded away in his temporarily half-crazed mind and which the past night and day had liberated" (Flags, 253). The undergarment he steals with his letters is a symbol of sexual conquest.[20] Like Horace, Snopes also turns from his epistolary lover to an actual woman who frustrates him—here Minnie Sue Turpin; and that juxtaposition of letters with lovers is complemented, finally, when Narcissa discovers on the eve of her wedding that the Snopes letters are missing and finds the new, "obscene" one "which she did not remember having received. The gist of it was plain enough, although she had not understood some of it literally. But on that day, she read it with tranquil detachment: it and all it implied was definitely behind her now" (Flags, 285). What Narcissa puts behind her as she enters her marriage is not auto-eroticism, however, but the epistolary image of herself as a sexual woman, the object of masculine desire. Horace may obscure that from her by poetic allusions, bad handwriting, and a lie about Belle, but Snopes bluntly if ungrammatically expresses it, and Narcissa clearly responds to and values it. What she fears from the loss of his letters is exposure of her secret self—precisely the whore he imagines and describes. She fears "the possibility that people might learn that someone had thought such things about her and put them into words," and she imagines that exposure as an actual loss of virginity, "the possibility that the *intactness* of her deep and heretofore *inviolate* serenity might be the sport of circumstance; that she must trust to chance against the eventuality of a stranger casually raising a stray bit of paper from the ground" (Flags, 285; my italics). When she forgets what she has done with the Snopes letters, as when she fails to understand Horace's, she is suppressing the erotic self-image and her vicarious relationship with the epistolary lovers it implies. Although she does burn Snopes' last and most sexually explicit letter, she continues to receive and to read letters from Horace, where she is idealized as a "still unravished bride" even after her marriage to Bayard. Bayard, of course, fathers her child then abandons her: he never writes her at all.

By such repetitions in the modifying contexts of his novel, Faulkner stitched together relationships between otherwise antithetic characters, measuring them against one another in terms of their modes of expression as well as their physical and emotional ties and binding together, however loosely in this form, the stuff of what Ben Wasson said was six novels written all together into one. Letters in particular provided access to the inner lives of Senders and Receivers alike and to their fictions of self, but the extent of the experiment is not at all clear from *Sartoris,* where passages having to do with letters, and some that echo imagery associated with letters elsewhere in the book, were cut before that novel was published. Restored in the Douglas Day edition of *Flags,* they reveal that part of what was deleted was intended as connective tissue. Horace's walk to the mail train and home after writing to Narcissa is one such scene (Flags, 341–347); Narcissa's reaction to Bayard's ride on the stallion in Chapter Two, 6, is another—this connected to the lost Snopes letters by the language of lost virginity that both scenes employ. Like her thoughts of the anonymous Snopes, thoughts of Bayard disturbingly invade Narcissa's well-guarded serenity. "His idea was like a tramping of heavy feet in those cool corridors of hers, in that grave serenity in which her days accomplished themselves; at the very syllables of his name her instincts brought her upstanding and under arms against him, thus increasing, doubling the sense of violation by the act of repulsing him and by the necessity for it. And yet, despite her armed sentinels, he still crashed with that hot violence of his through the bastions and thundered at the very inmost citadel of her being" (Flags, 134–135). To this is added her memory of Bayard's ride, which returns to her "like a recurring echo in her violated corridors." In succeeding images, horse and rider are co-adjoined as a sexually threatening centaur: she thinks of "the mad rush of the beast and its rider [as] a bronze tidal wave" which "sucked," "spewed," "spent its blind fury and ebbed," leaving the man "prone" while "the horse stood erect like a man" (Flags, 135). In addition to portraying Narcissa's character, and her combined sexual fear and fascination, the language of her response to the lost letters and to the violent ride links the men who prompt those responses, the one by his anonymous written words, the other by his deeds. In spite of Snopes' peripheral part in the plots of the novel, his association with Narcissa's husband-to-be, as well as with her brother, creates a troubling undercurrent of frustrated sexual desire in all of their relationships to her and links each of her suitors to each other one: Horace and Snopes by their letters, Snopes and Bayard by their sexual threat, and Bayard and Horace by the series of contrasts that culminates in the birth of Narcissa's son, Benbow Sartoris, who bears both of their names. These elastic, internal connections between characters stretch out of the novel as well.

Problems of form brought with them corollary questions requiring decisions and answers of their own as, turned homeward, Faulkner began to transform actual people and events into the apocryphal ones of his fictional world. It was a problem of personal distances. In addition to a pattern that would accommodate the cosmos he imagined, he was searching for a place to stand and a voice in which to speak that would keep him *in* the novel he was modeling on his family and region and simultaneously *out of* it; for ways to immerse himself in his personal experience of his home and yet maintain the artistic distance necessary to creation; for the means to make his book "personal," as he said in the *Sartoris* introduction, without limiting the imaginative space he required as he "improved on God." [21] The novel reflects that dilemma in the several characters who share the same problems of expression Faulkner was working to resolve through them. The oral fabulators turn the fictional facts he based on actual events into apocryphal legends of their own, sustained in the novel solely by them in their stories. The extremes of the compositional problem he embodied in the sexually frustrated letter writers: Horace, whose "wild and delicate futility . . . roamed unchallenged through the lonely region into which it had at last concentrated its conflicting parts" (Flags, 339), and Snopes, who "crouched over his desk . . . with jealousy and thwarted desire and furious impotent rage in his vitals" (Flags, 249). In their relations to Narcissa, they represent ideal love and base sensuality, respectively, and their separation into discrete, antithetical entities occupying the same ground is typical of strategies that divide lovers into dreamer and doer in Faulkner's writing from *The Marionettes* onward. Here, of course, neither lover is an active doer, or seducer, in the manner of Shade of Pierrot, for example; but each of the letter writers, with Bayard Sartoris as his active counterpart, is further divided, internally, by the complementary conflict between writing and desire: between a necessarily disguised text and the fantasy life of the ineffectual man it attempts to conceal. Broadly conceived, Horace's obscure, confessional letters and Snopes' plain-speaking, anonymous ones represent alternative approaches to autobiographical writing that Faulkner was confronting as he worked on *Flags*. Neither extreme suited his personal need. Horace produces a too-intimate, unreadable letter—a flawed curiosity, like his vase, designed for self-contemplation. Snopes composes, and then edits himself entirely out of, a letter-text that he and his reader both are desperate to keep from publication.

This strategy too suffered from the editing of *Flags*. Tenuous even there, patterns of self-criticism not entirely erased were foreshortened and obscured so that Faulkner's often comic depiction of the problems of autobiographical writing largely disappeared from his first nearly autobiographical novel. Snopes' fourth letter to Narcissa is a significant example. In Chapter Two, 4, in *Flags*, but not in *Sartoris*, Snopes writes a first draft of a letter to Narcissa, makes a "careful copy," and burns the draft (Flags, 95). When the bank closes, he returns to the Beard hotel, which is described in detail as a haven exclusively for bachelors. In *Flags* and in *Sartoris*, he finds Virgil in the out-house there and takes him to his room, where he dictates from his fair copy. Virgil transcribes the whole letter, including the fictional super-script, "Code number forty-eight. Mister Joe Butler, Saint Louis, Mis-souri," and the fictional signature, "Yours truly Hal Wagner. Code number twenty-four" (Flags, 99, 100). Snopes edits the letter by cut-ting away the superscript and the subscript, addresses an envelope to Narcissa with his left hand to disguise his writing, and burns the fair copy. He mails the letter on the night train. Faulkner inserted this epi-sode into the manuscript as a block of seven pages.[22] Within the in-serted episode he gave Snopes aspects of his own editorial practice: Snopes drafts and fair-copies his writing as Faulkner customarily did his own, and he trims "sheets of foolscap" (Flags, 99) in the way that Faulkner trimmed the bottom from legal-size sheets to make them uniform in length at pages 185–196 in the manuscript of the novel. Apparently this was common practice for him: he did the same with legal-size sheets when he typed his typescript from the manuscript of *Flags* and again when he revised *Sanctuary*.[23]

Faced in 1928 with a Harcourt, Brace contract that called for 110,000 words to be cut from the typescript of *Flags*, Ben Wasson may have decided that the opening letter-writing passages in Chapter Two, 4, were redundant, as he or another editor may also have found the scenes describing Horace's sexual frustrations and Narcissa's fears gra-tuitous or in bad taste. By his own account, and Wasson's, Faulkner had nothing directly to do with the changes in the autumn of 1928. *Flags* shows, however, that the letters deleted for *Sartoris* uncover inte-rior states of mind that link Snopes, Horace, and Bayard; the uncut sequence of Snopes' letter making suggests that, in addition to secretly giving Snopes characteristics of his own compositional practices, Faulkner was portraying the larger contexts of the author-publisher relationship as he knew it in 1927. Having given one of his letter writ-ers the name of his publisher, Horace, he gave the other one aspects of Liveright's editorial function. Together they parody his own serious concern for his text and the authority over the text that he believed was his as its author. In February 1927, he had objected to Liveright about the deletion of sexually explicit passages from the galley proofs of *Mosquitoes*; in October, when he sent Liveright the typescript of *Flags in the Dust*, he was as much concerned with the manner of its printing as Byron Snopes is with the copy Virgil Beard makes of his ungrammatical and badly punctuated letter to Narcissa. In fact, given the importance to the novel of the purposely miswritten Snopes let-ters, Faulkner might have been referring directly to them when he told Liveright, "I am enclosing a few suggestions for the printer: will you look over them and, if possible, smooth the printer's fur, cajole him, some way. He's been punctuating my stuff to death; giving me gratis quotation marks and premiums of commas that I dont need" (SL, 38).

Some of the problems of authorship depicted in *Flags* are of a piece with self-directed comedy and inside jokes elsewhere in the canon: Faulkner's writing Julian Lowe into and then out of *Soldiers' Pay,* for example, and naming himself in *Mosquitoes.* In *Flags* the relation of author to printer-publisher is parodied in Snopes' relations with Virgil Beard. Snopes dictates his letters to preserve anonymity, but the dictator is dictated to by the blackmailing copyist, who threatens to reproduce his letters in a pirated edition: "I remember ever' one of them letters," Virgil tells Snopes. "I bet I could sit down and write 'em all again. I bet I could" (Flags, 100–101). In this comic reversal, the literal printer threatens the author with public exposure; the author pays not to have his work republished, then steals back first editions from his reader. As part of his European persona, Faulkner had grown a beard in 1925, and he drew himself bearded in his Paris letters, where he said that his Aunt Vannye "could see right through it to the little boy" (SL, 25). Snopes' Virgil Beard is an ironic amaneunsis who is also a little boy; he writes with Snopes' pen, but his handwriting "divulged no individuality whatever" (Flags, 58), and Snopes employs him to conceal rather than to reveal himself as Narcissa's ardent correspondent.

Montgomery Ward Snopes, I.O., and Flem also are mentioned in *Flags,* and Phil Stone claimed the Snopes clan was a comic invention of his, a claim supported by Faulkner's dedicating *The Town* to Stone, who *"did half the laughing for thirty years."* But Byron Snopes' letter writing has point and meaning beyond the rise of the redneck in the South that Stone saw in the Snopes stories. There is autoerotic pleasure in writing and reading anonymous love letters, heightened by the impossibility of consummation, including the vicarious consummation of a written reply. Narcissa keeps letters she cannot answer; Snopes pleads conventionally for answers he has arranged never to receive. In the *Sartoris* introduction Faulkner spoke of writing the novel in terms of "reproduction, in its true way, the aesthetic and the mammalian." [24] In the novel, in Snopes' letters, he imagined the end of such letter writing as impotence. When Narcissa announces her engagement, pen and penis fail the letter writer together: "Married, married," Snopes thinks, and Faulkner explains, "Adultery, concealed if suspected, he could have borne; but this, boldly, in the world's face, flouting him with his own impotence . . ." (Flags, 249). His attack on the penman, Virgil Beard, combines stifled self-expression with sexual self-abuse: "Snopes was trying to say something in his mad, shaking voice, but the boy screamed steadily. He had lost all control of his body and he hung limp in the man's hand" (Flags, 251). The masturbatory image echoes an earlier, veiled one in Chapter Two, 4, when Virgil emerges from the outhouse "silently and innocently" (Flags, 98) to write another of the amatory letters he so precisely remembers. In both scenes the transcriber is involved in the autoerotic byplay of letters with the Sender and Receiver.

Likewise, Snopes' robbery of the Sartoris bank strikes at young Bayard through old Bayard, who becomes "an object upon which the Snopes could vent the secret, vicarious rage of his half-insane mind" (Flags, 249). His breaking into Narcissa's house, bedroom, and dresser drawer constitutes a vicarious rape, in which, however, the assailant is victim: instead of breaching the walled "garden" of her person (Flags, 244), Snopes leaps from Narcissa's bedroom window into her "shallow, glassed flower pit"; instead of ecstasy, "nausea swirled in him"; instead of holding Narcissa, Snopes clutches her undergarment in his hand; and it is not she but he who lies "moaning a little while his blood ran between his clasped fingers" (Flags, 256). Like Horace, he too flees Jefferson for another woman, but his further letter writing is banned symbolically by the law, which bars him from access to Narcissa even by mail: "As he crossed the square he saw the night watchman, Buck, standing beneath the light before the postoffice, and cursed him with silent and bitter derision" (Flags, 257). When he tries to replace Narcissa with Minnie Sue Turpin, she makes marriage a condition for sexual submission and Snopes is thwarted a final time, forced into isolation as he is also into silence.

Letters remained a significant part of Sartoris materials almost as long as Faulkner continued to tell the Sartoris story. The Snopes letters reappear in the story "There Was a Queen"; there is a partly transcribed correspondence between Miss Jenny and Johnny in "All the Dead Pilots," and Johnny's death is announced in an ironic letter in that story; and in *The Unvanquished* there are letters to and from an earlier generation of Sartorises in "Raid," "Vendee," and "Skirmish at Sartoris." Private writing is a controlling motif of the 1932–33 screenplay "War Birds," where Johnny Sartoris' diary is employed as a device to date the action, reveal states of mind in the hero, and communicate his experience of the war to his wife and son. If Bruce Kawin is right, both *Flags* and the film script are indebted to a 1926 book serialized in *Liberty* magazine, *War Birds: The Diary of an Unknown Aviator*,[25] but the letters of *Flags* just as likely were prompted by Faulkner's own letters. He had written letterlike gift books of his own for inaccessible women the previous year, and as he worked on *Flags* he wrote

Horace Liveright about the novel, mixing fact and fiction in his letters as he was doing in his manuscript. In a funny, self-assured letter in July 1927, Faulkner explained his having drawn a $200 draft on Liveright's bank as "a case of dire necessity." Piling one misfortune on another, he told his publisher that he had, in fact, lost $300 gambling in Memphis but would not have drawn even the $200 draft except that the whiskey he had buried in his garden against such emergencies had been smelled out and dug up by "one of our niggers," who had sold a little, been caught, and so lost the rest. Set upon by ill chance and circumstance, he had "turned to" Liveright only because "what with the flood last spring, southern people have no cash money for gambling debts." It was, he admitted, "quite a yarn." Of his novel he said, "I believe that at last I have learned to control the stuff and fix it on something like rational truth" (SL, 37). Liveright honored the draft in the end, but rejected the novel, bringing to an end in their correspondence Faulkner's self-confident tone and easy tale telling. In his ensuing letters the debt and the book are ominously linked. On November 30, 1927, he referred to the $200 as "that super-advance" (SL, 39); in February 1928, he asked that Liveright not hold the manuscript in lieu of "the what-ever-it-is I owe you," and he said in a postscript, "I mean, to pay you the money as soon as I place the rejected mss. I know a New Yorker cannot conceive of anyone being able to live day in and day out, yet without ever having as much as a hundred dollars or ten dollars, but it is not only possible in the provincial South; damn near 90% of the population does it. If I can place this mss., I will be able to pay you; at least I'll have incentive to light in and bang you out a book to suit you—though it'll never be one as youngly glamorous as 'Soldiers' Pay' nor as trashily smart as 'Mosquitoes'" (SL, 39–40). Early in March he wrote Liveright, "I have got going on a novel, which, if I continue as I am going now, I will finish within eight weeks. Maybe it'll please you" (SL, 40). By then he was done writing letters to Liveright, but the details of his "yarn," and the letterly context in which it had been set, he appropriated for the new book, where they are used to portray Jason Compson's destruction at the hands of his own ill chance and circumstance in *The Sound and the Fury*.

## [ iii ]

Like the poems, sketches, stories, and novels that he inserted, incorporated, and borrowed from for subsequent work, Faulkner's letters are part of what was for him that matchless resource: his own written words on the page. Thoughts and feelings committed to the letter page defined complex epistolary personae, and with them became the stuff of letters and of stories yet to come, notes toward a future fiction. In a letter from Paris in 1925 he had described his Aunt Vannye as "very nice, of the purest Babbitt ray serene" (SL, 22), and he borrowed that phrasing, and perhaps a sense of her Babbittry, for *The Sound and the Fury*, where Uncle Maury writes to Jason about a "bonanza—if you will permit the vulgarism—of the first water and purest ray serene" (SF, 279). Faulkner's "yarn" to Horace Liveright about gambling debts, bank drafts, and whiskey likewise was ready to his hand when, in the winter of 1928, he closed the door between himself and "all publishers' addresses and book lists" and began to write the story of the Compsons with what he called "that emotion definite and physical and yet nebulous to describe: that ecstasy, that eager and joyous faith and anticipation of surprise which the yet unmarred sheet beneath my hand held inviolate and unfailing, waiting for release." [26] Like Faulkner in his epistolary relationship with his New York publisher, Jason is betrayed on April 6, 1928, by telegrams from "one of the biggest manipulators in New York" (SF, 238), loses the same $200 gambling when the cotton market closes forty points down (SF, 303), and blames his lack of ready cash on the same 1927 flood (SF, 292). His injuries are compounded by Uncle Maury's drawing a draft on the bank account he administers for his mother, and the $200 recurs, as it does in the Liveright letters, as the amount Caddy sends each month for Quentin's upkeep: what Faulkner borrowed from Liveright and then could not repay, Jason receives from Caddy and loses.

Also like Faulkner's correspondence with Liveright, the fictional telegrams Jason sends and the letters he receives from Caddy, Lorraine, and Uncle Maury are elements of an epistolary dialogue in which identity is crucially at issue, and it is a measure of the injury Faulkner sustained when Horace Liveright rejected his manuscript that Jason's fictional letters, cast in the same terms as the author's, portray him as an incomplete, even anonymous self. As if he were a postal clerk—a job Faulkner had in 1922 and hated—Jason's mail contains messages for other people, checks made out in others' names, and baleful misaddresses such as Lorraine's "Dear daddy" (SF, 240). Caddy's child support check arrives six days late, and the telegrams from New York are delivered too late in the day for him to capitalize on them. In his self-imposed isolation, these letters and the telegrams Jason sends span no space or time, make no connections. They communicate absence. His telegram to Caddy is a cryptic lie; his wire to his broker, written after the market has closed, confesses the paranoid provinciality he has tried to conceal by hiring a broker in the first place. "Buy," he orders in his penultimate wire, written too late to send. "Market just on point of blowing its head off. Occasional flurries for purpose of hooking a few more country suckers who haven't got in to the telegraph office yet. Do not be alarmed" (SF, 304–305).

These are not isolated examples. In *The Sound and the Fury* there are twenty-one specific letters and telegrams, and the delays, misdirections, and interceptions to which they are subject portray characters, move the plots of the novel, and convey the themes of failed communication and broken identity proposed by the sound and fury in the title. More than any others in the canon, the characters of *The Sound and the Fury* help to write and read the novel. Nine letters are transcribed: Jason's three letters and four of the seven telegrams he receives and sends, the Compson wedding announcement, and Quentin's imaginary letter to Mrs. Bland. Her unread invitation to him is untranscribed, as are his two letters to Shreve, Uncle Maury's two to Mrs. Patterson, Caddy's to Miss Quentin, and two that Mrs. Compson says she has written, one to Quentin and one to Caddy. Quentin's letter to his father on June 2, 1910, is literally unwritten in that it contains only the symbolic key to his trunk of clothes and books. Small wonder at the end of this virtual casebook of letter forms and situations that Mrs. Compson should say of Miss Quentin's disappearance, "At least she would have enough consideration to leave a note. Even Quentin did that" (SF, 373).

The pervasive presence of so many and such varied letters constitutes a major motif of the novel, written complement to the structures of speaking and saying with which the narrators and the author simultaneously struggle. This is a central issue in Faulkner's work at this time. André Bleikasten has said of *The Sound and the Fury* that "it led him to the experience of the impossible":

> According to Faulkner himself, failure was the common fate of all writers of his generation: "All of us failed to match our dream of perfection." Whether the blame falls on the artist or on his medium, language, everything happens as though the writing process could never be completed, as though it could only be the gauging of a lack. Creation then ceases to be a triumphant gesture of assertion; it resigns itself to be the record of its errors, trials and defeats, the chronicle of its successive miscarriages, the inscription of the very impossibility from which it springs.
>
> Hence an increased self-reflexiveness. Novels tend to turn into extended metaphors for the hazardous game of their writing. . . . the novel becomes the narrative of an impossible narrative.[27]

As a particularly self-reflexive form of writing, letters are subject to the same hazards Bleikasten ascribes to the novel, and they portray creation in *The Sound and the Fury* negatively, in terms of impossibility. From the third page of the book, when Benjy is caught on the fence delivering Uncle Maury's letter to Mrs. Patterson, letters exist in the contexts of secrecy: of covert relationships, surreptitious writing, and furtive delivery. They are the mediums of social and sexual transgressions, punished in the novel by extremes of isolation that even letters cannot overcome. They subject Senders and Receivers to violations of their thought and person, render them vulnerable to appropriations of property and to physical harm. They are documents of frustrated desire, as intriguing, almost, in their secret silences as the secrets of the novel itself.

The first letters in the novel are Uncle Maury's illicit love letters to Mrs. Patterson, the first complications accruing from letters their misdelivery by Benjy, the first letter outcome Mr. Patterson's attack on the illicit letter writer. In the pattern of contrasts in the book between the loved and the unloved, nonvirgins and virgins, what Caddy accomplishes in the opening pages by successfully delivering a letter to Mrs. Patterson, her impotent brothers significantly fail to achieve. The writing, the delivery, and the punishment accretively recur—an increasingly important configuration by which the past is repeated in the various presents the book entails. Especially is this true of Quentin's and Jason's presents, but Benjy is not exempt despite his incapacity to write, or even speak. Mr. Compson points out to Quentin that in sending Benjy to Mrs. Patterson Maury proved himself "too poor a classicist to risk the blind immortal boy in person he should have chosen Jason because Jason would have made only the same kind of blunder Uncle Maury himself would have made not one to get him a black eye" (SF, 217). Yet Benjy is, in fact, a particularly suitable agent of Maury's frustrated philanderings. His given name is the same as his uncle's, Maury; and his inability to say the name Caddy when he attacks the Burgess girl through the open gate echoes his inability to bear his uncle's written words of love through the fence to Mrs. Patterson. Ironically like his uncle, he "addresses" the wrong woman, but by accident; his mute appeal, misinterpreted by Mr. Burgess, is analogous to Maury's undelivered message, intercepted by Mr. Patterson; and his castration, like his uncle's punishment, is for a sexual transgression. On April 6, 1928, Jason in fact does deliver a letter of Maury's to a lady, his mother, Caroline Compson—and successfully from Maury's point of view, for it gains him access to her bank account that Jason so jealously administers.

If Maury is punished for illicit, misdelivered letters to Mrs. Patterson, Quentin is tormented on June 2, 1910, by conventionally formal letters delivered but unread. These are the wedding announcement

and Mrs. Bland's invitation to a picnic. Both invitations bring Quentin
into the presence of a Harvard *"blackguard,"* as he calls Herbert Head
(SF, 152), where his ineffectuality is expressed by contrast to Herbert's
and Gerald Bland's masculinity. Both are favorites of dangerous maternal women, Herbert of his mother-in-law, Gerald of his mother; both
drive impressive cars—Mrs. Compson writes to Quentin about Herbert's (SF, 115), and he rides in Gerald's; and both are seducers of
young women. In the Bland party on June 2, Miss Holmes reminds
Quentin of home, Miss Daingerfield of its dangers. For Quentin,
the dangers of home are substantial ones, significantly bound in his
imagination to letters. Forewarned of the engagement by his mother's
letter about Herbert, Quentin fears to open the wedding invitation:
"Mr and Mrs Jason Richmond Compson announce the marriage of
their daughter Candace to Mr Sydney Herbert Head on the twenty-
fifth of April one thousand nine hundred and ten at Jefferson Mississippi. At home after the first of August number Something Something
Avenue South Bend Indiana. Shreve said Aren't you even going to
open it? *Three days. Times. Mr and Mrs Jason Richmond Compson"* (SF,
115). Like a jilted lover, he imagines the wedding invitation as a death
notice to which are accorded funeral rites: "Aren't you even going to
open it? *It lay on the table a candle burning at each corner upon the envelope
tied in a soiled pink garter two artificial flowers"* (SF, 115). The invitation is
the center of one of his earliest and most insistent memories on June
2, 1910, the crux of tormenting associations of sex with death, lost in-
nocence with sexual crimes, and feminine sexuality with filth. In his
first waking moments, thoughts of the boat race at New London lead
him to "the month of brides, the voice that breathed *She ran right out of
the mirror, out of the banked scent. Roses. Roses. Mr and Mrs Jason Richmond Compson announce the marriage of.* Roses. Not virgins like dogwood, milkweed. I said I have committed incest, Father I said. Roses.
Cunning and serene" (SF, 95). Fragments from this are the sources of
his full recollection of "women so delicate so mysterious Father said.
Delicate equilibrium of periodical filth between two moons balanced"
(SF, 159), and of his concluding memory of his conversation with his
father where he argues his incestuous love of Caddy and foretells his
suicide. In this way, the wedding announcement serves as a central
text from which major themes of the section emanate, a crux in the
memory productive of other memories.

In accordance with the laws and conventions of epistolary discourse, the remembered invitation, so conventional in its own form
and content, also is the generative source of other letter texts. As painful as Quentin's letter memories and associations are, they prompt him
to write immediately himself. At 7:59 A.M. Shreve interrupts Quentin's

reverie to announce Chapel—"Bell in two minutes" (SF, 95).[28] Between 8:15 A.M., when "the quarter hour sounded," and 8:30, when "the half hour went" (SF, 99, 101), Quentin says that he "wrapped the trunk key into a sheet of paper and put it in an envelope and addressed it to Father, and wrote the two notes and sealed them" (SF, 99–100). The unwritten letter to his father he stamps and mails at the post office at 8:30; the note to Shreve he stamps and retains, as he also temporarily retains the note he will give Deacon about his clothes with instructions to deliver it to Shreve the following day.[29] The key, the unmailed suicide note, and the secret bequest postpone the destructive action they describe. As writing—and nonwriting, in the case of the letter to Father—they are the antitheses of creation: inscriptions, to use Bleikasten's term for the novel, of the very failure of selfhood and impossibility of self-assertion from which they spring. They capitalize ironically on the law that letters span space and time, creating the figurative absence out of which Quentin enigmatically communicates his intention and which he makes literal by his drowning.

If Quentin is in love with Death, as Faulkner said in his 1945 "Appendix: Compson" (SF, 411), he is equally in love with his own writing about it. All morning on June 2, 1910, he carries his unmailed letters to Shreve, touching them through his coat on the trolley and as he searches for Deacon (SF, 110, 118) and feeling them "crackle through my coat" at the bridge (SF, 114).[30] At 11:15 Quentin gives Deacon one letter to deliver, and at 11:30 he tells Shreve to expect it (SF, 122, 125), but the second, stamped and sealed, is still in his pocket when he returns to Cambridge on the trolley in the evening: "I got off before we reached the postoffice. They'd all be sitting around somewhere by now though, and then I was hearing my watch and I began to listen for the chimes and I touched Shreve's letter through my coat, the bitten shadows of the elms flowing upon my hand. And then as I turned into the quad the chimes did begin and I went on while the notes came up like ripples on a pool and passed me and went on, saying Quarter to what? All right. Quarter to what" (SF, 212). For the troubled letter carrier, the conjunction of writing and drowning proposed by the language of the scene is only temporarily postponed by his avoiding the Cambridge post office. In a gathering of images significant to him, he simultaneously hears his watch, listens to the chimes, and touches the letter as shadows touch his hand. Like the last light he sees from the train, "supine and tranquil upon tideflats like pieces of broken mirror" (SF, 211), the bell "notes . . . like ripples on a pool" contain narcissistic images of himself, cast as writing on water, the recognizable analogues of the two "notes" written and sealed at the beginning of the day. "Notes" are bells only four times on June 2,

1910: once in the bakery with Julio's sister (SF, 158), and three times when Quentin returns to Cambridge (SF, 212, 219, 222). The five other instances of the word refer to letters (SF, 100, 125, 130, 175, 182).[31] Like the drowned man's shadow, which has been "watching for him in the water all the time," as "Niggers say" (SF, 111)—and like the image of himself as Sender inscribed in the text of his suicide note—these "notes" bide in the "pool" in the very shadow of his imminent drowning. The final scene is framed by audible bells and audible letters: "The last note sounded. . . . I put on my coat. Shreve's letter crackled through the cloth and I took it out and examined the address, and put it in my side pocket. . . . I'd have to go by the postoffice . . ." (SF, 222). Quentin leaves his watch for Shreve in the Harvard room that is no longer his own, and departs to mail his letter to that address. His last note will speak to Shreve—as the monologue of his last day does to the reader of the novel—from the dead, spanning the distance his drowning creates between the time-tormented Harvard dormitory and the house of death with its "roof of wind" (SF, 98) in the timeless caverns and grottoes of the sea.

What Quentin has written there is not revealed, nor are his letters read by their Receivers. Revealing himself as he does by his "spoken" thoughts and memories, he keeps his epistolary image secret. The key in the letter to his father will confirm Mr. Compson's conception of Quentin as a gentleman, known by the clothes and books in the trunk. The clothes he wills Deacon will clothe an anti-Quentin: a living fiction, created by a letter; a mock-Harvard man with southern manners; a Negro master of disguise who, as a Negro, is someone Quentin already thinks of as his own "obverse reflection" (SF, 106). His one transcribed letter is the invented one to Mrs. Bland. Composed in the midst of painful memories of Caddy's wedding, it parodies both the discourse convention and the proprieties of social letter form. "My dear Madam," he begins, "I have not yet had an opportunity of receiving your communication but I beg in advance to be excused today or yesterday and tomorrow or when" (SF, 132). If he fails to read her invitation, it is because it threatens him. The power of her letter is suggested by her subsequent claim that his trouble with the law is connected: "That's what you get for not reading my note," Mrs. Bland says (SF, 182). She is "Semiramis" (SF, 125), her note a dangerously authoritative inscription like the wedding announcement, associated in Quentin's mind with an exotic flower that recalls his "Roses. Not virgins like dogwood, milkweed" and the troubling honeysuckle. "Letter on the table by hand," Quentin thinks, "command orchid scented coloured" (SF, 132).[32] If he fails to reply, it is because he refuses on June 2 to commit his most private self-image to writing where he can be read, as he also refuses to read contradictory images of himself in others' letters. "I could see the letter before I turned the light on," he says when he returns to his Harvard room. "[I] took Mrs Bland's letter and tore it across and dropped the pieces into the waste basket" (SF, 213).

The letters that Quentin refuses to read or record, Jason openly violates on June 6, 1928, but to the same self-destructive ends. Like Quentin, Jason fears his epistolary persona and the images of himself in others' letters to him, but his misuse of letters typically takes more devious forms. For example, when he shares his letter from Uncle Maury with his mother, he is violating his uncle's written injunction against telling her about his business bonanza and the draft on her bank account. Yet Jason gives her the letter to read before he has read it himself, suggesting it is to her that Maury actually has written. Neither the salutation, "My dear young nephew," nor the signature, "Your affectionate Uncle, / Maury L. Bascomb" (SF, 277, 279), describes the actual relationship of mutual contempt between Sender and Receiver, and the flattering references to Mrs. Compson in the body of the letter are designed to move her more than to persuade her cynical son. Maury portrays himself as the last of the Bascombs, pursuing "the ultimate solidification of my affairs by which I may restore to its rightful position that family of which I have the honour to be the sole remaining male descendant; that family in which I have ever included your lady mother and her children" (SF, 278). The phrasing is completely in accord with Mrs. Compson's pride of name, and Maury appeals directly to her self-image as an aristocratic lady when he writes of "your Mother's delicate health and that timorousness which such delicately nurtured Southern ladies would naturally feel regarding matters of business, and their charming proneness to divulge unwittingly such matters in conversation . . . It is our duty to shield her from the crass material world as much as possible" (SF, 279). By addressing his letter to Jason, Maury recognizes the son's nominal authority in his mother's financial affairs; by implicitly addressing Mrs. Compson, he circumvents that authority. And Jason knows it: when he gives Mrs. Compson the letter to read first, he acknowledges his uncle's strategy without putting his own authority to the test. As he tells himself, "there wasn't any need to open it. I could have written it myself, or recited it to her from memory, adding ten dollars just to be safe" (SF, 250). Yet by betraying even the false confidentiality of his uncle's letter, Jason also betrays himself and his mother, whom Maury thereby robs. As old Uncle Job says of Jason, "Aint a man in dis town kin keep up wid you fer smartness. You fools a man whut so smart he cant even keep up wid hisself . . . Dats Mr Jason Compson" (SF, 311–312).

Jason's letters from women are still more striking examples of his ironic self-betrayals, and they demonstrate still more decisively the potential power of the Sender over the Receiver in an epistolary relationship and the commitment that letterly discourse imposes on both parties. Like the letter from Uncle Maury, the women's letters Jason receives and reads on June 6 constitute recurrent challenges to his identity, contradicting or only ironically matching roles he has imagined and plays for himself: the upstanding citizen of Jefferson, the long-suffering head of the Compson family, the sophisticated man of parts with a mistress in Memphis. In effect, the letters impose contrary definitions and enforce patterns of behavior from which he tries to defend himself when he misappropriates, robs, rewrites, reseals, and mishandles them. They reveal him a thief who steals from his sister and niece, a forger of checks who cheats his own mother, a lover ashamed of his beloved. Clearly he understands the power of their letters and fears them. He answers Caddy's imperious letter with a cryptic lie: "All well. Q writing today" (SF, 239); he opens and robs her letter to Miss Quentin; and when he has read Lorraine's love letter he burns it.

> I make it a rule never to keep a scrap of paper bearing a woman's hand, and I never write them at all. Lorraine is always after me to write to her but I says anything I forgot to tell you will save till I get to Memphis again but I says I dont mind you writing me now and then in a plain envelope, but if you ever try to call me up on the telephone, Memphis wont hold you I says. I says when I'm up there I'm one of the boys, but I'm not going to have any woman calling me on the telephone. Here I says, giving her the forty dollars. If you ever get drunk and take a notion to call me on the phone, just remember this and count ten before you do it. (SF, 240–241)

In the one-sided epistolary situation that Jason here describes, the laws of letters are rewritten to accommodate his fragile self-image and gratify his vicarious sexual imaginings. Lorraine may write love letters to "Dear daddy" but not call him; he will visit her as "one of the boys" but not write. In conjunction with the corollary restrictions he imposes on Caddy's and Quentin's letters, these are neither lawful nor letterly. Caddy is forbidden to visit but must write letters to Jason with checks he pretends to destroy; Quentin receives letters from Caddy, which Jason intercepts and purloins. In the vulnerability of the absent letter writers, and of the letters as letters, Jason finds a tenuous security. Nonetheless, as a party to this correspondence he is at risk according to the dictates of his own laws. When Quentin breaks into his room and his money cache, for example, she reenacts his breaking into her letter for the check and avenges the theft: letterlike, when he finds it on Sunday morning, his metal box with its broken lock contains papers but no money.

In one sense, as his correspondence shows, Jason's is a world circumscribed and beset by women: his mother and Quentin who receive letters, Lorraine and Caddy who write them. Because the women Senders and Receivers are present in the letters that Jason mistreats, theirs are among the most dangerous in *The Sound and the Fury* and the most significant—here and in the canon of letters in the novels. Recent feminist criticism of the epistolary novel would suggest that Caddy's and Lorraine's transcribed letters are forgeries in that they are the work of a man, William Faulkner, writing in the guise of a woman.[33] There literally is a letter forgery in the novel: the check Jason writes in Caddy's name and reseals in her letter for his mother to burn. But whether or not they are forgeries in themselves, Caddy's letter and Lorraine's are among the first *transcribed* letters by female characters in the early canon, and two of only a very few by women transcribed anywhere in Faulkner's work. Women may read the letters of men, and often according to convention they keep them, but their own writing seldom is quoted. In *The Sound and the Fury*, however, Lorraine's note portrays the Sender and her Receiver in roles Jason himself has solicited by permitting her to write and paid for with the forty dollars. "Dear daddy wish you were here. No good parties when daddys out of town I miss my sweet daddy" (SF, 240). In the childish text with its childish coquette, Jason reads himself as an authoritative presence: father to her daughter, seducer to her innocent child. These personae suggest the perverse sexual relationship between Jason and Lorraine, and the scene of reading in Jason's business office suggests its financial basis. For Jason, love is a business arrangement, and Lorraine's is a sexually gratifying business letter from a "good honest whore" (SF, 291) to her customer. The power of her letter lies in its ability to excite Jason; its authority over him is suggested by his frustrated response. In Lorraine's absence, he satisfies his vicarious desire for her by assaulting Quentin, his niece and ward, the figurative daughter he forces to his will. Quentin literally is the child-whore Lorraine pretends to be in her letter, the sexual truant who charges, "It's his fault . . . He makes me do it" (SF, 324). The two women frequently are associated in Jason's mind: in his reverie on Lorraine as a "good honest whore," for example. In the scene in the back-room office where Jason and Quentin contest possession of Caddy's letter, he physically abuses her and, by giving her only ten dollars of the fifty that Caddy sends her, robs her of the same amount he paid Lorraine:

"When I turned to come back she was out of sight behind the desk. I ran. I ran around the desk and caught her as she jerked her hand out of the drawer. I took the letter away from her, beating her knuckles on the desk until she let go" (SF, 264). If Quentin has no "sweetie that can write" (SF, 263), as Jason says, neither has Lorraine, and when he is robbed of his financial power by Quentin, Jason simultaneously forfeits his sexual potency as well. In frustrated pursuit of his niece on Easter Sunday he imagines himself impotent in bed with Lorraine, "lying beside her, pleading with her to help him" (SF, 383).

In the context of Faulkner's experiments with reflexive forms in the late 1920s, and his developing sense of the potential of simultaneous multiple perspectives, such letters properly are read less as forgeries than as vital intratexts, writing that in significant ways is analogous to the stories-in-stories told orally by men and women alike, and like those stories possessing the power to portray character through the uniqueness of individual points of view. Miss Jenny's story of Carolina Bayard in *Flags* is one example; Temple's self-consciously fictive story of her night at the Old Frenchman Place in *Sanctuary* is another. But particularly is this true of the letters in *The Sound and the Fury*, where the solipsism of the first three chapters is reinforced by the presence in each of secret letters that substitute for Sender and Receiver and by the letter secrets that devolve from them. André Bleikasten argues from the evidence of the 1933 introduction to *The Sound and the Fury* that the novel is a "*transnarcissistic* object, meant to establish a connection between the narcissism of its producer and that of its consumer." [34] Bleikasten finds that the novel was a substitute for the "beautiful and tragic little girl" Faulkner said he never had, and that "from the writer's mind she has slipped into the narrator's; from being Faulkner's private fantasy she becomes the obsessive memory of the Compson brothers, without ever really assuming shape and substance in the space of fiction." [35] Letters, of course, also are generated by absence. Caddy's letter in this respect is analogous to the novel itself: it is a text that substitutes for her in the book as the text of the book substitutes for her in the mind of the author. Literally in a novel where she neither speaks in her own voice nor acts except in her brothers' memories, Caddy's letter to Jason represents her attempt to write herself into being.

It is an artifact of her, made in her image and mailed from her exile; unlike the other artifacts of Caddy—the sound of her name, for example, her slipper, and her daughter Quentin, who reenacts her mother's childhood in the Compson garden—the written one, rather than stimulating a past memory, appeals for her recognition in the present. It, too, is a business letter, containing a check. Its content is generated and shaped not by Jason's sexual fantasies, as the letter from Lorraine is, nor by his nominal status as a business associate, as the letter from Maury is, but rather by his reluctance to answer women's letters and his mistreatment of Caddy's previous letters to him and to Quentin.

> I had no answer to my letter about Quentin's easter dress. Did it arrive all right? I've had no answer to the last two letters I wrote her, though the check in the second one was cashed with the other check. Is she sick? Let me know at once or I'll come there and see for myself. You promised you would let me know when she needed things. I will expect to hear from you before the 10th. No you'd better wire me at once. You are opening my letters to her. I know that as well as if I were looking at you. You'd better wire me at once about her to this address. (SF, 236)

Unlike Lorraine's acquiescent note and Maury's flattering letter, this bears no salutation and no signature. But it is inscribed with power: it makes present demands on the Receiver that he answers defensively with deceptions, forgeries, and the destruction of other letters.

Bleikasten's discerning analogy for Caddy is Eurydice, but in this letter she is Demeter searching for a Persephone in the power of mock-Pluto, a greedy god of wealth, who interposes himself in the correspondence between mother and daughter. Quentin tells Jason, "I'm bad and I'm going to hell, and I don't care. I'd rather be in hell than anywhere where you are" (SF, 235), but he makes her days a present hell, and it surely is significant that Caddy's first concern on Good Friday is that Quentin not be ill-clothed for Easter and the celebration of the Resurrection. Persephone-like Quentin tells Jason, "I want my mother" (SF, 230), but in a novel where mothers and daughters are irretrievably separated—by Damuddy's death and Mrs. Compson's pride—flight with the circus man promises no reunion. Caddy's letter to Jason is a work of mourning—to adopt a phrase that Bleikasten applies to the novel itself[36]—and it duplicates Quentin's attempt to retrieve a lost relationship. The letter is a hopeless appeal for answering letters that will complete her and her daughter as partners in the epistolary discourse: "I had no answer to my letter . . . no answer to the last two letters I wrote her . . . Let me know at once or I'll come there . . . You promised you would let me know . . . I will expect to hear from you . . . wire me at once . . . wire me at once about her . . ." The appeal itself is powerless to move the man Caddy says "never had a drop of warm blood" (SF, 259). Rather, the power of the letter resides in Caddy's imminent presence in it: she writes, "You are opening my letters to her. I know that as well as if I were looking at you"; and she names herself on the $200 check. It is that check Jason forges for his mother to burn, and that forgery is both the substitute for Caddy by which he exploits her and an effigy by which he erases her name. His answering telegram is a mechanical message that likewise mutilates Quentin's name, by encoding it: "All well. Q writing today" is taken to be a business strategy, as indeed it ironically is.

In the sequence in which Jason handles and mishandles them, letters from women progressively lose power in the text of the novel. Caddy's threatening letter enforces a response; Lorraine's note is read and then burned. Caddy's second letter, to Quentin, is neither transcribed nor carefully read. Jason has "a hunch . . . that it was about time [Caddy] was up to some of her tricks again" (SF, 250), but he is interrupted twice trying to open the tricky letter (SF, 242, 243) and again before he can read it (SF, 262). When Quentin insists, "It's mine. I saw the name" (SF, 264), Jason devalues it literally by giving it to her without the enclosed money order.

> "How much is it?" she says.
> "Read the letter," I says. "I reckon it'll say."
> She read it fast, in about two looks.
> "It dont say," she says, looking up. She dropped the letter to the floor. (SF, 265)

In an attempt to regain the stolen money, and symbolically to re-institute the discourse, Quentin offers to write her mother, as Jason's telegram promises she will, according to Jason's own rules for letters: "Mother will pay you. I'll write her to pay you and that I wont ever ask her for anything again. You can see the letter" (SF, 266). But Jason already has the money, and there is no value to him in censoring letters he already sees. When in his back-room office he forces Quentin to endorse Caddy's $50 money order, he brings all women's writing—and reading—under his subjection.

> "Will you let me see it?" she says. "I just want to look at it. Whatever it says, I wont ask for but ten dollars. You can have the rest. I just want to see it."
> "Not after the way you've acted," I says. "You've got to learn one thing, and that is that when I tell you to do something, you've got it to do. You sign your name on that line."

She took the pen, but instead of signing it she just stood there with her head bent and the pen shaking in her hand. Just like her mother. "Oh, God," she says, "oh, God."

"Yes," I says. "That's one thing you'll have to learn if you never learn anything else. Sign it now, and get on out of here." (SF, 267)

When Jason forges Caddy's check on a St. Louis bank, and reseals it in her letter to deliver to Mrs. Compson (SF, 269), the subjugation of women's letters is brought to a close. Caddy's daughter is prevented from reading the money order; Caddy's mother likewise cannot read her check—because her "eyes are giving out" (SF, 269). She makes no attempt to read Caddy's letter (SF, 272).

Simultaneously, the force of Jason's own writing is dissipated and the power of his reading frustrated. His mode of expression is the forgery and the lie; his medium the impersonal telegram, tapped out electrically by another's hand and bearing no trace of the Sender's identity. Throughout Jason's day, his intrigues with letters intersect at cross-purposes his visits to the telegraph office: he gains control of letters at the expense of his wires to and from the New York agent, and he blames his losses on letters. As he says at the telegraph office in the afternoon, "It was one point above the opening. I had already lost thirteen points, all because she had come helling in there at twelve, worrying me about that letter" (SF, 281). Ultimately, he loses the $200 in the cotton market that he gained by Caddy's $200 check: when the news comes that the market closed at 12.21, Jason thinks, "forty points down. Forty times five dollars; buy something with that if you can" (SF, 303). Literally now, writing and reading letters fail Jason, and with them his investments. The next-to-last wire from his broker he carries in his pocket unread, as evidence that New York is using the telegraph office to defraud (SF, 282). A wire that arrives at 3:30 is delivered at 5:10, too late to be read profitably: "Sell, it says. The market will be unstable, with a general downward tendency. Do not be alarmed following government report" (SF, 304). Jason's answering wire is written too late to be delivered.

"Send this collect," I says, taking a blank. Buy, I wrote, Market just on point of blowing its head off. Occasional flurries for purpose of hooking a few more country suckers who haven't got in to the telegraph office yet. Do not be alarmed. "Send that collect," I says.

He looked at the message, then he looked at the clock. "Market closed an hour ago," he says.

"Well," I says. "That's not my fault either. I didn't invent it; I just bought a little of it while under the impression that the telegraph company would keep me informed as to what it was doing." (SF, 304–305)

Jason is present in this wire as its Sender, the self-portrayed "country sucker" hooked by his misuse of his own telegrams from New York. The final telegram he sends, the last in Jason's chapter and the last of the letters in the novel, no one reads: it is a closed text that returns letters to the secrecy with which they begin in *The Sound and the Fury.* "I wrote the other one out and counted the money. 'And this one too, if you're sure you can spell b-u-y'" (SF, 305).

What Jason writes beyond the fragment he spells for the messenger and to whom he addresses himself in the only one of his wires that he pays for himself are not recorded. His last telegram echoes the previous, undeliverable one to New York, but certainly it is not to his broker that he sends the cryptic word "b-u-y" this time. *Buy* is Jason's word for sexual love as well as for business, and in the context of the many overlapping telegrams and letters that he handles on June 6, and the disappointments and vicarious pleasures they bring him, it may be that this wire is to Lorraine, the most accessible and acquiescent of his correspondents, who plays to his authority as "daddy." With the market down forty points and Jason out $200, his profit on the day is the $40 he took from Quentin. Lorraine is a businesswoman of letters, and forty dollars is her price: he has told her, "Buy yourself a dress with it" (SF, 241). Quentin, in fact, is Jason's business—he calls her "my job" (SF, 246)—and she appears half-dressed, tears a dress Jason bought her, and wears the dress of a Gayoso Street whore (SF, 228, 233, 289). Caddy's concern about Quentin's "easter dress" prompts Jason's wire to her that the cotton speculators take to be "a code message to buy" (SF, 239). In Memphis, where Jason is "one of the boys," he plays the free spender who believes "money has no value; it's just the way you spend it. It dont belong to anybody, so why try to hoard it" (SF, 241). The same self-justification of sexual expenses covers business losses, as well. He pays for his telegram in the same spirit that he does Lorraine's dress, and moments after writing it out his thoughts turn again to Lorraine in self-justification of their relationship. "I'd like to see the colour of the man's eyes that would speak disrespectful of any woman that was my friend it's these damn good women that do it I'd like to see the good, church-going woman that's half as square as Lorraine, whore or no whore" (SF, 307). If Jason's first telegram is a figurative "code message to buy," it may be that "b-u-y" in his last is a code.

By its very secrecy, the secret telegram encourages speculation, but it is appropriate—if this last letter is in fact to Lorraine—that Jason's chapter of the novel should end with a secret telegram to a whore as Ben's begins with a surreptitious love letter to an adulteress. Letters serve the book in this way as points of mutual reference for all letter writers, letter readers, and letter carriers, bridging the distances between the chapters as well as the physical separation of the characters that letters conventionally attempt to overcome. They extend the theme of sound and fury, and they portray the terrible opposite of those—the mute silences of interrupted discourse and the deathly quietude that falls upon characters vainly "trying to say." They frame with private writing the private monologues of the brothers Compson, which themselves partly owe their language and form to Faulkner's own letters and his letterlike private writing during the years when he was learning the laws of both canons and the possibilities inherent in them for integrations.

# IV. Letters at Hand

"Now he (Quentin) could read it, could finish it—the sloped whimsical ironic hand out of Mississippi attenuated, into the iron snow."
—*Absalom, Absalom!*, 377

## [ i ]

With the integration of letters into *The Sound and the Fury*, Faulkner mastered a fictional device he had been working with since he included Cadet Lowe in *Soldiers' Pay* to write the letters he does, as he does—perhaps to un-write Faulkner's own unheroic and unwriterly identity as cadet. Quentin's and Caddy's letters in *The Sound and the Fury* are far more sophisticated devices: artifacts of their most intimate selves, written from their exile, their letters embody them as the absent spirits of the Compson family and home. In a present to which past honor is lost, Quentin writes nothing that can be answered; lost herself, Caddy pleads for answering letters that there is no one left to write. In the brief period between 1925 and 1929, letters, for Faulkner, had assumed the status of familiar tools for telling stories. Like symbol and allusion, which he likewise had readily at hand, they were part of the stock in his carpenter shop, and on the firm foundation of his fully lettered work he built confidently and well. In the shifting canon that evolved at this time, peripheral issues of one book were expanded in another and central devices of one were modified or replaced in the next according to need. So in *Sanctuary* Horace returns from Kinston to Jefferson, his florid letters to Narcissa no longer at issue as they are in *Flags*. In the story "There Was a Queen," however, the Snopes letters turn up again, now as the motive force in Narcissa's illicit sex life. Here the letters seem the generative force in the writing of the story, but many of the short stories Faulkner wrote at this period, the major phase of his story-writing career, are lettered in notable ways. Better than half of the stories dating between 1928 and 1932 employ correspondence in ways that range from incidental devices of language and plot to central issues bearing on character and theme. The novels, too, continued to be lettered. In *Absalom, Absalom!*, perhaps the climactic book of Faulkner's career after *The Sound and the Fury*, letters contribute centrally to the telling and retelling of what Quentin calls "the rag-tag and bob-ends of old tales and talking"

(AA, 303), and the laws of letters shape narrative speculations that shape the book itself.

Inescapably, Faulkner's own writing exerted the first influence on successive books: inescapably because, even more than his reading, his own writing represented the conscious awareness of the craft of fiction as he had practiced it himself. As he wrote more letters, and wrote them more into his fictions, he came to rely on them not only as stock in his carpenter shop but also, frequently, as a stock device. The unpublished story "Moonlight" is an instructive example of the breadth of Faulkner's borrowings from himself, and of his sense of the narrative potential and the limitations of inserted letters. Faulkner remembered "Moonlight" as "about the first story I ever wrote" and dated it "around 1919, 1920, or 1921."[1] The story turns on whether or not a young couple should take advantage of an available empty house to make love; the characters Cecily Binford and the boy named George anticipate Cecily Saunders and George Farr in *Soldiers' Pay*.[2] A revised version of "Moonlight," dating from the autumn of 1928 when Faulkner was finishing the typescript of *The Sound and the Fury*, includes a letter from the renamed Susan to an unnamed sixteen-year-old boy, promising "I will be yours tonight even if tomorrow not good-bye but farewell forever" (USWF, 497). The revision may owe something to Sherwood Anderson's *Winesburg, Ohio:* in the story "Nobody Knows" George Willard receives a note from Louise Trunnion saying "I'm yours if you want me"; in "Godliness" Louise Bentley writes a similar letter to John Hardy.[3] But the letter situation in the revised "Moonlight," and some of the language of the story, are more obviously indebted to *Soldiers' Pay*, where Cecily writes to George Farr to arrange an assignation of the kind Susan's childish letter parodies (SP, 146). That note, with Cecily's "nervous spidery script sprawled thinly across it" (SP, 213), excites George in the way that the protagonist of "Moonlight" is excited by "a scrap of cheap scented pink note paper scrawled over with sprawling purple ink" (USWF, 498). Apparently, when he revised the story Faulkner thought of the letter as a device to bring the boy and girl together in a dramatic way, as Cecily's note does in the novel, but he uses it to undercut their romantic preconceptions. The boy takes the miswritten letter as a sign that he and Susan are adults; the reader reads there that they are children.

In this way, the story that anticipated the novel subsequently was reshaped according to a method developed for the longer work. The revised "Moonlight" is far from a successful story, however, despite the enabling device of the letter. It was rejected by *Scribner's* in 1928, as it was by the magazines to which his agent, Morton Goldman, sent it when Faulkner returned to it again in the mid-1930s.[4] A more mature story that evolved from it, but without the letters, is "Hair," published in 1931 by *American Mercury* and collected in *These 13*. "Moonlight" supplies "Hair" the character Susan Reed, who like the Susan of the earlier story is an orphaned "niece" of Mr. and Mrs. Burchett (CSWF, 131; USWF, 497); Susan Reed's bad reputation derives from Cecily's sexual daring and Susan's invitation to her teenage lover. But Hawkshaw, the barber, is forefronted in "Hair," and the Cecily-Susan character is made an unexpressive and enigmatic figure of sexual rumor who neither speaks nor writes. Letters in "Hair" are used, instead, to convey information from the traveling narrator to Gavin Stevens about Hawkshaw's faithful attendance on his dead fiancée, Sophie Starnes. Significant to the narrative pattern of theory and countertheory in the story, the speculations developing from his letter are contradicted at the end of the story by Hawkshaw and Susan's marriage during the drummer's absence from Jefferson.

The letters that Faulkner inserted and deleted at need from this grouping of related stories are characteristic in form and function of the many letters in the stories he wrote at this time for national magazines. Of the thirty-eight stories he attempted to market between December 1927 and January 1932, twenty-four employ letters or refer to letter situations.[5] These comprise a convenient body of writing in which to investigate the several ways Faulkner called on letters and letter conventions in the major phase of his short-story career. No story is an epistolary one consisting entirely of letters and, in some, letters are only an incidental device. There is bare mention of letters in "The Leg," where a picture mailed to Everbe Corinthia and inscribed with an unprintable phrase identifies Davy as her demon lover; the Jefferson post office is a setting in "Death Drag"; a transcribed military document supplies the title "With Caution and Dispatch." A larger group of stories, including "Hair," relies on letters to tie together aspects of plot, provide background information, and span geographical distances between characters. In "Smoke" Granby Dodge's secret tax payments and unsigned notes help indict him for murder; in his desperation to find Davy, in "Divorce in Naples," George manages to send a letter from a prison where there is neither paper nor pencil; Wilfred Midgleston's letter to the editor of the *New York Times* is one artifact of reality in the fantasy story "Black Music"; in "Ad Astra," in complement to themes set forth by the subadar, the German writes letters refusing his barony, and asks the narrator to write his wife telling her "this life iss nothing" (CSWF, 426). In "The Big Shot," letter discourse is used as a metaphor: when Dal Martin thinks of a way to overcome the difference in social position between himself and Dr. Blount, "it was as though it were all finished, like two compared letters, question and answer, dropped at the same instant into the mail box" (USWF, 519).

Several other stories employ letters, with varying results, as the means of working out plots and portraying character and theme. In November 1928, a *Scribner's* editor wrote Faulkner, "I was not able to get a great deal out of 'Bench for Two,' although your device was perfectly understandable."[6] Faulkner worked on the story subsequently, and in 1933 Morton Goldman sold it to *American Mercury*, titled "Pennsylvania Station," for $200 (SL, 76). The story was still murky—in 1948 Faulkner thought it might not be good enough to include in *Collected Stories* (SL, 274)—and the "device" was part of the problem. "Pennsylvania Station" turns largely on complications deriving from letters; the transient who tells the story of his sister's buying a coffin tells of communicating with her by mail. Yet she neither reads nor writes. Her letters are written for her and read to her by a neighbor, who enlarges on what she reads as she reports it; her son fails to mail a letter she dictates to the neighbor, then forges one in her name, which she certifies she wrote herself; and her brother invents a letter from the profligate son, whose only letter to his mother is the funeral wreath he mails when she dies. A marginally better letter story is "Idyll in the Desert," published in a limited edition by Random House in December 1931. The narrator is a government mail rider in Arizona, whose appointed rounds afford him knowledge of the tuberculars at isolated desert camps about whom he tells. A mail carrier, he is also both Sender and Receiver in a complex of correspondences that make and move the plot. He is intermediary between Dorry Howse and his lover, "Mrs. So-and-so in New York," whom his telegram brings together (USWF, 405); he is agent for the woman's husband, whom he keeps informed of her illness when Dorry abandons her; and he fakes registered envelopes for the husband's support money so that she will believe it is from Dorry. When Mrs. So-and-so dies, drastically changed by her illness, he verifies her identity to her husband by a series of wires.

The mail rider's letters for lovers and husbands, and the need to forge them, convey the themes of separation and betrayal which, with the correspondence, establish links between "Idyll" and three letter stories associated by their use of a tyrannical parent.[7] In "Elly," the least of these, Elly defends herself against her grandmother's charge that her lover is a Negro by writing notes to the deaf old woman on the backs of old dance cards—the medium of correspondence suggesting, perhaps, the dark, back side of acceptable courtships. In "A Rose for Emily," the best of the three, Emily's "thwarted . . . woman's life" (CSWF, 127) and her withdrawal from society following her father's and Homer Barron's deaths are expressed, in part, by her mail. When the mayor writes regarding her taxes, she replies with "a note on paper of an archaic shape, in a thin, flowing calligraphy in faded ink, to the effect that she no longer went out at all. The tax notice was also enclosed, without comment" (CSWF, 120). As with her letter, so with her home. Her writing is as expressive of her life alone in the old house as her house is of the corpse in the upstairs room. The narrator's language when he describes the "once . . . white" house with its "stubborn and coquettish decay" (CSWF, 119) is deliberate: it recalls the faded letter written there, the archaic writer, and her decaying lover. A letterly detail later in the story isolates both the house and its occupant from the town: "When the town got free postal delivery, Miss Emily alone refused to let them fasten the metal numbers above her door and attach a mailbox to it" (CSWF, 128). Literally, she refuses an address, putting herself beyond the appeal of all letters, and so beyond the need to respond. Tax notices, thereafter, are "returned by the post office . . . , unclaimed" (CSWF, 128).

The third story of the group is "Miss Zilphia Gant," a study of abnormal female psychology, as Faulkner understood it, that has some obvious connections to "A Rose for Emily," among other stories of its kind.[8] Here Faulkner used letters as the medium of psychological replacement according to epistolary laws and conventions he understood very well. After her husband forsakes her, for example, Zilphia corresponds with him vicariously by writing "guarded significant letters to agony columns, mentioning incidents which only he could recognize" (USWF, 379). The figurative replies are her weekly letters from the Memphis detective agency, for which "the postmaster rallied her on her city sweetheart" (USWF, 379). Like the wedding announcements in the Memphis paper, which excite her to "violate her ineradicable virginity again and again with something evoked out of the darkness immemorial and philoprogenitive" (USWF, 379), the Memphis letters are erotic substitutes for the absent husband, now remarried. "By means of the letters she knew how they lived. She knew more about each than the other did. She knew when they quarrelled and felt exultation; she knew when they were reconciled and felt raging and impotent despair. Sometimes at night she would become one of the two of them, entering their bodies in turn and crucified anew by her ubiquity, participating in ecstasies the more racking for being vicarious and transcendant of the actual flesh." (USWF, 379–380). The detective's letters tell Zilphia that the new wife is pregnant, when the child will be born, and about the birth and the mother's death. By means of these letters she is able to adopt or steal the child herself, thereby becoming a mother, as in her dream, "without a man" (USWF, 379). With the lovemaking and conception figuratively accomplished, Miss Zilphia retreats into isolation with her foster-daughter as her mother had with her, and "the letters from the city sweetheart ceased" (USWF, 381).

Of this story Faulkner said, in a letter to Alfred Dashiell at *Scribner's* in late 1928, "'Miss Zilphia Gant' may be too diffuse, still; I don't know. I am quite sure that I have no feeling for short stories; that I shall never be able to write them, yet for some strange reason I continue to do so, and to try them on Scribners' with unflagging optimism" (SL, 42). That the reason was primarily financial is suggested by a funny, self-effacing letter to *Post* editor Thomas B. Costain, who had suggested that Faulkner visit the offices of the magazine in Philadelphia. When Faulkner returned the proofs of "Mountain Victory," he addressed Costain as "Mr Coston" and assumed the familiar epistolary guise of hard-pressed provincial. "About coming East," he wrote, "I'd have to sell the Post about three more stories next month before I could afford the trip. I have had to do a lot of repair work on my house, which has not been touched in that way to speak of since it was built in 1848. So at present I am living on corn field peas, let alone hoping to go anywhere. But if I ever do get up that way again, I shall look forward to seeing you all with a great deal of pleasure, if not profit." [9] Costain responded in kind at the end of the month, writing, "We feel it would be a matter of mutual benefit if we could have a talk with you about your work, so we are hoping that you will be diligent enough to send us the necessary number of manuscripts in the specified time." He added, "I imagine the cutting you have done on the galley proofs will suffice." [10]

Without question Faulkner did write stories for the money magazine publication offered, and he was willing to cut and shape them to editorial standards not necessarily his own. But for a long time editors tended to agree with the assessment of his work that he offered Dashiell at the beginning. A letter from a *Scribner's* editor in November 1928 suggested, "The trouble with your writing . . . is that you get mostly the overtones and seem to avoid the real core of the story. It would seem that in the attempt to avoid the obvious you have manufactured the vague. You are skirting around drama and not writing it." [11] A letter the next month, praising "Miss Zilphia Gant" as "by far the most coherent thing of yours I have seen," offered the observation that Faulkner was "like a distance runner trying short sprints." [12] The truth of that judgment is suggested by his notable success in creating novelistic effects in short stories as much as by the difficulty he had placing them, and letters were part of that success. Three stories that illustrate the point, lettered in different ways and to different ends, are "Victory," "All the Dead Pilots," and "There Was a Queen."

"Victory" is a very long story and was longer still before Faulkner extracted the material of "Crevasse," probably in the spring of 1931 when he was planning the composition of *These 13*, where both were published.[13] It does not appear on the short story Sending Schedule, and there is no evidence it was offered for publication to a magazine. Long though it is, the story covers a surprisingly long period of time—the nine years from Alec Gray's enlistment in 1914 to the Christmas Eve in 1923 when the Canadian émigré Walkley encounters him selling matches in Piccadilly Circus. Duration is suggested in "Victory," as in "A Rose for Emily," for example, by events rather than dates and by the episodic structure of the story and the broken chronology of the scenes that give the sense of extended time characteristic of the best of Faulkner's short fictions. Presumably, Gray enlists in the first year of the war, since his grandfather believes he will be home before Christmastide (CSWF, 442). It is 1921 when he returns to France, three years after the Armistice (CSWF, 456), and he attends two subsequent Armistice Day celebrations (CSWF, 458, 459) before meeting Walkley. The undated fragments of monthly letters between Gray and his family, and the several long interruptions in their correspondence, mark events at the war and at home in Scotland that establish contrasts between Gray's past and present lives. They do so, however, not by what they say but by what they are. Rather than revealing the successive change in Gray, his letters conceal him in formulaic phrasing that, like the title "Victory," is ironically expressive. The letters hide his physical hurts in repetitions: *"I am well," "I am well," "I have been sick but I am better now," "my hurt is well," "I am well"* (CSWF, 444, 447, 448). Such stolid understatements give the appearance of dutiful humility, but in the contexts of Gray's actual wounds and heroic or vengeful acts they suggest the *"pride and vainglory"* that Gray's father warns his son against (CSWF, 447). When the father writes, *"Never miscall your birth, Alec. You are not a gentleman,"* Gray answers by sending his "medal, and his photograph in the new tunic with the pips and ribbon and the barred cuffs" (CSWF, 447–448). His concern for appearances, so evident in the forms of his letters, shows itself after the war in the pressed suit and regimental scarf he wears to sell matches, and prompts his final letter to his mother. He spends his last money on a black silk dress for her, and writes again, *"I am well. Love to Jessie and Matthew and John Wesley and Elizabeth"* (CSWF, 456).

Such stories are made to the complex reflexive patterns that Faulkner used for novels, where multi-faceted events in time and place are presented with the semblance of simultaneity. This accounts for the ease with which he included independent stories in novels from the mid-1930s onward: "Wash" in *Absalom, Absalom!,* for example, the Snopes stories in the Trilogy, and the Sartoris and McCaslin-Beauchamp stories in the story novels, *The Unvanquished* and *Go Down, Moses.* "All the Dead Pilots" and "There Was a Queen," conversely, seem to have been inspired by novels. Together with the companion piece, "Ad Astra," both are part of the Sartoris material Faulkner was working with early in 1927—*Flags in the Dust,* certainly, and probably in the case of the story about Narcissa's letters, *Sanctuary.* Respectively, they fill gaps in the Sartoris history and bring Sartoris stories forward into the present. Whereas "Victory" uses letters to achieve novelistic effects, "All the Dead Pilots" and "There Was a Queen" seem to have been generated by the various letters in the lettered Sartoris novels.

In the first of these, letters provide the form of the story, in the second the substance. Faulkner chose as narrator of "All the Dead Pilots" a military censor, who extends the theme, borrowed from the subadar in "Ad Astra," that "they are dead, all the old pilots, dead on the eleventh of November, 1918" (CSWF, 511). Granting this, his concern is to express their heroism in a diminished present. His story is a "composite: a series of brief glares in which, instantaneous and without depth or perspective, there stood into sight the portent and the threat of what the race could bear and become, in an instant between dark and dark" (CSWF, 512). The photographic image is commensurate with the narrator's attempts to develop a synchronized flash camera,[14] but the "composite" at the end of the story is composed of letters, not pictures, or rather, of letters that make a picture. Crippled by the loss of a leg, the narrator officially cripples correspondence, defacing personal letters with his paper cutter, pot of glue, and red ink. He is one of the many voyeurs in Faulkner's fiction: the letters he reads and ruins give him access to the private lives in the story he tells and, finally, provide him a way of telling the untellable. The censor transcribes four letters found together in the same mail when Johnny Sartoris is killed: Johnny's last letter to Aunt Jenny, Major Kaye's letter to Jenny announcing Johnny's death, and parts of two letters from Jenny to Johnny returned to her with his personal effects. Together they form the composite. The first two contain the "transparent and honorable lies" about war the narrator has previously described (CSWF, 512): Johnny's *"I am all right about going to church,"* for example, and Kaye's *"it may be a comfort to you that he was buried by a minister"* (CSWF, 529, 530). The last two are fragments, censored in their transcription not for military reasons but for the formal imperatives of the story itself, and suggesting by their censored form not the danger of letters to the war effort but the limited understanding of war in letters from home. The censor quotes this from one of Jenny's letters: *". . . let those foreign women alone. I lived through a war myself and I know how women act in war, even with Yankees. And a good-for-nothing hellion like you . . ."* And this from another: *". . . we think it's about time you came home. Your grandfather is getting old, and it don't look like they will ever get done fighting over there. So you come on home. The Yankees are in it now. Let them fight if they want to. It's their war. It's not yours"* (CSWF, 531). Jenny's words are returned to her with letters from the living and the dead. Mocked by Johnny's life in France as the narrator knows it, by his heroism, and by his death, they stand for a chasm of misunderstanding they cannot span. But it is the limits of the four letters individually, this juxtaposition reveals, that necessitate the narrator's composite, which is in fact a picture made with fragments of letters, reflexive analogue of the story itself. "And that's all," he concludes. "That's it. The courage, the recklessness, call it what you will, is the flash, the instant of sublimation; then flick! the old darkness again. That's why. It's too strong for steady diet. And if it were a steady diet, it would not be a flash, a glare. And so, being momentary, it can be preserved and prolonged only on paper: a picture, a few written words that any match, a minute and harmless flame that any child can engender, can obliterate in an instant" (CSWF, 531).

It was the enigmatic durability of written experience in letters rather than its fragility that generated "There Was a Queen" from the deep pool of materials with which Faulkner was working in the winter and spring of 1928. It is possible that parts of "All the Dead Pilots" existed before *Sartoris*, but Hans Skei points out that the earliest record of the story, on the Sending Schedule, is February 5, 1930.[15] "There Was a Queen" dates from *Scribner's* rejection letter, July 2, 1929. In that letter, Dashiell objected specifically that the Sartoris "background . . . comes up and overwhelms the early part of the story."[16] In the large context of Compson-Sartoris-Benbow materials Faulkner was shaping that winter and spring, however, that background is precisely what gives special force to the Snopes letters and the means Narcissa employs to retrieve them. Faulkner returned to Oxford from New York in December 1928. In January 1929 he began work on *Sanctuary* and that winter and spring revised the Quentin section of *The Sound and the Fury*. The edited version of *Flags in the Dust* was published as *Sartoris* on January 31. In this complex of new writing and revision, aspects of Horace Benbow's sexual obsession that were deemphasized in *Sartoris* were attached to Quentin Compson; *Sanctuary* may have influenced the revision of *The Sound and the Fury* as well as being influenced by it and by *Flags*.[17] In "There Was a Queen" Faulkner extended and expanded upon published and unpublished materials from this vortex. Narcissa's attachment to the Snopes letters is reclaimed from *Flags/Sartoris* but colored now by aspects of her character, implicit there, that Faulkner was developing in the *Sanctuary* manuscript. In the Sartoris novels, the lost letters evoke her "distaste and dread . . . that the intactness of her deep and heretofore inviolate serenity might be the sport of circumstance; that she must trust to chance against the eventuality of a stranger casually raising a stray bit of paper from the ground" (Flags, 285). In "There Was a Queen" she tells Jenny, "I was crazy for a while. I thought of people, men, reading them, seeing not only my name on them, but the marks of my eyes where I had read them again and again. I was wild. When Bayard and I were on our honeymoon, I was wild. I couldn't even think about him alone. It was like I was having to sleep with all the men in the world at the same time" (CSWF, 739–740). This passage borrows from both Sartoris-Benbow sources. Narcissa's guilt demonstrates the truth of Horace's recognition, in *Sanctuary*, that "there's a corruption about even looking upon evil, even by accident; you cannot haggle, traffic, with putrefaction" (SR, 125). Her imagining herself sleeping with "all the men in the world at the same time" recalls Horace's final letter to Narcissa in *Flags*, where he borrows from *Don Juan* to express his sexual frustration. Don Juan's wish, "That womankind had but one rosy mouth / To kiss them all at once from North to South," furnishes Horace's wish that spring be concentrated in one place "like Byron's ladies' mouths" (Flags, 399), which itself echoes Byron Snopes' description of Narcissa's mouth in a letter Horace delivers to her (Flags, 244). In a still more sexually charged context, in the 1930 story "Divorce in Naples," the bosun goes to the same source to describe George's longing to have all the women at once, paraphrasing "unwitting and with unprintable aptness Byron's epigram about women's mouths" (CSWF, 882).

In addition to the same characters, the language and the psychology of sexual repression in "There Was a Queen" are the same as in these novels, and they relate the story to others submitted for publication at this time: "The Leg," "Miss Zilphia Gant," "Elly," and "A Rose for Emily." The letters themselves are central in a special way. In the "background," they are the source of Jenny's and Narcissa's differences about how a lady behaves; in the foreground, the laws of letters shape Narcissa's sexual attitudes and guide her sexual activity. The erotic force of the Snopes letters and Narcissa's sense of the anonymous Sender as a vicarious lover are much more fully developed here than in the novels. But stronger still is her sense of her own presence in the letters as named Receiver, and as the fascinated reader and re-

reader who marked the texts with "the marks of my eyes where I had read them again and again." The intimacy of the relationship, as the Sender and Receiver mutually depict it, brings the federal agent to Narcissa, "trying to find out where the man had gone," as she tells Jenny, "thinking I must know, since the man had written me letters like that" (CSWF, 740). The agent is searching for Snopes. Narcissa is in search of a written image of herself, hoarded from her husband's view while he lived and secretly nourished in her widowhood. This she reclaims when she takes back the letters in Memphis. She trades her physical body for an epistolary persona, thereby rendering the vicarious experience real. What Snopes and Narcissa imagined together separately in their one-sided epistolary discourse, Narcissa and the man aptly designated an "agent" enact together. The price is the letters themselves. Narcissa considers herself the social superior of both the illiterate letter writer and the Yankee Jew. Both in these contexts are "low," and they represent to her the carnal Everyman who invaded her marriage bed: by enacting a fantasy about one stranger with another, Narcissa figuratively does sleep "with all the men in the world at the same time" as she images herself doing on her honeymoon. When she justifies herself to Jenny, she tells her, "Men are all about the same, with their ideas of good and bad. Fools" (CSWF, 741).

In this conflux of related work, the Snopes letters in "There Was a Queen" reveal Narcissa Benbow as Faulkner imagined her after *Flags in the Dust*—in ways that remember the ironic association of Narcissa with Temple Drake in *Sanctuary* and look forward to the Temple of *Requiem for a Nun*. The distinguishing facts of Temple's life in *Sanctuary* are her rape, her confinement at Miss Reba's, and her public appearance in court at Lee Goodwin's trial. Narcissa's self-regard in all of the Sartoris-Benbow texts, her deep-seated, self-righteous concern there for propriety, and her hypocritical manipulation of the law and lawyers in *Sanctuary* make it fitting in "There Was a Queen" that the illicit Memphis lover she subverts is an agent of the law rather than Temple's Memphis gangster, that she arranges her own violation rather than being abducted, and that she spends two nights in a Memphis hotel rather than weeks in a Memphis brothel. It is no broad variation in their sexual behavior that Temple has Red in her bed as Popeye's surrogate, for Narcissa too has a surrogate lover: she sleeps with all mankind through the agency of Snopes' letters, and with Snopes through the federal agent. Nor should we wonder that Narcissa gives her body to keep her letters, and the wild dreams they evoke, from public exposure, when in *Sanctuary* the corn cob, source and symbol of the nightmare Temple describes to Horace, is produced in open court and made the object of obscene speculation in Jefferson. In "There Was a Queen," Faulkner was using the epistolary medium of *Flags/Sartoris* to convey characters and themes he was setting forth by different means in *Sanctuary*. And he did the same regularly with these materials. "They were mine," Narcissa says of the Snopes letters in "There Was a Queen," "I had to get them back" (CSWF, 741); and in *Requiem*, where Temple is blackmailed with letters Faulkner invented for that novel, she tells Gavin, "all that matters is that I wrote the letters" (RN, 127).

[ ii ]

Given the record of Faulkner's work on *Sanctuary* in 1929 and 1931, it hardly needs saying that it, too, was shaped by intertextual contexts. The two texts of the book virtually are two novels: the original one the story of Horace Benbow, extended from *Flags in the Dust*; the revised one the story of Temple Drake.[18] Of course both the stories are in both versions of the novel, but there are substantial and significant differences between them, including their being differently lettered. From *Flags* to the original *Sanctuary*, Faulkner retained Horace's letters to this sister in form and function. Two days before her marriage to Bayard, Horace delivers a letter to Narcissa's bedroom (SO, 17), as he does a Snopes letter in *Flags* when he tells her he is marrying Belle (Flags, 243). The Snopes letters are briefly described in the original *Sanctuary*, together with Narcissa's "detached equanimity" when she reads them, and, when she loses them, her oddly "maternal" passion "at the idea of having letters addressed to her read by someone she did not know" (SO, 74). When Horace writes to Belle for a divorce, his detachment is such that it is as if her name on the envelope were "scrawled there by a hand that had no actual relation to his life" (SO, 220). Faulkner brought the original manuscript to closure, as he did Horace's story in *Flags*, with a transcribed letter from Horace to Narcissa and, here, her brief reply. The long, self-accusatory letter about his cowardice at the Goodwin trial, and his unhappy return to Belle, concludes with the plea that Narcissa help Rudy Lamar in his name. "I want you to find that woman yourself; tell her that I must give up the case because I do not think I am good enough, and that I am putting it in the hands of the best criminal lawyer I can find, for an appeal, and that she is not to worry. Do this, my dear" (SO, 283). Narcissa's response is as calculated a betrayal of Horace's trust as her revelations about his case to the county attorney, Eustace Graham. "I received your letter," she writes. "Your message to that woman I cut off and mailed to her at the jail. I imagine she got it" (SO, 284). Literally, she has edited Ruby out of Horace's letter to her, and out of their lives. Six pages later, after Popeye has been jailed in Birmingham and hanged, the manuscript ends. Less than two years later, when the revised *Sanctuary* was published in February 1931, all of this lettered matter had been deleted, this time by Faulkner himself.

Why Faulkner deleted the letters and why he revised at all have much to do with the closeness of *Sanctuary* to *Flags*.[19] The letters are a device belonging to the multiple stories-in-stories of Faulkner's first Yoknapatawpha novel—to Horace's relations to Narcissa and Belle; and to Narcissa's vicarious relation to Snopes, and through his letters to Horace and Bayard. These logically carried into *Sanctuary* in early 1929 as part of the baggage the characters brought with them, but in the interim Faulkner's conception of Horace and Narcissa had changed. It would change again by the time he received the *Sanctuary* galleys from Hal Smith in November 1930, for he already had extended their stories in other work then and had expanded on matter accruing to them. The Snopes letters in the original *Sanctuary* are incidental background matter; by July 1929, Narcissa's attachment to them had been appropriated as the occasion for her improbity and the resultant death of Jenny Du Pre in "There Was a Queen."

The next year they were gone from the novel. The letters Horace writes in the original *Sanctuary* represent a more complex revision. To begin with, they portray him more as the victim of his own singular failings, as in *Flags*, than of circumstance and the contingencies of existence, as in the published novel. His last letter to Narcissa is framed by expressions of his cowardice, his ineffectuality as a lawyer, and his betrayal of Ruby and Lee. The long central section describes his unhappy relationship with Belle and her daughter, Little Belle, and his sense of his paradoxical relation through them to all women. "I thank God that no bone and flesh of mine has taken that form which, rife with its inherent folly, knells and bequeathes its own disaster, untouched. Untouched, mind you. That's what hurts. Not that there is evil in the world; evil belongs in the world: it is the mortar in which the bricks are set. It's that they can be so impervious to the mire which they reveal and teach us to abhor; can wallow without tarnishment in the very stuff in the comparison with which their bright, tragic, fleeting magic lies" (SO, 282). This passage is of a piece with deleted passages of dream work, in which Horace associates Belle with his own dead mother by an allusion to Emma Bovary's death (SO, 60), and in cutting them both Faulkner diminished Horace's role as the central consciousness of the book and put him at a further remove from the "wild and delicate futility" of the character depicted in the letters in *Flags*. In the revised book, Horace still is helplessly attracted to and repelled by destructive women, such as Narcissa and Belle, by destroyed women, such as Ruby, and by Little Belle and Temple, who represent the potential for both. But this has less of the pitiable about it and more of human fatality in a stillborn world that Faulkner described in both versions of *Sanctuary* as "stark and dying above the tide-edge of the fluid in which it lived and breathed" (SO, 219; SR, 215). To support this theme, the descriptions in Horace's letter of Belle's meeting him in her bedroom at Kinston and his telephone call to Little Belle at her houseparty were retained in the revision, expanded and recast as exposition. Narcissa's letter of reply was cut simply because there no longer was a letter to reply to.

Certainly Faulkner's attitude toward his art and himself as artist had changed when he came to the *Sanctuary* galleys from the time when he let Ben Wasson do as he would with *Flags in the Dust*.[20] In his 1932 introduction to the novel, he said he could not let the book "shame *The Sound and the Fury* and *As I Lay Dying*" (ESPL, 178). But perhaps it was not solely the advances he had made in his art, or even the combination of artistic pride and financial need in the late autumn of 1930, that impelled these and the numerous other alterations of language and forms. Granting for the moment the persuasive surmise that Faulkner cut Horace's part of the book because aspects of the character as he had shaped it two and even four years before were too close to the man he had then been himself[21]—granting this, it may be that in the late fall of 1930 a letter from the semiautobiographical character claiming pride in his childless state was too close, in a way that other intimate material in the novel was not, to the writer whose wife had a daughter by her first husband and was then enduring a particularly difficult pregnancy.[22] Another of Horace's letters in the galleys, to Belle asking for a divorce, might also have reminded the author painfully of himself and of letters he had written himself in the months between January and May 1929 when he was writing the book. In the original *Sanctuary*, Horace puts off writing Belle from the night he first thinks of it, when Ruby tells him Temple was at the Frenchman Place, until the night Snopes tells him Temple is in a Memphis brothel; when he writes the letter it is not mailed until the morning of the night he returns from Miss Reba's, sick with visions of sexual aberration in a stillborn world. In the interim, his sister Narcissa accuses him of threatening her own reputation in Jefferson by carrying on an affair with Ruby Lamar and pressures him to return to Belle. His need to free himself from Narcissa, and all tormenting women, turns him again to his unwritten letter. "I'm going to Europe, Horace said. Soon as this business is finished. This damned country. I'll write Belle for a divorce and——he lay for a tense moment, then he started to swing his feet to the floor, but refrained. I'll write tomorrow. I couldn't even write a

sane letter to anyone now" (SO, 199). The time in the novel is May and
June 1929, and Faulkner wrote that passage about divorce sometime
before he finished his manuscript on May 25 of that year. Estelle's divorce had been granted April 29: she was emotionally drained by it,
insecure in Oxford in the role of divorcee, and Faulkner was under
pressure, particularly from Estelle's sister, to marry her immediately.[23]
It was then that he wrote the undated letter to Hal Smith asking for
$500, and explaining that he was marrying "for my honor and the san-
ity—I believe life—of a woman. . . . It's a situation which I engendered and permitted to ripen which has become unbearable, and I am
tired of running from devilment I bring about."[24] Despite the inversion
of divorce, in this scene from the novel, and Faulkner's own marriage,
Horace's determination to run and Faulkner's to stay, the excuse Horace
gives for putting off writing a letter to Belle echoes precisely the excuse Faulkner gave Smith for the turbulence of the letter he did write.
"This sounds a little insane," he said, "but I'm not in any shape to
write letters now."[25] Of course Horace does return to Belle at the end
of the novel, and Faulkner must have known when he brought the
book to an end a month after Estelle's divorce that he would marry
her—"both want to and have to," as he wrote Smith.[26] In this context,
Horace's letter to Narcissa may well express—in the passages about
his unhappiness with his divorced wife and her daughter—some
of William Faulkner's forebodings about his impending marriage.
Horace writes, among other things, of "that unfailing aptitude of
women for coinciding with the emotional periphery of a man at the
exact moment when it reaches top dead center, at the exact moment
when the fates have prized his jaws for the regurgitated bit" (SO, 281).
Once again, the very personal matter of his own life and letters crossed
genres, but this time without objective distancing, and this time he
recognized and deleted it himself before the novel was published two
years later.

The more commonly recognized form of intertextuality, involving
the absorption of one writer's work into that of another, is everywhere
apparent in Faulkner's work from the beginning of his career. *Sanctuary* resonates with borrowings that range from familiar adaptations of
Eliot's poetry through allusions to Sir James Frazer and Greek and Roman mythology to the very specific and repeated references in the
novel to Flaubert's *Madame Bovary*.[27] To the latter case, in particular,
some speculative additions having to do with letters may be made.
The book that bookish Horace Benbow carries in his pocket when
he and Popeye confront each other across the pond in the opening
scene of the revised *Sanctuary* is not identified, but the conjunction of

Popeye's interest in the book (SR, 4) and Horace's description of him soon following suggest that it might be *Madame Bovary:* "He smells black, Benbow thought; he smells like that black stuff that ran out of Bovary's mouth and down upon her bridal veil when they raised her head" (SR, 7). If Horace knows Flaubert's book well enough to quote it, he knows the book in his pocket well, too. In the original *Sanctuary* when Horace leaves Belle, he puts Little Belle's photograph in his pocket with a "dog-eared volume" (SO, 19), which reappears twice more in contexts analogous to this with Popeye. The photograph is "propped against a book on the table" (SO, 59) on the night Horace dreams that Belle suffers Bovary's macabre death throe and remembers Popeye's smelling black. The book and the photograph are juxtaposed again when Horace recalls Ruby's story about Temple at the Old Frenchman Place (SO, 143); and when Temple tells of seeing herself as a bride in a coffin, her unconscious allusion to Bovary prompts Horace to project her experience on Little Belle: he imagines Little Belle/Temple watching "something black and furious go roaring out of her pale body" (SO, 220; SR, 216). Appropriately enough, Faulkner seems to have borrowed a book by an old Frenchman to put into Horace's pocket at the Old Frenchman Place. It is the artifact from which some of his most dreadful and revealing allusions and associations are drawn.

If Flaubert's book is in Faulkner's literally, it may be that other writing from that book is present also—specifically, the letter Rodolphe writes to Emma to break off their love affair in Book Two, Chapter Eight, of *Madame Bovary.* The letter is a calculated piece of deception and self-justification from a gentleman to the young married woman who has been his lover, and it would have appealed to Faulkner as a suggestive document in a book of his own filled with false lovers and hypocritical relationships, especially one as fully lettered as the original *Sanctuary.* Rodolphe's strategy is sly self-deprecation: he has been dragging Emma to the abyss, he is tormented by the grief that would come to her if she knew his true nature, and he will punish himself by exile for his crimes against her. "I am going away," he writes. "I don't know where. I am too close to madness to think." He asks only that she "remember the unfortunate man who caused your undoing. Teach my name to your child; let her repeat it in her prayers." [28]

Horace's sincere letter to Narcissa that Faulkner cut from the conclusion of the *Sanctuary* galleys is the antithesis of this, and his letter asking Belle for a divorce is not transcribed in either version of the book. Gowan's letter to Narcissa, however, might have been modeled on Rodolphe's.

*Narcissa my dear*

　　*This has no heading. I wish it could have no date. But if my heart were as blank as this page, this would not be necessary at all. I will not see you again. I cannot write it, for I have gone through with an experience which I cannot face. I have but one rift in the darkness, that is that I have injured no one save myself by my folly, and that the extent of that folly you will never learn. I need not say that the hope that you never learn it is the sole reason why I will not see you again. Think as well of me as you can. I wish I had the right to say, if you learn of my folly think not the less of me.*

G. (SR, 126)

All letters are fictions, but none more consciously so than this. Gowan's epistolary persona literally is Rodolphe, a fictional fiction of himself as Sender. Like Rodolphe, he is unworthy of his correspondent's love, tormented by the thought she might learn of his true nature, and consoled by the knowledge he has harmed no one but himself. He too punishes himself by exile; he too asks to be thought well of. And he too is a hypocrite: a callow Rodolphe, who understands the extent of his folly as having *"passed out twice"* (SR, 83) and jilts a woman he has not wronged. Jenny calls his letter "a delicate operation on the human heart without anaesthetic" (SR, 126), but the hypocrisy of the letter lies in the fact that it should be written to Narcissa at all, rather than to Temple. If Temple is the figurative "sister" of Emma Bovary in the novel,[29] Narcissa and Temple are closely associated as inverted images of one another, and in the pattern of surrogates for love and lovers that pervades *Sanctuary* it is no surprise to find a letter written to one woman belonging properly to another. Gowan's letter undoes his crime against Temple by making him the romantic hero of a novel by Flaubert. Couched as an acknowledgment of unspecified *"folly,"* the letter employs epistolary strategies and a language that in fact erase all trace of Gowan Stevens from it. Having no *"heading"* it has no return address and so can be neither answered nor acknowledged. Gowan wishes it had no date. Figuratively, it is the *"blank page"* he describes, a self-negating artifact phrased in twelve negatives, including the Sender's contention that *"I cannot write it."* It is not even signed with his name. Gowan leaves his identity as a gentleman and his identity with Temple when he abandons her at the Frenchman Place. Frightened of facing her, and of facing the "people who knew him, who might know him" (SR, 83), he faces Narcissa instead in the epistolary guise of a fictional character.

　　Faulkner supported this motif by leaving Temple no address to which Gowan or Horace can write. There is no forwarding address at the university post office in Oxford where Horace seeks her: instead, like Gowan, he finds her name scrawled suggestively on the wall of the lavatory at the railway station. That impossible address is extended to the Old Frenchman Place, where Temple is raped in a barn used by the bootleggers as an outhouse, and to Miss Reba's brothel when Virgil Snopes and Fonzo Winbush confuse the "lattice-work false entry" (SR, 185) at her front door with the same. The house with no front door has no place for mail: the only letter delivered to Reba's is the "torn scrap of paper . . . from a handbill" (SR, 201), left there for Horace by Snopes and containing only another address, of another brothel. The conjoined images of excrement and false entry, however, are perversely suggestive of the aberrant sexual violations to which Temple is subjected, and the lack of a front on the house makes concrete the figure for sexual intercourse that Faulkner elsewhere names *"the beast with two backs"* (SF, 184) after Rabelais and Shakespeare. Reba's house is a temple of prostitution—sign and symbol of its own function[30]—and when Horace says he will subpoena Temple there, Reba says she wants "no jay cops up here with no letters for nobody" (SR, 261). This detail was added to the revised *Sanctuary*, as was the description of Eustace Graham as a former mail carrier (SR, 254), a job which helps to account for his ability to make contact with Temple when Horace fails to bring her to the trial as his witness.

## [ iii ]

Asked at Virginia in 1957 about the "sensationalism" of *Sanctuary*, Faulkner called it an "incidental tool" and went on to remind his audience that "the carpenter don't build a house just to drive nails. He drives nails to build a house."[31] He might have been speaking of the letters in the novel, as well. For the novelist as carpenter, the house of fiction took many forms. In his best work, as Noel Polk has said of the *Sanctuary* revisions, Faulkner steadfastly refused to repeat himself.[32] But as the forms of his fiction changed under his shaping hand, so did the serious uses he found for "incidental tools," experimenting at need according to the formal imperatives of the work that engaged him. The imaginative integrity of the builder included knowing the limits and potential of his materials, and it informed the principles of construction he avowed. Cash Bundren puts the matter into more imaginative terms, suggestive of Faulkner's remarks about literary form, when he says in *As I Lay Dying*,

Folks seem to get away from the olden right teaching that says to drive the nails down and trim the edges well always like it was for your own use and comfort you were making it. It's like some folks has the smooth, pretty boards to build a courthouse with and others dont have no more than rough lumber fitten to build a chicken coop. But it's better to build a tight chicken coop than a shoddy courthouse, and when they both build shoddy or build well, neither because it's one or tother is going to make a man feel the better nor the worse. (AILD, 224)

Henry James would have understood. He too thought of the novelist as a builder, and in the preface to *The Portrait of a Lady* he found that book a "neat and careful and proportional pile of bricks . . . a structure reared with an 'architectural competence.'"[33] Faulkner had built well in *Sanctuary*, and in his own introduction to the book in 1932, he said that he had rebuilt still better. "I tore the galleys down and rewrote the book," he wrote near the end of the piece. "It had been already set up once, so I had to pay for the privilege of rewriting it, trying to make out of it something which would not shame *The Sound and the Fury* and *As I Lay Dying* too much and I made a fair job" (ESPL, 178).

There followed from *Sanctuary*, in 1932 and 1936, two novels with the working title "Dark House," both built partly with incidental letters but both marking, in the application and then in the theoretical concern with letters and epistolarity, significant advances over earlier work. I shall have more to say in Chapter V about the allusive letters of *Light in August*. For the moment it is enough to point out Faulkner's increased understanding in *Light in August* of the absolute power of the letter as letter, which provides the background of letter theories expressed by the characters and investigated, with other mysteries, in *Absalom, Absalom!*, the most fully and profoundly lettered of Faulkner's novels.

Letter conventions are observed in *Light in August* even in the most incidental situations, unconsciously, perhaps, but still unavoidably. When McEachern comes to the orphanage for Joe, for example, he twice asks specifically for his correspondent, Miss Atkins, whose letters have summoned him there (LIA, 133–134). The anonymous note thrown through Hightower's window tied to a brick, "commanding him to get out of town by sunset and signed K.K.K." (LIA, 66), is a middle stage in the community's progressively violent reactions to his preaching, his wife's behavior, and his remaining alone in Jefferson with a Negro cook. In another instance, an unwritten letter is paired with a written one as opening and closing strategies in a pattern of betrayals. Early in the novel, Lena asks Lucas to send for her by "mouthword" because, as she says, "he ain't any hand for letters" (LIA, 17). He portrays this failing, and indicts himself, in the miswritten letter to the sheriff, "in which he had succeeded for an instant in snaring his whole soul and life too" (LIA, 413): *"Mr Wat Kenedy Dear sir please give barer My reward Money for captain Murder Xmas rapp it up in Paper 4 given it toe barer yrs truly"* (LIA, 412). The point is not only that Burch is uneducated, or even greedy, but that he is literally anonymous. A subscript explains, *"not Sined but All rigt You no who"* (LIA, 413). Finally, it may be that material from Faulkner's 1927 bank draft letter to Horace Liveright found its way into *Light in August* in an incidental way, as it did, more significantly, in *The Sound and the Fury*. The "yarn" about buried alcohol dug up by "one of our niggers" (SL, 37) suggests the scene where Joe closes out his liquor business by digging up and destroying his own alcohol. Parts of the same Faulkner letter provided details for Jason Compson's self-inflicted moral bankruptcy.

But in *Light in August*, Faulkner was experimenting seriously with the power of letters as letters over Sender and Receiver, and with the consequences of the letterly discourse for both. Joe Christmas discovers almost casually in Chapter 11, in the first phase of his affair with Joanna Burden, that she is a letter writer with an extensive correspondence.

> He had never seen her sitting save one time when he looked through a downstairs window and saw her writing at a desk in the room. And it was a year after he had remarked without curiosity the volume of mail which she received and sent, and that for a certain period of each forenoon she would sit at the worn, scarred, rolltop desk in one of the scarceused and sparsely furnished downstairs rooms, writing steadily, before he learned that what she received were business and private documents with fifty different postmarks and what she sent were replies—advice, business, financial and religious, to the presidents and faculties and trustees, and advice personal and practical to young girl students and even alumnae, of a dozen negro schools and colleges through the south. (LIA, 220)

In Chapter 12, in the second phase, the woman who by day writes in the respectable epistolary guise of "a combined priest and banker and trained nurse" (LIA, 244), by night reveals "An avidity for the forbidden wordsymbols; and insatiable appetite for the sound of them on his tongue and on her own" (LIA, 244). Faulkner added the description of Joanna as "priest . . . banker . . . nurse" to the Christmas flashback in the manuscript of the novel, perhaps to create just such a contrast,[34] for in this second phase of their relationship, Joanna and Joe become correspondents as well as lovers. She summons him to her with notes concealed in a hollow fence post, feeding her fantasies by telling him to come at a certain hour, or by a certain route, or to a certain place. These notes of love are the dark antitheses of her letters of advice to educated Negroes, and Joe is the dark double of those correspondents, the forbidden lover to whom she whispers, "Negro! Negro! Negro!" (LIA, 245). At those times the epistolary fantasies in the notes extend to her person, "her body gleaming in the slow shifting from one to another of such formally erotic attitudes and gestures as a Beardsley of the time of Petronius might have drawn" (LIA, 245). From the outset, Joe thinks of Joanna as a double self, a woman trying to be a woman, making love like a man, and her androgyny finds a complement in her letter writing. As she writes her conflicting personae alternately into her business letters and her intimate notes to Joe, so she becomes the double self that she writes there. Each set of letters has the force to define her in a contrary way, and Joe thinks of her now as "two creatures that struggled in the one body like two moongleamed shapes struggling drowning in alternate throes upon the surface of a black thick pool beneath the last moon" (LIA, 246).

Faulkner perhaps was drawing on private writing as he had in *The Sound and the Fury* to portray the uncontrollable inner life of the Sender in such passages and scenes, but he also was working to create contexts for their most forceful effects. In Chapters 11 and 12, letters and letterwriting are the tools by which Joanna's principled obsession with Negroes is expressed and Joe most deeply bound to her and impelled. Her obsession derives from the youthful trauma, described to Joe at the end of Chapter 11, when she first saw the Negro as a "black shadow in the shape of a cross" and her father told her, "You must struggle, rise. But in order to rise, you must raise the shadow with you" (LIA, 239, 240). Structurally, this story-within-the-story marks the end of the first phase of her affair with Joe and the beginning of the second: it bridges the time between the two and juxtaposes her lettered relations to Negro college students and to Joe. Following what Joe calls her "surrender . . . in words" (LIA, 227), her letter writing changes dramatically. It is a different "Negro" she addresses in her tryst letters, in a different persona, and rather than raising him up the notes summon Joe to "corruption" (LIA, 246).

Such is the authority of the epistolary Self-as-Word in *Light in August* that the Sender literally is shaped to her own written image: she writes herself into being as a Beardsleyan Salome. In the third place of their affair, by exerting the authority of the letter over its Receiver, Joanna rewrites Joe and herself back into the Receiver and Sender of her initial, formal correspondence with Negro colleges. As the theme of lost identity in the novel should suggest, there are inherent dangers in this for both parties in the correspondence. Faulkner makes clear that Joe is the victim rather than the instrument of Joanna's corruption, as he is also the reader rather than the self-fantasizing writer of letters; but he is also less their creature, and in the third phase his misreadings of Joanna's notes, and his own psychic inability to meet their demands on him, doom both correspondents. At her climacteric as a woman, Joanna still sends notes to the Negro cabin as to a Negro's address, but the maternalistic guise of the woman who gave practical advice in her letters reasserts itself as the persona of the self-styled mother-to-be who tells Joe, "I am with child" (LIA, 252). When he answers the first of these as a "bridegroom" (LIA, 253), she proposes instead of lovemaking that he "take over all her business affairs—with the negro schools" (LIA, 254). Literally, she asks him to write for her, to be Sender of her letters to Negroes as well as Receiver, and to share with her the burdens of her racial obsession. Joanna's strategy is designed to sustain her in her passionate commitment to Negroes by distancing the "Negro" object of her passion, and if Joe will not write for her to students, he can become one of the students to whom she safely can write. This is the sense of her second note, which Joe again answers as a lover, this time without reading it and without realizing "that he was bound just as tightly by that small square of still undivulging paper as though it were a lock and chain" (LIA, 257). As if locked and chained, he carries the note with him, still unaware of its power, and still without reading it even when "it sprang open of its own accord, as though inviting him, insisting" (LIA, 259). The danger to him is implicit in Faulkner's description of Joanna: Joe "saw that she wore steelrimmed spectacles which he had never seen before. He stood in the door, his hand still on the knob, quite motionless. It seemed to him that he could actually hear the words inside him: *You should have read that note. You should have read that note* thinking, 'I am going to do something. Going to do something'" (LIA, 260–261).

Joanna has become to Joe tyrannical mother, one of several such women Faulkner characteristically described in this way. Miss Zilphia Gant is one, and another is the imaginary woman with "iron-gray hair and spectacles" Temple Drake tries to become to control the "little black . . . nigger boy," Popeye, in *Sanctuary* (SR, 212).[35] As Zilphia fulfills her sexual fantasies through letters and resolves her hysteria by acquiring a child, so does Joanna call Joe to her letters and invent a pregnancy; as Temple distances Popeye by imagining him a Negro school boy and herself a "teacher," so Joanna insists Joe go to a Negro school where he will have to "tell niggers that I am a nigger too" (LIA, 262). She would un-man him; he in turn unsexes her. "'You haven't got any baby,' he said. 'You never had one. There is not anything the matter with you except being old. You just got old and it happened to you and now you are not any good anymore. That's all that's wrong with you'" (LIA, 262). Prophetically, this denies Joanna access to either of the epistolary personae through which she has expressed herself in her letters and her life. It is neither as lover nor as mother but as prophetess that she now tells Joe, "Maybe it would be better if we both were dead" (LIA, 263).

When her letters begin again, they are more authoritative still, and more dangerous, and the alteration in Joanna is explicit in her texts as it is also in her physical description. "He would now remember the hollow fencepost as something of which he had heard told, as having taken place in another life from any that he had ever lived. Because the paper, the ink, the form and space, were the same. They had never been long; they were not long now. But now there was nothing evocative of unspoken promise, of rich and unmentionable delights, in them. They were now briefer than epitaphs and more terse than commands" (LIA, 263). The contrary characteristics of "unspoken promise" and brief "epitaphs" describe the evolution of the relationship between Joe and Joanna, and not coincidentally they correspond to two conventional conclusions to epistolary love affairs: Joanna's letters written in the second phase lead to sex, those in the third to death. In the end, both parties to the correspondence are helpless in the power of its laws: Joanna cannot write herself simultaneously as a woman and a servant to an abstract cause, Joe can neither aid her nor free himself from her attempts to be both through her letters to him. Regina K. Fadiman has said that, in adding the Christmas flashback to *Light in August*, Faulkner was concerned to have Joe play out in his affair with Joanna three major events of his childhood, "each representative of one aspect of the unholy trinity that governs his fate. . . . Christmas's hatred of prayer and all forms of religion, and his repugnance for Negroes, which he acts out in his compulsive struggles with women."[36] Joe's letters from Joanna in Chapters 11 and 12 are a compelling element in that pattern. Joanna's last, epitaphlike notes invite him to rites of expiation and prayer and recall him to his childhood with the McEacherns. Figuratively, they span past and present: it is to break that final bond with the past, and destroy the identity her letters impose on him as present Receiver, that Joe kills their Sender. The murder is not self-asserting, of course, but self-denying, and the fatality of the crime, everywhere emphasized in the long flashback that concludes with the lettered chapters, is not free of the influence of letters even after they have ceased. On that night, Joe "did not know if she had left a note for him or not, expected him or not" (LIA, 266), but it is the entire body of Joanna's letters to him, their impact on him, and the collective memories of his past they embody that fatefully draw him to her room to stand waiting while her pistol misfires. What epistolary self-assertion there is for Joe comes belatedly, and futilely, in the form of his only letter in the book: the single phrase "raggedly written, as though by an unpractised hand," left at the Negro church for the sheriff (LIA, 309). Again, as with Lucas Burch, the present letter verifies a past prophecy. Joe's inability to say who or what he is bears out the Negro yard man at the orphanage who tells him, "You dont know what you are. And more than that, you wont never know" (LIA, 363); and this is remembered in his "unprintable" and "unsigned" letter—an untranscribed writing that neither expresses nor names a Sender and exerts no authorial authority over the Receiver. Like his sometime partner, sometimes called Joe, who also writes anonymously to the sheriff, Joe Christmas "ain't any hand for letters."

[ iv ]

The context in which Faulkner began work on the second novel titled "Dark House" in February 1934 is a precedent canon of stories and novels into which he had written letters in a variety of forms and functions for a decade. The subject matter of the new project was generated by the 1931 short story "Evangeline," which opens with a telegram about a ghost and uses a full range of incidental letters and letter strategies to move the plot and maintain connections between the characters. The manuscript of the novel began with letters, as well: among the first pieces added to the "Evangeline" material was Mr. Compson's letter to Quentin about Rosa Coldfield, which opened an early version.[37] By January 31, 1936, when he signed the last page of the manuscript of *Absalom, Absalom!*, Faulkner had inserted that letter into his novel, divided into two parts, together with six others he transcribed: Charles Bon's letter to Judith Sutpen, and two unwritten letters Bon imagines Thomas Sutpen sending him; the lawyer's letterlike diary, his letter to Henry Sutpen at college, and a summary of his letter to Bon. These and many more, either actually sent and received or invented by narrators in support of their own tellings, are the recurrent objects of description and subjects of speculation in a novel so thoroughly and profoundly lettered that no simple catalog of the archive can do it justice. For example, the same letters regularly reappear: Mr. Compson imagines a body of letters in Chapter IV that may or may not have existed in fact, which Quentin re-imagines in Chapter VII and Shreve adopts and expands on in Chapter VIII. Bon's letter to Judith, transcribed at the end of Chapter IV, is the point of reference for the whole one hundred pages of Mr. Compson's narrative in Chapters II, III, and IV; Mr. Compson's letter to Quentin about Rosa, which frames Quentin's and Shreve's telling in Chapters VI through IX, is described repeatedly in Chapter VII as an object of meditation. So much are these letters the substance of oral transmission in the text, and so much the structural and thematic loci of the telling, that they often are the substance as well as the sources of its mysteries. Quentin speculates that, because he is "a barracks filled with stubborn back-looking ghosts" (AA, 12), Rosa writes him the "summons, out of another world almost" (AA, 10), with which her demonizing and the novel begin. At the center of the book, Quentin reads Bon's letter, sees his "shadow" cast upon it, and hears his "dead tongue speaking" (AA, 129). At the conclusion of the novel he reads in the last half of his father's letter Mr. Compson's hope that Rosa *"has herself gained that place or bourne where the objects of the outrage and of the commiseration also are no longer ghosts but are actual people to be actual recipients of the hatred and the pity"* (AA, 377). Like this last one, each other letter also is a "fragile pandora's box of scrawled paper," filling the novel as this one does Quentin's Harvard room with the "violent and unratiocinative djinns and demons" (AA, 258) that the narrators confront in their telling.

In this sense, the transmission of the letters is a paradigm for the transmission of the narrative. The many passages and scenes in which Charles Bon's letter to Judith Sutpen is read and reread, and the problems of reading it for the characters, approximate the problems of reading the novel itself.[38] In *Absalom, Absalom!*, however, Faulkner's consideration of reading unavoidably extended also to problems of writing—of letter reading and letter writing specifically, and the laws that determine the resources and limits of letters as expressive narrative devices. This he entrusted in part to his characters, who test their understanding against parts of the text written by one of them as they do against stories they tell and are told. In so doing the characters in *Absalom, Absalom!* use letters and develop theories of epistolarity in the same ways and to the same ends that Faulkner had done in his precedent fiction. That self-critical exercise in turn extended his own understandings—of the power of letters to span historical time as well as space, for example, and of the determined circularity of epistolary discourse—and on these discoveries he continued to build.

In Mr. Compson's three-chapter-long meditation on Bon's letter, he finds himself unable to explain the relationship that binds "this girl," "this father," "this brother," and "this lover" (AA, 99–100). He says, "It's just incredible. It just does not explain. Or perhaps that's it: they dont explain and we are not supposed to know" (AA, 100). Decidedly, Mr. Compson's preconceptions about the larger than life figures he contemplates through Bon's letter color his reading.[39] But it also must be said that he is reading a personal letter in 1909 addressed in 1865 to Judith Sutpen: he is not the intended Receiver Bon imagined and portrayed.[40] He has the facts of the letter, but cannot bring them to life. Striving to make the story of Charles and Judith explain, he first says that in autumn of 1859 Henry "seduced her along with himself from that distance between Oxford and Sutpen's Hundred, between herself and the man whom she had not even seen yet, as though by means of that telepathy with which as children they seemed at times to anticipate one anothers' actions" (AA, 99). Bon visits Sutpen's Hundred at Christmas 1859 and again briefly the following summer. When the letter in his hand reminds Mr. Compson of love letters, he substitutes for telepathic seduction letters from Bon to Judith in that summer of 1860, and from Henry and Bon both that autumn when they meet again at the University. At Christmas 1860, Henry and Bon ride away together. Mr. Compson speculates that, in the spring of 1861, "probably Henry wrote Judith where they were and what they intended to do" (AA, 119), and that during the war there would have been "no word from [Bon] save through Henry that he (Bon) was alive" (AA, 121). At the moment, when Mr. Compson gives Quentin Bon's 1865 letter to read, he still is concerned with the restraint and opacity of that solitary text, and he invents still more letters. "Now you can see why I said that he loved her," he tells Quentin.

> Because there were other letters, many of them gallant flowery indolent frequent and insincere, sent by hand over that forty miles between Oxford and Jefferson after that first Christmas—the metropolitan gallant's idle and delicately flattering (and doubtless to him, meaningless) gesture to the bucolic maiden—and that bucolic maiden, with that profound and absolutely inexplicable tranquil patient clairvoyance of women against which that metropolitan gallant's foppish posturing was just the jackanape antics of a small boy, receiving the letters without understanding them, not even keeping them, for all their elegant and gallant and tediously contrived turns of form and metaphor, until the next one arrived. But keeping this one which must have reached her out of a clear sky after an interval of four years, considering this one worthy to give to a stranger to keep or not to keep, even to read or not to read as the stranger saw fit, to make that scratch, that undying mark on the blank face of the oblivion to which we are all doomed, of which she spoke——(AA, 128–129)

The epistolary contexts here imagined do two things: first, they valorize Bon's letter as the single one kept, and therefore the most significant one written; second, by making it a fragment of an extended epistolary dialogue to which Mr. Compson has no access, they account for his inability to understand it. Judith keeps Bon's letter as an artifact of their love—to make "that undying mark on the blank face of . . . oblivion," Mr. Compson says; Mr. Compson explains how that letter came into existence and why it is the enigmatic artifact that he finds it to be.

To Quentin and Shreve, the Bon-Judith correspondence is a more than plausible invention: being of an age with the correspondents they "overpass to love, where there might be paradox and inconsistency but nothing fault nor false" (AA, 316). It is one of the patterns of the book that Quentin and Shreve assemble Sutpen materials from the "rag-tag and bob-ends of old tales and talking" (AA, 303) to which they later give significant form. The story of Wash Jones is an example. In Chapter VI, spurred by Shreve's urging that he *tell about the South*" (AA, 174), Quentin recalls to himself Sutpen's return from the war, his seduction of Milly, his murder, and the manner of Judith's life at Sutpen's Hundred thereafter. Like Faulkner, perhaps, he is reflecting on stories he knows and privately considering the ways they might fit what he is planning to tell. Near the end of Chapter VII, when he breaks in on Shreve's "playing" with these facts, he focuses his previous reflections: recounting the story he says he heard from his father, he gives his material very much the same form William Faulkner did in the 1933 story "Wash," from which the novel in part derived.[41] This is not to say that Quentin *is* William Faulkner, but that as the fictional teller, and reteller, of Faulkner's published fictions he employs Faulkner's own devices and strategies of narration. So with the correspondence Quentin and Shreve borrow from Mr. Compson's imagining.

Quentin returns to the Bon-Judith correspondence in Chapter VII to put it into context, retrieving the letters from his father's narrative, adding to them letters from Henry, and re-imagining the motives for the writing and its impact. According to Quentin, Henry's letters from Oxford in autumn 1859 introduce Bon's name to Judith and to Sutpen; in the winter and spring of 1860, after his Christmas visit, Bon writes to Judith each week from Oxford; Henry arranges by letter for Bon's second visit that summer, when Sutpen goes to New Orleans. When Sutpen comes home with the gravestones during the war, he and Judith both know that Bon will write to propose marriage when Henry will permit it. Having heard his father's theory that letters do not explain, and Judith's that they verify reality, Quentin fits his father's narrative practices to Judith's epistolary theory by inventing letters in support of a credible pattern. In this he is guided literally by his father. Shreve delivers Mr. Compson's letter by hand at the beginning of Chapter VI:

> Then on the table before Quentin, lying on the open text book beneath the lamp, the white oblong of envelope, the familiar blurred mechanical *Jefferson Jan 10 1910 Miss* and then, opened, the *My dear son* in his father's sloped fine hand out of that dead dusty summer where he had prepared for Harvard so that his father's hand could lie on a strange lamplit table in Cambridge; that dead summer twilight—the wistaria, the cigar-smell, the fireflies—attenuated up from Mississippi and into this strange room, across this strange iron New England snow. (AA, 173)

Letter and textbook form a palimpsest: facts are read through the letter, which itself is a mixture of fact and fiction about Rosa's funeral and Mr. Compson's speculations on death and the afterlife. The image of the palimpsest accords with the fictional history Quentin "reads" in and through this letter and those his father earlier invented, which he now re-imagines.

Such is the force of this letter that it is forecast at the outset of Mr. Compson's narrative in Chapter II, where the actual September evening in Mississippi is described as an anticipation of the memory the letter will release. Clearly, it is less its meaning than this capacity of the physical text to evoke a prior scene of narration that gives it its present power. Quentin reads only the first half in Chapter VI and the second half only at the end of the book in Chapter IX. Seven times as the story of Bon and Judith unfolds in Chapter VII, his father's letter is described as the object of his meditation. Quentin's hands frame "the rectangle of paper folded across the middle and now open, three quarters open, whose bulk had raised half itself by the leverage of the old crease in weightless and paradoxical levitation, lying at such an angle that he could not possibly have read it, deciphered it, even without this added distortion. Yet he seemed to be looking at it, . . . his face lowered a little, brooding, almost sullen" (AA, 217–218). The narrative and the letter open out together: with his father's hand figuratively between his own, he conjures Rosa and the Sutpens from that text, "talking apparently (if to anything) to the letter lying on the open book on the table between his hands" (AA, 255). It is "pandora's box": half-open before him, it gives up its "djinns and demons" all through the long night of his telling. Near dawn, in the final pages of Chapter IX, when he reads the second half of the letter, it becomes a window, like the window that wakes him in June in *The Sound and the*

*Fury.* Through the windowlike letter, he sees himself and the South juxtaposed:

> Quentin did not answer [Shreve], staring at the window; then he could not tell if *it* was the actual window or the window's pale rectangle upon his eyelids, though after a moment *it* began to emerge. *It* began to take shape in *its* same curious, light, gravity-defying attitude—the once-folded sheet out of the wistaria Mississippi summer, the cigar smell, the random blowing of the fireflies. . . . *It* was becoming quite distinct; he would be able to decipher the words soon, in a moment; even almost now, now, now. . . . Now he (Quentin) could read *it*, could finish *it*—the sloped whimsical ironic hand out of Mississippi attenuated, into the iron snow: . . . (AA, 376–377; my italics)

In Chapter VIII Shreve incorporates the Bon-Judith-Henry letters that Mr. Compson and Quentin imagine with others of his own invention into a theory of calculated self-authoring by which Charles Bon presents himself to Sutpen through letters to Judith in order to force Sutpen to acknowledge him his son.[42] In this Shreve is guided by Quentin's letter and his telling, and through him by Mr. Compson and Judith. "My dear son," is precisely the salutation Bon hopes to evoke from his own father by his letters to Judith: self-verification by a letter is what Judith appeals for when she gives Grandmother Compson the scrap of Bon's letter as an artifact of love—"because it would have happened," she explains, "be remembered even if only from passing from one hand to another, one mind to another" (AA, 127).[43] Of Bon's hopes for a letter from Sutpen in the winter and spring of 1860, Shreve says:

> Maybe he thought it would be in the mail bag each time the nigger rode over from Sutpen's Hundred, and Henry believing it was the letter from her that he was waiting for, when what he was thinking was *Maybe he will write it then. He would just have to write "I am your father. Burn this" and I would do it. Or if not that, a sheet, a scrap of paper with the one word "Charles" in his hand, and I would know what he meant and he would not even have to ask me to burn it. Or a lock of his hair or a pairing from his finger nail and I would know them because I believe now that I have known what his hair and finger nails would look like all my life, could choose that lock and that paring out of a thousand.* And it did not come, and his letter went to her every two weeks and hers came back to him, and maybe he thought *If one of mine to her should come back to me unopened then. That would be a sign.* And that didn't hap-

pen: and then Henry began to talk about his stopping at Sutpen's Hundred for a day or so on his way home and he said all right to it, said *It will be Henry who will get the letter, the letter saying it is inconvenient for me to come at that time; so apparently he does not intend to acknowledge me as his son, but at least I shall have forced him to admit that I am.* And that one did not come either and the date was set and the family at Sutpen's Hundred notified of it and that letter did not come either . . . (AA, 326–327)

In this virtual casebook of epistolary possibilities, unwritten letters are transcribed as imagined *("I am your father. Burn this"; "Charles"),* symbols are imagined as letters (a lock of hair, finger nail parings), and letters are imagined as symbols *("If one of mine to her should come back unopened then. That would be a sign").* Acknowledgment of one correspondent is imagined coming through another *("It will be Henry who will get the letter").*

In Shreve's reading to them, the letters at hand do explain, and do so according to generic laws of their own that make possible in his narrative the most calculated strategies of self-expression and self-protection and the most intricate manipulations of characters. With Quentin, Shreve shapes a credible whole from letter writers and their letters. When there are too few of either, he supplies more. As he imagines it in Chapter VII, the imaginary New Orleans lawyer tortures Eulalia with faked letters written in a language she cannot read, gets Bon to the university, and writes to bring Henry together with Bon. Eulalia's hatred of Sutpen is transferred to the lawyer's letter about him, which is not "perused but consumed, leaving her sitting there with a black crumbling blank carbon ash in her hand" (AA, 305). The diary he keeps is a two-sided discourse about Judith, of such privacy and immediacy that the generative ideas and the act of writing and rewriting even to the punctuation, are described together with the inscription. The lawyer writes and replies to himself: his unwritten *"daughter? daughter? daughter?"* is written as *"Query: bigamy threat, Yes or No. Possible No. Incest threat: Credible Yes* and the hand going back before it put down the period, lining out the *Credible,* writing in *Certain,* underlining it" (AA, 310). His letter to Henry closes with instructions on how it should be read, and a calculated equation of its scenes of reading and writing by which Henry is equated with Bon. *"So take this, Sir, neither as the unwarranted insolence which an unsolicited communication from myself to you would be, not as a plea for sufferance on behalf of an unknown, but as an introduction (clumsy though it be) to one young gentleman whose position needs neither detailing nor recapitulation in the place where this letter is read, of another young gentleman whose position requires neither detailing nor recapitulation in the place where it was written"* (AA, 315).[44] In the summer of 1860, Shreve suggests, the lawyer intercepts Bon's letters from Henry and Judith. In effect, Bon must dismiss the interfering lawyer before he can write for himself, in his own person, the letter that Judith gives Grandmother and Quentin reads. He does so when the lawyer advises him by mail how to exploit Judith, writing "a letter, two or maybe three pages of your humble and obedient e and t and c that boiled down to eighteen words *I know you are a fool, but just what kind of fool are you going to be?* and Bon was at least enough of a not-fool to do the boiling down" (AA, 337).

What Bon writes to Judith and what Quentin in particular makes of what he reads there have much to say about Faulkner's own increased understanding of letters and epistolarity as they bear upon the structure and meaning of his novel. The text of the letter is nearly three pages, written, Bon says, in stove polish stolen from the Union army, on French notepaper stolen from a gutted Confederate mansion. He is writing about writing, at the end of Henry's four-year prohibition, as well as about writing of love: he guides Judith's reading *("You will notice," "Imagine us"),* he portrays himself writing *("I must stop")* and he imagines himself in a dialogue with Judith as she reads him *("Stop what? you will say. Why, thinking, remembering—remark that I do not say, hoping")* (AA, 129, 131). In the space between letters, shared hardship is their bond. He is present in the letter as one of the *"scarecrows with one of those concocted plans of scarecrow desperation"* whom he asks Judith to imagine stealing stove polish (AA, 130); she is present, as Receiver, as one of those women, *"lady or female either, below Mason's and Dixon's in this year of grace 1865"* to whom the word *"hunger"* is *"sheer redundancy"* (AA, 129). In the physical components of his letter as they represent those hardships, he finds *"a curious and apt commentary on the times and augur of the future"* (AA, 129). At the center of the letter, Bon places the message for Judith: *"We have waited long enough."* He concludes with the promised prophecy: *"I cannot say when to expect me. Because what IS is something else again because it was not even alive then. And since because within this sheet of paper you now hold the best of the old South which is dead, and the words you read were written upon it with the best (each box said, the very best) of the new North which has conquered and which therefore, whether it likes it or not, will have to survive, I now believe that you and I are, strangely enough, included among those who are doomed to live"* (AA, 131–132). Lacking "date or salutation or signature" (AA, 129), the letter exists, as Charles Bon says it was written, in *"a period without boundaries or location in time"* (AA, 131). Indeed, it is unbounded itself, having neither a conventional beginning nor an ending. From Judith's reaction to this enigmatic text, Mr. Compson's memory of it, and Quentin's reading, Faulkner posited in *Absalom, Absalom!* what was for him a new law of letters having implications for authorship, ownership, and the authority of the letter in historical time. Jacques Lacan phrases this in the "formula" that concludes his discussion of Poe's story "The Purloined Letter": "the sender, we tell you, receives from the receiver his own message in reverse form. Thus it is that what the 'purloined letter,' nay, the 'letter in sufferance' means is that a letter always arrives at its destination."[45]

By a "letter in sufferance" Lacan means "a letter held up in the course of delivery." He argues it is specious to assume that "a letter has completed its destiny after fulfilling its function": he distinguishes between the "holder" and the "possessor" of a letter, and describes the "proprietorship" with which the "holder" temporarily is endowed. This suggests a corollary law of ownership: "Might a letter on which the sender retains certain rights," he asks, "not quite belong to the person to whom it is addressed? or might it be that the latter was never the real receiver?"[46] The formula, with these corollaries, has special relevance for Bon's letter to Judith, which is passed by her into Grandmother Compson's keeping to read or not read as she likes, and subsequently to Mr. Compson, who passes it in turn to Quentin, the latest Receiver and the only one in the novel who is shown actually reading its text. Judith disclaims ownership when she gives up the letter; Bon gives up his right of ownership when he dies. But the possibility of a yet to be completed destiny makes it a "letter in sufferance," held in proprietorship by the Compsons.

As there are subsequent readers who interpret the letter, so there is a second Sender who helps shape it—Henry Sutpen himself—who is bound to Bon in all things, including writing. Immediately upon reading Bon's letter, while his father speculates on the scene of writing as one of "defiance and . . . ultimatum," Quentin has a vision of its consequences at the scene of its first reading: Henry and Bon "facing one another at the gate," and Judith waiting "in a wedding dress made from stolen scraps" (AA, 132). That vision is evoked by Quentin's empathetic reading, and when Faulkner returns in Chapter VIII to the circumstances of its writing, he gives Shreve and Quentin together a vision that derives from their mutual empathy with each other and the characters of their story. "They were both in Carolina and the time was forty-six years ago, and it was not even four now but compounded still further, since now both of them were Henry Sutpen and both of them were Bon, compounded each of both yet either neither, smelling the very smoke which had blown and faded away forty-six years ago from the *bivouac fires burning in a pine grove . . ."* (AA, 351).[47] In the first part of that long passage (AA, 346–350), Bon sees Sutpen in Carolina in March of 1865, sees in Sutpen's face "recognition, and that was all" (AA, 348), and tells Henry that they have waited long enough for the war to resolve their dilemma for them. *"And then Henry would begin to say 'Thank God. Thank God' panting and saying 'Thank God,' saying 'Don't try to explain it. Just do it' and Bon: 'You authorize me? As her brother you give me permission?' and Henry: 'Brother? Brother? You are the oldest: why do you ask me?' and Bon: 'No. He has never acknowledged me. He just warned me. You are the brother and the son. Do I have your permission, Henry?' and Henry: 'Write. Write. Write.' So Bon wrote the letter, after the four years, and Henry read it and sent it off"* (AA, 349). The passage makes clear how intimately Henry is involved with Bon in the composition of the letter that he will kill Bon for writing. He *authorizes* it: he urges its writing, he is its first reader, and he mails it. In this, he is co-Sender with Bon as he is also co-Receiver with Judith and therefore co-owner of the letter with them both, implicated through that involvement in their conjoined destinies as they are in his. After their deaths, the "letter in sufferance" is his and, as Lacan suggests such letters must, it finds its way back to him.

Bon writes his last letter to force Sutpen's hand through Henry, who is portrayed in the letter with its Sender as one of Bon's *"scarecrows."* The message, *"We have waited long enough,"* is for Henry as well as for Judith: Bon tells him as much when he asks permission to write. Yet in the interim between the composition of the letter and the end of the war, Bon changes himself from Henry's *"Brother"* into *"the nigger that's going to sleep with your sister"* (AA, 358), and Henry guards the Sutpen gate, as his father decrees he must, from the black brother whose letter he authorized. Now the letter has fulfilled its dual function, as loveletter and as the instrument of paternal acknowledgment: when the text comes into Quentin's hands, it fulfills its destiny by returning to its original destination. On the night Quentin reads Bon-Henry's letter to Henry-Judith, he finds the "shadowy, almost substanceless" Bon in "the faint spidery script not like something impressed upon the paper by a once-living hand but like a shadow cast upon it which had resolved on the paper the instant before he looked at it and which might fade, vanish, at any instant while he still read" (AA, 93, 129). Under the spell of the presences the letter evokes, he has his vision of Judith and of Henry and Bon at the Sutpen gate, and that night he goes to Sutpen's Hundred, passes the gate, and confronts Henry for himself. Bon's text speaks of life—*"you and I are, strangely enough, included among those who are doomed to live"* (AA, 132)—but Henry speaks to Quentin of death:

*And you are——?*
*Henry Sutpen.*
*And you have been here——?*
*Four years.*
*And you came home——?*
*To die. Yes.*
*To die?*
*Yes. To die.*
*And you have been here——?*
*Four years.*
*And you are——?*
*Henry Sutpen.* (AA, 373)

Forty-four years after Bon writes to Judith, the letter containing his shadow returns to its co-Sender at its first destination in the person of a final reader impelled there by the vision his reading evokes. As in Lacan's formula, "the sender receives from the receiver his own message in reverse form"; here, Quentin's dialogue with Henry, which begins as it ends, *"And you are——? Henry Sutpen,"* the mirroring halves framing the words *"To die. Yes. / To die? / Yes. To die."* In a final reversal of the 1865 scene at the gate, the black sister, Clytie, now guards the Sutpen door against a white brother, the figurative "Quentin-Henry" (AA, 334), who finds in an upstairs bedroom not a bride in her gown but the murderer of that unwed bride's husband-to-be, his "wasted hands crossed on the breast as if he were already a corpse" (AA, 373).

The circularity of epistolary discourse complements such patterns of doubling and repetition throughout the novel by binding Senders and Receivers of letters to each other, exerting that authority in historical time as well as space.[48] Faulkner was working in *Absalom, Absalom!* with the multiple identities of historical characters re-created in the present, and with the ways those inventions shape the present narrators.[49] Through the access that history provides to private letters and documents, and the letter theory he arrived at as he worked, Faulkner found the means of expressing both the legendary characters and the legendmakers. In himself, Henry is the tripartite persona that, according to the laws of letters, is present in all epistolary discourses: he is at once a prior reader of Bon's letter, its literal Sender, and its Receiver-to-be. In Lacan's terms, he has retained certain terrible "rights" to the letter he authorizes, including the right to an answering message: he is the "real receiver" Lacan posits, who proves that "the 'letter in sufferance' means . . . that a letter always arrives at its destination." It is, after all, neither Bon nor Judith but Henry who is *"doomed to live,"* and it is the letter that dooms him as it also foretells his doom. Quentin's sense of the letter as "the intact ash of its former shape and substance" (AA, 128) pictures both the altered man he will find at Sutpen's Hundred that night and the manner of his death in the December conflagration.

Perhaps it is Quentin's sense of the fatality of the letter's circular course, and the complementary prophetic dimension to which Bon himself alludes, that brings him to his own *"apt commentary on the times and augur of the future"* in the closing pages of the novel. Sutpen's Hundred is his own destination as well as the letter's, a symbol of the doomed South to which he bears the letter with its message of doom to confront Henry. At the end of Chapter IX, where the journey begun in Chapter VI is concluded, Quentin turns from his memory of the interview with Henry Sutpen to Poe's scholar of "forgotten lore" in "The Raven," and to his tormented vision of his future, "thinking 'Nevermore of peace. Nevermore of peace. Nevermore Nevermore Nevermore'" (AA, 373).[50] In this dual context of Henry's coming home to die and the words of Poe's prophet-bird, Quentin reads the final half of his father's letter about Rosa, the "Cassandralike" poetess laureate of Jefferson (AA, 22) who has predicted that he will not return to the South but will remember her story and write about it. It is Mr. Compson's hope that Rosa will be reunited with her ghosts in heaven. But if Quentin finds a prophecy for himself in the conjunction of these literary and letterly images, it is more akin to the tormented understanding that comes to the student at the end of Poe's poem, for whom the Raven's eyes "have all the seeming of a demon that is dreaming, / And the lamp-light o'er him streaming throws his shadow on the floor; / And my soul from out that shadow that lies floating on the floor / Shall be lifted—nevermore!" Bon's raven shadow falls across the House of Sutpen in this way, as it also is imprinted on his letter. Metaphorically, the foreboding shadow of the Sutpens and the Sutpen legend as he has created it lies just as darkly on Quentin. He knows himself "older at twenty than a lot of people who have died" (AA, 377), and when Shreve asks, "Why do you hate the South?" Quentin replies "quickly, at once, immediately; 'I dont hate it,' he said. *I dont hate it* he thought, panting in the cold air, the iron New England dark; *I dont. I dont! I dont hate it! I dont hate it!*" (AA, 378).

# V. Broken Letters

". . . all that matters is that I wrote the letters."    —*Requiem for a Nun*, 127

## [ i ]

Charles Bon's letter to Judith is a troublesome text in a number of ways—as a historical document, as an autobiographical one, and, generically, as a letter. This is so not least because of its incompleteness, which generates and sustains the interest of its readers at the same time that it frustrates their attempts at a definitive reading. Janet Gurkin Altman has suggested that "to write a letter is to map one's coordinates—temporal, spatial, emotional, intellectual—in order to tell someone else where one is located at a particular time and how far one has traveled since the last writing. Reference points on that map are particular to the shared world of writer and addressee: underlying the epistolary dialogue are common memories and often common experiences that take place between the letters."[1] In the case of Bon's letter, however, the coordinates Altman identifies are either deleted—the letter has no date, salutation, or signature—or suppressed. The world Bon shares with his addressee exists in the four-year space of war between letters rather than in shared personal experiences, and the psychological needs that spur Bon to write from that space and time *"without boundaries or location"* are expressed only enigmatically in the assertion, *"We have waited long enough"* (AA, 130). Because so little is clear from the shadowy text itself, so much of its meaning must be reconstructed by his subsequent readers from available facts and their own reasonable inventions: the epistolary courtship, Henry's prohibition against writing, Judith's response to the letter, and her passing it to Grandmother Compson after Bon's death. The letter is an incomplete transmission, which its rereaders forty years later subjectively rewrite. If this incompleteness suggests the problems of reading the novel, it also suggests the limits of writing factual history, autobiography, and letters. In this chapter I should like to examine the restraints Faulkner imposed on himself by epistolary incompleteness in his fiction early and late, and the resource he made of the incomplete, the unwritten, the unread, and the unreadable. These are the "broken letters" of the canon.

In the form alone, a complete letter text contains a date, address, and return address, and the message is framed by an opening salutation and closing signature. It may include an addendum, or postscript. But even a complete letter is not solitary.[2] In the larger context of sending and receiving, the letter is not complete until it has been delivered, read, and answered, and even then according to Jacques Lacan it has not necessarily completed its "destiny." Moreover, it is in the nature of the individual letter text to be partial, however complete it may be in its form or as a unit of discourse. A letter is an autobiographical fragment, and letter writing is a matter of self-conscious selection, involving exclusion as well as inclusion and the construction of conscious and unconscious masks and personae that conceal as well as reveal. Small wonder that letters encourage the close reading and interpretation they do in epistolary novels,[3] or that being incomplete the explications of single letters often are incomplete themselves. Mr. Compson expresses the dilemma in the context of history when he tells Quentin, ". . . we exhume from old trunks and boxes and drawers letters without salutation or signature, in which men and women who once lived and breathed are now merely initials or nicknames out of some now incomprehensible affection which sound to us like Sanskrit or Choctaw; we see dimly people, the people in whose living blood and seed we ourselves lay dormant and waiting, in this shadowy attenuation of time possessing now heroic proportions, performing their acts of simple passion and simple violence, impervious to time and inexplicable" (AA, 100–101).

The inherent incompleteness of the Sender, the text, and the Receiver and the potential of letters to collectively finish themselves are qualities particularly suited to the needs of a novelist committed, as Faulkner was, to the contrapuntal integration of diverse materials and tellings in multifaceted forms. The incompletely written is by definition only partially readable, connotative rather than definitive, and it is not the least of the attractions for Faulkner that it lends itself to the mysterious, the suspected, the partially known. Letters evocative of these qualities take their place in the canon with other devices of narrative Faulkner used to arrest the motion of life by artificial means and to hold it fixed so that, being life, it might move again.

Seldom in Faulkner's fiction are letters the instruments of simple revelation and discovery. In addition to communicating information, they evoke speculative reactions and responses that turn their readers to new reconsiderations. Bon's unsigned letter, for example, brings forward the enigma of his identity rather than solving it. His presence is implicit in the ashen and shadowlike text, but the central "fact" of his blackness is communicated to Quentin at Sutpen's Hundred in an unrecorded part of the interview with Henry. In effect Bon never escapes the boundaries of his partial text except in the imagination of his readers. Even Rosa never sees him except as a "shadow" in a photograph, or even feels the weight of his body in his coffin (AA, 146–147). The man whose letter prompts Judith to make a wedding gown is the man-as-writing rather than the letter writer himself, and it is that figure, and her epistolary relationship with him, that she tries to validate by giving the letter to Grandmother Compson. That Bon is as incomplete as the letter by which he attempts to complete himself. Faulkner's deletions of salutation and signature complement the theme of incest: a brother may not address his sister as lover. But, literally, Bon has no name to sign: his French surname is not his father's nor is it a word in his father's native language. In his letter to Judith, as in the re-creations of him that derive from that partial text, Bon is that anomalous nonself, the impalpable shadow-brother and Negro "shadow" doubly denied access to his white sister.[4] Moreover, his letter to Judith is the only recorded fragment of an otherwise entirely imagined discourse. In the broken chain of letters that they intermittently share according to Mr. Compson and Quentin, only this is transcribed. His other letters to her are destroyed; her letters to him are lost or intercepted by the lawyer Shreve invents. Her only recorded writing is the epitaph on his gravestone: *"Charles Bon. Born in New Orleans, Louisiana. Died at Sutpen's Hundred, Mississippi, May 3, 1865. Aged 33 years and 5 months"* (AA, 190). Significantly, the epitaph is patently wrong about Bon's antecedents: according to Sutpen, Bon was not born in New Orleans but the West Indies, and in that fact is the secret of his racial identity. As Judith herself will tell Grandmother Compson, no such "block of stone with scratches on it" is sufficient to verify a life (AA, 127). Yet except for his letter, fragment though it is, the Compson narrators and the novel reader know little more of Bon's existence than Rosa, who conjures from *"the circumambient air"* of the Sutpen garden the shade she calls *"Charles Bon, Charles Good, Charles Husband-soon-to-be"* (AA, 148).

The uses to which Faulkner put letters and letter fragments such as these in *Absalom, Absalom!* look forward into the canon as well as back, and they locate points of reference between that book and others earlier and later. In particular, the themes of miscegenation, incest, and the search for a father are conveyed in *Go Down, Moses* by the letterlike fragments of correspondence between Buck and Buddy McCaslin in the commissary ledgers. Faulkner says of these historical documents, where often the twins' handwriting appears on the same page, that it is "as if, long since past any oral intercourse, they had used the diurnally advancing pages to conduct the unavoidable business of the compulsion which had traversed all the waste wilderness of North Mississippi in 1830 and '40 and singled them out to drive" (GDM, 263). The epistolary form is adopted first on the ledger page devoted to Percival Brownlee. Buck's entries for March 3, 5, and 6, 1856, initiate a written dialogue between the brothers, consisting of cryptic questions and answers in misspelled and grammatically incorrect English, that approximate epistolary discourse. It reads, in part:

> *6 Mar 1856 Cant plough either Says he aims to be a Precher so may be he can lead stock to Crick to Drink*

and this time it was the other, the hand which he now recognised as his uncle's when he could see them both on the same page:

> *Mar 23th 1856 Cant do that either Except one at a Time Get shut of him*

then the first again:

> *24 Mar 1856 Who in hell would buy him*

then the second:

> *19th of Apr 1856 Nobody You put yourself out of Market at Cold Water two months ago I never said sell him Free him* (GDM, 264)

In this chain of discourse, Ike's rereading of the nearly identical texts is synchronic with their writing and reading three decades before. To approximate the process of Ike's reading for the reader of the novel, Faulkner simulates the differences in handwriting by subtle differences in epistolary usage: Buck dates his messages using cardinal numbers (*"6 Mar," "24 Mar"*), Buddy uses, and misuses, the *-th* suffix of ordinals (*"Mar 23th," "19th of Apr"*). By this means, and with the narrator's directions, historical investigations at an early period are overlaid with historical investigations at a later one, so that, as Ike searches the ledgers for his own heritage, he and the novel reader uncover simultaneously the secret of miscegenation and incest that Buck and Buddy discover and express in the privacy of their letterlike writing. These also are matters beyond "oral intercourse."

The value of letters here lies in their innate capacity to conceal as well as reveal, and in the ledgers subsequently transcribed, the twins again turn to epistolary forms for privacy.[5] Following Buck's exposition of old Carothers' death and the freeing of Roskus, Fibby, and Thucydus, the mystery of Eunice's suicide is cast as letterly discourse:

> *Eunice Bought by Father in New Orleans 1807 $650 dolars. Marrid to Thucydus 1809 Drownd in Crick Cristmas Day 1832*

and then the other hand appeared, the first time he had seen it in [this] ledger to distinguish it as his uncle's . . . :

*June 21th 1833 Drownd herself*

and the first:

*23 June 1833 Who in hell ever heard of a niger drownding him self*

and the second, unhurried, with a complete finality; the two identical entries might have been made with a rubber stamp save for the date:

*Aug 13th 1833 Drownd herself* (GDM, 267)

By their epistolarity rather than as messages of disclosure, the strategies of concealment prove doubly revealing. The twins' empathy for each other is intensified by their literally writing on the same page of the letter text they share as Senders and Receivers of these incomplete notes, and this extends to Ike, who reads on succeeding pages of the ledger as in a genealogical postscript the names and dates of Tomasina and her son Turl and the cryptic words *"Fathers will"* (GDM, 269). For Ike, and for the reader of the novel, it is not only Brownlee and the other McCaslin slaves but Buck and Buddy, and finally old Carothers McCaslin himself, whom Faulkner says "took substance and even a sort of shadowy life with their passions and complexities too as page followed page and year year; all there, not only the general and condoned injustice and its slow amortization but the specific tragedy which had not been condoned and could never be amortized" (GDM, 265–266).

From this letterly core at the core of the ledgers, as enigmatic in itself as Charles Bon's letter to Judith and as incomplete, Isaac McCaslin reads the literally unspeakable crime of which his father and uncle wrote and in writing discovered for themselves. Like Bon's letter to Judith, the letters that hold the darkest secrets in the McCaslin ledgers are letters in sufferance, and Isaac is their destined final Receiver. As in *Absalom, Absalom!*, where Mr. Compson's partially read letter to Quentin is the focus of Quentin's meditation as he tells about the South, the transcribed ledger fragments in Part 4 of "The Bear" are the focal point of Ike's and Cass Edmonds' reconstruction of God's plan for the South. Thematically, Quentin and Isaac are related characters, and the association is strengthened in these scenes by the significant presence of letters in both.[6] Like Mr. Compson's letter, the ledgers also are a "pandora's box" (AA, 258) of miscegenation and incest, and Ike's attempt to repudiate his birthright is analogous to Quentin's agonized, ironical denial that he hates the South. If Quentin "sounds like father" as he meditates on the half-read letter in his hand, Isaac literally writes like Old Carothers, his handwriting in the ledgers "queerly enough resembling neither his father's nor his uncle's nor even Mc-Caslin's, but like that of his grandfather's save for the spelling" (GDM, 273). Even at the end of his life, in "Delta Autumn," Ike is no more free from that "bold cramped hand" (GDM, 269) than is Quentin, in the last year of his life, from Mr. Compson's "sloped whimsical ironic hand out of Mississippi attenuated" (AA, 377): he conceives of his grandfather's having spawned a future in which *"Chinese and African and Aryan and Jew, all breed and spawn together until no man has time to say which one is which nor cares"* (GDM, 364). Isaac and Quentin are readers bound by fragments of their father's letter writing to the region and the past that writing portrays and makes tangible to their imaginations. Isaac, at least, reads his destiny there. In the enigmatic words *"Fathers will,"* he finds evidence of his grandfather's willful crimes as well as old Carothers' recognition of Turl as his son. Buck and Buddy extend the terms of the will to include Turl's children, and it is their collective will that Isaac attempts to serve by paying bequests to James and Fonsiba, and finally to James' great-grandchild, Roth's son. When he recognizes the impossibility of expiating the sins he has read in the ledgers, he has much the same vision of the future to which Shreve comes when he tells Quentin, ". . . in a few thousand years, I who regard you will also have sprung from the loins of African kings." According to Shreve, "it clears the whole ledger" (AA, 378).

[ ii ]

The past imposes itself on the present through letters in another way in the stories of *The Unvanquished*, six of which date from 1934, in the early stages of Faulkner's work on *Absalom, Absalom!*. Clearly they were written for money. In one letter to Morton Goldman, in August 1934, Faulkner said, "As far as I am concerned, while I have to write trash, I dont care who buys it, as long as they pay the best price I can get; doubtless the Post feels the same way about it; anytime that I sacrifice a high price to a lower one it will not be to refrain from antagonising the Post; it will be to write something better than a pulp series like this" (SL, 84). Whatever his impatience with the stories in 1934, and with the *Saturday Evening Post*, it is just as clear that the stories are serious work.[7] There are transcribed letters in three of the stories: the forged orders that Ringo writes under Granny's direction in "Riposte in Tertio," the warning letter from Grumby and Matt Bowden in "Vendée," and Aunt Louisa's letters from Hawkhurst in "Skirmish at Sartoris." Together they convey something of the changed world that Charles Bon speaks of in his letter to Judith when he says that *"what*

*WAS is one thing, and now it is not because it is dead, it died in 1861, and
therefore what IS . . . is something else again because it was not even alive
then"* (AA, 131). In the broken world of the Civil War, letter writers
and readers appeal for order to epistolary conventions of the lost past
and struggle with departures from epistolary custom and usage that
derive from and express the exigencies of the present. A Mississippi
Negro boy writes letters in the name of Union generals, his lying writing sanctioned by a woman who abhors lies yet represents herself in
those letters under assumed names. The power of the forged documents is clear from the returns Granny reaps in Union mules; the
altered times are suggested by her vain faith in the standard that
"Southern men would not harm a woman, even if the letter failed to
work" (U, 171): as Matt Bowden makes clear in "Vendée," Grumby in
fact shoots her out of fear of a letter.

The warning note, with Bowden's postscript, is equally suggestive
of lost values. Pinned to the body of a Negro lynched by the gang,
Grumby's note reads: *"Last woning not thret. Turn back. The barer of this
my promise and garntee. I have stood all I aim to stand children no children. / G."* (U, 203). Grumby's "big crude printed letters" are in contrast to Bowden's postscript written "in a hand neat and small and
prettier than Granny's, only you knew that a man had written it," and
that handwriting conjures in Bayard's memory the actual "little black-
haired hands" (U, 203) of the writer. In its form and style, the postscript looks back to a more genteel and gentle time, but in fact it is a
footnote that validates the text of Grumby's message and depicts a still
more cruel version of the present reality in which children are threatened by the hands, and the handwriting of apparent gentlemen.
*"This is signed by others beside G., one of wh$^m$ in particular hav$^{ns}$ less
scruples re children than he has. Nethless unders$^{gnd}$ desires to give both you
and G. one more chance. Take it, and some day become a man. Refuse it, and
cease even to be a child"* (U, 203). When Bowden betrays Grumby, his
"little black-haired hand" holds a pistol (U, 204) instead of a pen.
Symbolically, Grumby's ill-written warning letter "answers" the forged
one for which he shot Granny. But if his first error is fearing "a piece
of paper on which someone had signed Bedford Forrest's name" (U,
207), as Bowden says, his fatal error is exchanging his own pistol for a
pen. Bayard and Ringo punish both errors by severing the hand that
pulled the trigger and wrote the note. When they fix Grumby's right
hand to Granny's grave marker, Uncle Buck McCaslin calls it "the
proof and the expiation" of his crime against her (U, 213).

Fragments of conventional letters serve the same end of ironically
undercutting antebellum standards of behavior in the sixth story of
the book, "Skirmish at Sartoris." Bayard Sartoris grows into young

manhood in *The Unvanquished* in what he calls "a world ordered completely by men's doings, . . . a world of burned towns and houses and ruined plantations and fields inhabited only by women" (U, 216). To this new world, some women adapt—Granny by forging military documents, Drusilla by going to war as a soldier in John Sartoris' troop. Conversely, Aunt Louisa clings to the "Southern principles of purity and womanhood" (U, 222) that she writes in her letters about Drusilla. These letters, artifacts of an irretrievable time, are barely readable by the people who receive them.

Louisa's first letter, in August 1864, reports Drusilla's disappearance from Hawkhurst but mistakenly assumes that she is with Granny and so will read it as well. The second, addressed to Granny from *"Hawkhurst, Gihon County, Alabama"* (U, 217) reveals that Drusilla has joined John Sartoris' troop and laments her rejecting what Bayard paraphrases as "the highest destiny of a Southern woman—to be the bridewidow of a lost cause" (U, 219). Bayard reads it at Christmas 1864.

> *Dear Sister:*
> *I think this will be news to you as it was to me though I both hope and pray it will not be the heart-rending shock to you it was to me as naturally it cannot since you are only an aunt while I am the mother. But it is not myself I am thinking of since I am a woman, a mother, a Southern woman, and it has been our lot during the last four years to learn to bear anything. But when I think of my husband who laid down his life to protect a heritage of courageous men and spotless women looking down from heaven upon a daughter who had deliberately cast away that for which he died, and when I think of my half-orphan son who will one day ask of me why his martyred father's sacrifice was not enough to preserve his sister's good name——(U, 218–219)*

The third letter, addressed to Mrs. Compson in Jefferson after the war, is an appeal to have the standards of propriety restored at Sartoris, where Drusilla is living in the same cabin with John Sartoris. Aunt Louisa and Mrs. Compson, and Mrs. Habersham who arranges the wedding, are anachronisms. They are the women whom Bayard says "never surrendered" (U, 216), but their antebellum values are no more viable—or inviolate—in 1864–65 than Louisa's second letter, which records them. "The envelope was worn and dirty," Bayard says, "and it had been opened once and then glued back, but we could still make out *Hawkhurst, Gihon County, Alabama* on it even though we did not recognize Aunt Louisa's hand at first" (U, 217). Louisa's one-sided correspondence is not answered, and so not affirmed. Instead, it contributes literally to the destruction of the lost past it attempts to sustain. The stove polish and French stationery of Bon's letters to Judith augur a new present for those *"doomed to live"*; Louisa's letters, written on wallpaper in an unrecognizable hand, are inscribed on remnants of the very ruins that once housed the values they espouse.

By transcribing only this undated and unsigned fragment, and recording the remainder of her correspondence in scattered ironic paraphrases, Faulkner destroys the continuity of Louisa's letters, undercuts the validity of their arguments, and strips them of the power to move events. Bayard finds them virtually unreadable. Like Quentin Compson, who is too young at twenty to recognize in Miss Rosa's "neat faded cramped script . . . a character cold, implacable, and even ruthless" (AA, 10), Bayard recognizes none of the unstated prewar assumptions shared by Aunt Louisa and her Receivers—that Drusilla "was now living in a word that Aunt Louisa would not even repeat but that Granny knew what it was" (U, 219), for example, or in her letter to Mrs. Compson that "there were times when the good name of one family was the good name of all" (U, 222). That such words as *sin* are unstated, and remain so, is a rule of life as Aunt Louisa knows and writes of it, and Bayard's inability to read her old-fashioned letters is a function of their partially written form as well as his inexperience with the world they depict. Appropriate to this failure of communication, the Christmas letter is addressed to a dead woman: Bayard reads it while he and Ringo are hunting Grumby, and the implied contrast between Grumby's note about children and Louisa's letter about her child brings the past into violent juxtaposition with the present. The last letter is addressed to a stranger, Mrs. Compson, who can read it and acts on it, but despite her visit to Sartoris, and Mrs. Habersham's after her, Louisa must come in person to impose the standards she has written of in her letters. Her letters do not serve *The Unvanquished* as a validation of the living past as letters do *Absalom, Absalom!* and *Go Down, Moses.* Bayard says, "I couldn't make any sense out of that one too and I still didn't know what Aunt Louisa was talking about and I didn't believe that Mrs. Compson knew either" (U, 223). Simply put, they are irrelevant at the end of the war. Broken in form and in content, they are used as artifacts of a broken world, to convey romantic and ephemeral values that in the present are no more permanent than speech. This Aunt Louisa confirms when she arrives, "already crying and talking just like the letters sounded, like even when you listened to her you had to skip around fast to make any sense" (U, 230).

[ iii ]

Broken letters are of a piece with other narrative devices and strategies by which Faulkner reproduced the motion of life in his chronicles, novels, and stories. His interest in the unspoken suggestion, the
allusive echo, and the portentous detail is conspicuous of synecdochic
assumptions that are rooted in his poetry and inform his most profoundly poetic fiction. The fractured shards of Ben's memory, to take
the great example of *The Sound and the Fury,* and the way he presented
them on the page typographically, he said were designed to represent
"that unbroken-surfaced confusion of an idiot which is outwardly a
dynamic and logical coherence" (SL, 44), and that chapter is itself but
one segment of a whole from which the central subject and center are
absent.[8] Of the typography of Ben's chapter, Faulkner said, "I purposely used italics for both actual scenes and remembered scenes for
the reason, not to indicate the different dates of happenings, but
merely to permit the reader to anticipate a thought-transference, let-
ting the recollection postulate its own date" (SL, 45). Incomplete letters serve in much the same way. Like the bits and pieces of Ben's
living memories, since Ben cannot lie, bits and pieces of letters document moments of absence, separate from the narrative present. Ben
records "facts" of his own apprehending, like pieces of a broken mirror: broken letters, however subjective by nature, bring with them the
analogous and demonstrable authority of the written. Their partial
forms and isolated facts glint in the text latent with import and portent. They induce memory in the reader, urge connection, bridge the
unstated. They represent indeterminate causes of consequent effects
dramatized in the lives of the characters, and as such encourage close
inspection, speculation, and belief. In the "productive confusion"[9]
of Faulkner's most controlled narratives, they provide the calculated
means for explorations in which the reader participates doubly, reading the partly written, the unread, and the unreadable in the text as
he or she reads.

Completely transcribed letters offer the reader a consciously considered, "completed" image of the Sender—even when the Sender is
writing compulsively from unconscious needs and extrarational motives.[10] In fiction, of course, the calculated art of the letter is the novelist's, and it is significant in this regard also that in Faulkner's fiction
relatively few letter texts are complete. The broken letters portray
Sender and Receiver in broken images, pieces of masks rather than
masks. Characters are depicted writing and reading letters, texts are
described, but Faulkner seems to have been as much interested in the
act of letter writing and the impact of the texts on Sender and Re-

ceiver as in the messages their letters contain. As in seventeenth-century genre painting—of Vermeer, for example—where the scene of writing or reading a letter becomes the occasion for an intimate moment of revelation,[11] Faulkner's fiction draws on the magical power of the letter as a profoundly significant object, accretive of laws and conventions uniquely its own. Transcribed or not, the fact that the text is a letter implies the psychological needs of the writer to write and forces on the Receiver the obligation to respond as he or she can. The impact of the letter on both correspondents shows its power, deepening the mystery of its motive even when the writing itself is unread.

The fascination of incomplete letters in the text is various. Miswritten letters encourage rewriting by the reader. Julian Lowe's comic letters to Margaret Powers have so little impact because Margaret and the novel reader easily translate their clumsy devices and disguises and read a meaning contrary to what they say. As a justifiable claim on *"reward Money for captain Murder Xmas"* (LIA, 412), Lucas Burch's letter to the sheriff is as groundless, when the reader has rewritten it, as its tortured phrasing is parodically representative of conventional epistolary forms. In *The Unvanquished*, Matt Bowden himself rewrites Grumby's *"last woning not thret"* as an actual threat that includes Grumby when he offers in his postscript *"to give both you and G. one more chance."* Letters not fully transcribed encourage particularly close reading. The parodic phrasing of Aunt Louisa's partial letter about Drusilla is sufficient to represent the standards of her place and time, but Bon's letter to Judith, in the far more complex and demanding contexts of *Absalom, Absalom!*, demands the novel reader's closest attention as it does Mr. Compson's and Quentin's. Like Bon's, Caddy's letter to Jason also is without salutation or signature, but neither Jason's name nor hers is possible there because of the antagonism between the correspondents: Caddy can hardly address "Dear Jason," or send her name where her name is not spoken. Her letter, like the novel, is a text in which she is present but absent, and Jason's answering telegram encodes their actual relationship in a lie: "All well. Q writing today" (SF, 239). In these instances, Faulkner cut the salutations and signatures from such letters with the same calculation, if not from the same motives, as Snopes does in his letters to Narcissa, and like Snopes in those anonymous letters, he freed his reader to re-imagine the Sender and Receiver from the unbounded text. The extreme of this strategy is Quentin's letter to his father on June 2, 1910, where he erases himself completely from his text: the letter literally is unwritten, but the blank sheet of paper and the key are profoundly expressive and demand interpretation even where the reading is impossible.

Unrecorded writing is still more enigmatic, and often in Faulkner's fiction the untranscribed letters are letters from women. Caddy and Lorraine do write letters that the reader of the novel reads, but neither text is complete. And Caddy and Lorraine are exceptions. Margaret Powers' answers to Lowe are not written in *Soldiers' Pay;* her letters to Dick are recorded in fragments mixed with phrases of present memory and desire as in dreams: "I miss you like the devil, Dick. Someone to sleep with? I don't know. Oh, Dick, Dick. You left no mark on me, nothing. Kiss me through my hair, Dick, with all your ugly body, and let's don't ever see each other again, ever. . . . No, we won't, dear, ugly Dick" (SP, 182). The only complete letter from a woman in the canon is Narcissa's to Horace at the end of the original *Sanctuary,* and that one Faulkner deleted when he revised the book in 1931. Even Rosa Coldfield's writing is untranscribed. The "poetess laureate" of Yoknapatawpha County (AA, 11), author of "a thousand or more" odes to southern soldiers (AA, 83), whose note to Quentin sets the novel in motion, leaves no scrap of her writing except the epitaph on Judith's gravestone: *"Judith Coldfield Sutpen. Daughter of Ellen Coldfield. Born October 3, 1841. Suffered the Indignities and Travails of this World for 42 Years, 4 Months, 9 Days, and went to Rest at Last February 12, 1884. Pause, Mortal; Remember Vanity and Folly and Beware"* (AA, 211). Even the epitaph is more significant for what is omitted than what is said: when Quentin recognizes her authorship, he recognizes that the indignities and travails, like the vanity and folly, are implicitly attributable to Sutpen, the father who pointedly is not named on the stone.

Why this should be so of women's letters in particular has more to do with the conventions letters bring with them into the fictional context than with the novelist's fear of writing like a woman.[12] There are, after all, women whose writing is transcribed, however stunted in form, and such women as Rosa and Addie Bundren speak convincingly and at length in their own voices. Apparently, he wished to keep women's private writing private for narrative reasons. Quentin begins to suggest something of Faulkner's strategy of evocative concealment when he explains his own twisted fascination with Caddy: "Because women so delicate so mysterious Father said" (SF, 159); Jason suggests that the danger of women's letters lies in the coercive power of their intimate revelations when he says, "I make it a rule never to keep a scrap of paper bearing a woman's hand, and I never write them at all" (SF, 240). Jason burns Lorraine's letter, and Quentin suppresses Mrs. Bland's by refusing to read it, but there is more to women's broken writing than unhealthy male voyeurism and fear. Their letters in Faulkner's fiction *are* mysterious, and they *are* dangerous to men. Cecily Saunders' notes to George Farr evoke her in ways that put him in subjection, and Joanna Burden's tryst notes are symptomatic of a condition that corrupts her and terrifies Joe. "It could not be said that [Joe] corrupted her. His own life, for all its anonymous promiscuity, had been conventional enough, as a life of healthy and normal sin usually is. The corruption came from a source even more inexplicable to him than to her. In fact, it was as though with the corruption which she seemed to gather from the air itself, she began to corrupt him. He began to be afraid. He could not have said of what. But he began to see himself as from a distance, like a man being sucked down into a bottomless morass" (LIA, 245–246).

None of Joanna's writing is transcribed, although she writes letters regularly for years. In the racist-sexist contexts of *Light in August*, her letters of practical advice to Negro colleges are doubly secret, from the reader because the messages are untranscribed and from the community of Jefferson in that, despite her personae as "priest and banker and trained nurse," the whole of her correspondence inscribes a forbidden familiarity between the races. If her racial sensibilities occasion letters of advice, surreptitious letters occasion her intimacy with Joe. Joe finds that "she revealed an unexpected and infallible instinct for intrigue. She insisted on a place for concealing notes, letters. It was in a hollow fence post below the rotting stable. He never saw her put a note there, yet she insisted on his visiting it daily; when he did so, the letter would be there. When he did not and lied to her, he would find that she had already set traps to catch him in the lie; she cried, wept" (LIA, 245). The implicit power of such letters can be seen by his subjection to them. "Sometimes the notes would tell him not to come until a certain hour, to that house which no white person save himself had entered in years and in which for twenty years now she had been all night alone; for a whole week she forced him to climb into a window to come to her" (LIA, 245). Windows are used in searches for and flights from sexual identity by Lena and Joe and Lucas Burch, and the requirement set forth in Joanna's untranscribed notes obliquely portrays her need to know herself in this way, and to be known. Doubly hidden—as she is self-revealed—in her hidden notes, Joanna makes Joe "seek her about the dark house until he found her, hidden, in closets, in empty rooms, waiting, panting, her eyes in the dark glowing like the eyes of cats" (LIA, 245). In the absence of a readable text, the power of such letters in the novel lies in the potency of their own generic laws. Joanna exerts her power as Sender over Joe as Receiver to literally discover herself to him. Joe suffers her power: he does not write but responds as the "Negro" lover she imagines until the night that he kills her, when "he did not know if she had left a note for him or not" (LIA, 266).

To use letters in this way is to ask of readers that they "read the unreadable."[13] In effect, this requires that broken and untranscribed letters must be read according to the laws of their genre and the conventions of their usage—within the fictional contexts they generate and sustain by their very incompleteness as letters. This formula has relevance for all of the letter situations in Faulkner's fiction, but for none more than the most passionately erotic epistolary love affair in the canon—in *Requiem for a Nun,* where Temple Drake's letters to Red summon him at last to Miss Reba's. Popeye shoots him there, as Temple says, at the moment "when all of him except just his body was already in the room with me and the door locked at last for just the two of us alone" (RN, 132). Not coincidentally, that phrasing is perfectly descriptive of the shared intimacy of the Sender and the Receiver of love letters and wonderfully expressive of the intensity of erotic substitution love letters have power to achieve.

## [ iv ]

Temple Drake's untranscribed love letters to Alabama Red are surely the most mysterious and enigmatic personal documents in all of Faulkner's fiction. The situation as Temple explains it to the Governor in Act Two, Scene I, of *Requiem* is this: "I wrote some letters that you would have thought that even Temple Drake might have been ashamed to put on paper, and then the man I wrote them to died, and I married another man and reformed, or thought I had, and bore two children and hired another reformed whore so that I would have somebody to talk to, and I even thought I had forgotten about the letters until they turned up again and then I found out that I not only hadn't forgot about the letters, I hadn't even reformed—" (RN, 131). We do not know what Temple wrote to Red. Gavin, Gowan, and the Governor never read her letters; Popeye according to Gavin cannot read them at all, being illiterate; and Red's brother Pete, who does read them, returns them without reporting what they say. It is Nancy's opinion that, whatever is in the letters, "it was already there in whoever could write the kind of letters that even eight years afterward could still make grief and ruin. The letters never did matter" (RN, 159). Again, according to Gavin, Nancy "can't read or write either" (RN, 103), but she may know part of the truth, being as she is the dark alter image of Temple. Temple herself says, "I met the man, how doesn't matter, and I fell what I called in love with him and what it was or what I called it doesn't matter either because all that matters is that I wrote the letters—" (RN, 127).

Temple's lost letters are letters in sufferance and in suffering. They originate in love and longing, end in death, and return to her to reinscribe that pattern in the narrative present. They move the plot of the novel inexorably from sexual blackmail to the murder of Temple's child and the execution of Nancy Mannigoe. They are the substance of Temple's confession in the Governor's chambers, the source of her agony, the recognizable but absent center of the book. They are central to the lives in the novel, and the deaths, and they require of readers that they read motive forces from what literally is not written—that they write for themselves from the evidence of the unreadable not only what Temple wrote to Red but also how she wrote it and why. Inquiries into such questions about Temple's privately kept private writing lead deep into the book—and outside it, on a bridge of literary and personal letters, to Faulkner's reasons for writing letters into Temple's story in the revised contexts of *Requiem* and for writing them as he did.

If we do not know precisely what Temple wrote, what she wrote about from the Manuel Street brothel where Popeye kept her prisoner and the ways she presented herself to Red are implicit in the way she describes her letters. She says she knew the "right words. Though all you would have needed probably would be an old dictionary from back in Shakespeare's time when, so they say, people hadn't learned how to blush at words. That is, anybody except Temple Drake, who didn't need a dictionary, who was a fast learner and so even just one lesson would have been enough for her" (RN, 130). The "right words" produce what she calls "good letters": lewd, of course, but fragments of emotionally charged autobiography for all of that, designedly confessional and totally unrestrained, transcriptions truer than flesh. Written in the aftermath of lovemaking with Red, and "two or three when it would be two or three days between" (RN, 128), the letters contain sentiments the more intimate in that they can never be spoken, Popeye being always present. But they are generated by more than the lovers' separation. Temple's isolation from the world is hellish, her solitude unnatural, and her writing an appeal for community in the underworld within the world from which she feels herself an exile. Her letters are fueled by the ironic freedom from social constraints that her bondage provides. In these contexts of magnified feeling, her uninhibited imagination displays her in extreme poses of sexual invitation commensurate with sexual mores of Manuel Street. They are mirrors: she explains to the Governor that writing was "something to do, be doing, filling the time, better than fashion parades in front of the two-foot glass with nobody to be disturbed even by the . . . pants, or even no pants. Good letters—" (RN, 128). The "goodness" of the letters cuts two ways. First, it distinguishes the epistolary from her several public self-images: from "Temple Drake, the foolish virgin" (RN, 113), from Temple Drake the "reformed whore" (RN, 131), and especially, being "good letters," from "Temple Drake [who] liked evil" (RN, 117). By these inversions, ironically, the letters valorize an otherwise inexpressible self that they never disclose. Written out of the trauma of a grotesque sexual violation, Temple's letters keep inviolable, because unreadable, the Temple Drake who "fell what I called in love."

If her letters are mirror texts, they mirror more than herself. They are also allusive, and the appeal to literary standards outside the book also valorizes Temple's private epistolary image. Temple quotes Macbeth's "Tomorrow and tomorrow and tomorrow" speech in Act Two, Scene III, of *Requiem,* and Faulkner alludes to the same speech in the prologue to Act Two, where he says that the Anglo-Saxon pioneer in the Mississippi wilderness "strutted his roaring eupeptic hour, and was no more" (RN, 177, 90). His fondness for Shakespearean allusion and Temple's insistence on Shakespeare's words here and in her letters present the possibility that in this half-play, half-novel of multiple mirrorings there is a specific Shakespearean precedent for the letter writing and for the resulting complications. In *King Lear,* Lear's daughter Goneril, herself the alter image of good Cordelia, proposes adultery and murder in a love letter to Edmund that perfectly shows her evil nature. "If your will want not," Goneril writes in Act IV, Scene VI, punning on the word *will* (lust), "time and place will be fruitfully offered" for Edmund to kill her husband, Albany, and bed her. Should Albany survive Goneril's murderous design, the sexual design will fail as well: "Then am I the prisoner," she tells her lover, "and his bed my jail, from the loathed warmth whereof deliver me, and supply the place for your labor." When Edmund's half-brother Edgar intercepts this "post unsanctified / Of murderous lechers," he delivers it, and the lovers, into Albany's hands. The letters at the center of *Requiem* and *Lear* bring into focus both the parallels to the play in Faulkner's novel and his characteristic inversions, and they remind us that letters bring with them into the texts where they are written and read generic laws that function consistently across a broad range of situations. The conjoined categories of sex and death in the play are familiar as the overture and outcome by which Temple's last letter to Red is defined, and like hers Goneril's is a letter in sufferance that disastrously returns to her. Temple is, in fact, a prisoner in Popeye's bed, delivered periodically from its "loathed warmth" by Red, who takes Popeye's "place" and supplies his "labor"; her letters, like Goneril's, come into the possession of her lover's brother, Pete, who threatens, as Edgar does, to show them to her husband. But Temple is the victim of Popeye's evil, Goneril the agent of her own and Edmund's, and even though murder is done in *Requiem* there is no indication that Temple recruits Red to kill Popeye. In the scene with the Governor, Temple's letters are ignored; Goneril's return to convict her. When Albany confronts the "murderous lechers" in *Lear*, Act V, Scene III, he threatens to put Goneril's written words back into her mouth, then delivers her misdirected letter himself, not as an erotic invitation now but as Edmund's death warrant. "Shut your mouth," he orders his wife, "or with this paper I shall stop it. Hold, sir, / Thou worse than any name, read thine own evil."

Why Faulkner made Temple Drake a letter writer when he returned to her story in *Requiem for a Nun* is still another matter, one that depends on another context. If he drew on Shakespeare's *King Lear* for letter situations, his novel is not modeled on the play, and it is modeled less closely on his own precedent work than might be expected by the cast of characters he brings back. He told an audience at the University of Virginia that he had not thought of Temple's future life with Gowan Stevens until after he had written *Sanctuary*,[14] and when he told Hal Smith in October 1933 that he was working on a novel "about a nigger woman" to be called *Requiem for a Nun*, he compared it to *As I Lay Dying* rather than to *Sanctuary* (SL, 75). There are no love letters in *As I Lay Dying* or in *Sanctuary*. In the latter book, instead of writing erotic love letters from the solitude of her room, Temple hurls herself at Red at the roadhouse, "her mouth gaped and ugly like that of a dying fish as she writhed her loins against him" (SR, 232). In *Flags in the Dust*, it is true, Byron Snopes writes amatory letters to Narcissa, and in "There Was a Queen" Narcissa arranges a sexual assignation to get them back. But the untranscribed letters in *Requiem* apparently were an invention independent of these precedents. It was one in which art imitated life. When Faulkner resumed work on the novel in 1949, he was deeply involved in an erotic correspondence of his own, with Meta Carpenter. By the time the novel was well begun he was engaged in another, with Joan Williams, and a third, with Jean Stein, would follow in 1954. This correspondence is the second, personal context of Temple's letters to Red.

In a 1981 interview with Meta Carpenter Wilde, Panthea Reid Broughton notes that her relationship with Faulkner "was characterized more by separation than by togetherness,"[15] and Broughton's chronology of the relationship makes clear what Ms. Wilde's book, *A Loving Gentleman*, implies—that after 1935–1936, when Faulkner and Meta Carpenter were first together in Hollywood, their love affair was maintained largely by letter.[16] Temple's surreptitious letters to Red, and perhaps even the fact that they are not transcribed, must owe something to the secrecy with which Meta and Faulkner's other lovers had to write to him, and to his well-founded fear of their letters being discovered. Wilde reports that she wrote Faulkner in Oxford in care of Phil Stone;[17] Faulkner proposed that Joan Williams address her letters to a character from *Requiem*—the founder of Yoknapatawpha County, Alex Holston—and he had to tear up her first letter because his mail was not safe.[18] He burned almost all of the others he received from her.[19] There was real danger in such letters from women. In October 1952 Faulkner wrote to Saxe Commins: "Hell's to pay here now. While I was hors de combat, E[stelle] opened and read Joan Williams' letters to me. Now E. is drunk, and I am trying to nurse her before Malcolm sends her to a hospital, which costs like fury and does no good unless you make an effort yourself. I cant really blame her, certainly I cant criticise her, I am even sorry for her, even if people who will open and read another's private and personal letters, do deserve exactly what they get" (LDB-II, 94). There are different versions of this story: Estelle Faulkner wrote Commins in February 1954 that "Billy is completely enamoured, and Joan professes her love in no uncertain terms—*Bill had Malcolm open and read her letters to him*—and Mac, shocked, gave them to me—I returned them to Bill, but he knows that Jill and I know" (LDB-II, 135). Malcolm himself told James W. Silver a story of "Faulkner lying on his bed drunk and naked, listening to a love letter haltingly read to him by a Negro servant, with Estelle coming into the room, taking the letter, and sitting on the bed's edge, dramatically rendering it for her husband."[20] Malcolm also told Silver that he and his sister had intercepted and copied a letter from Joan to use in the event of a divorce.[21] Like all lovers who assume that their letters will be cherished, Wilde expresses the hope that Faulkner kept hers, and she knows that he would have had to keep them in secrecy. *"Did you bury them, Bill? Are they in some secret cupboard somewhere, bound with decaying string, each letter in its proper envelope?"*[22] In addition to reinforcing the conventions of privacy in personal correspondence, the power of women's erotic letters and their potential to cause suffering are implied by these contraventions of privacy. Together they suggest why Temple reacts as she does when her letters to Red turn up again and Pete threatens to show them to Gowan.

If Faulkner had Meta's and Joan's secret letters to him in mind when he kept the content of Temple's secret, the imaginative language of her letters to Red and some sense of their content are suggested by existing fragments of his own. Wilde told Broughton that Faulkner revealed himself openly in his letters to her. "Thinking back," she said, "he could envision the romantic scenes we had had together and out of that would come the memories that would help him to put other things in writing. He really could write love letters."[23] The method she describes is the same that produces Temple's "good letters" in the aftermath of lovemaking with Red, and what Temple implies about hers is confirmed by the sexually explicit passages of Faulkner's that Wilde quotes in her book. Author and character are writing within the same epistolary convention, and their "good letters" imply crossings between the canon of actual letters and the untranscribed fictional ones that move the novel. Faulkner portrayed himself to Meta in what Temple calls the "right words": in an early letter, she is "my heart, my jasmine garden, my April and May cunt; my white one, my blonde morning, winged, my sweetly dividing, my honey-cloyed, my sweet-assed gal."[24] A poem written in epistolary form includes both salutation and signature. The names denominate sexual organs.

*To Mrs. Bowen. Sweet, the maiden's mouth is (not) cold, (by a damn sight)*
*Her breast blossoms are simply red; (I know why they're red)*
*Her hair, mere brown or gold (one where, even less brown than gold*
*Since no sun kisses there, but only one of earth's sons seeks delight*
*When lover's dark limbs cover the beloved's white)*
*Fold on simple fold (she holds and he is holed)*
*Binding (let it be "heads" then, if the censors require it) her head.*
   *(Yes, "heads" then, if necessary for the censors)*
   *(When we're in bed)*
     *(The same bed, that is)*
       *Respectfully,*
   *Mr. Bowen*[25]

Throughout their correspondence, the portrayed self is designedly substitute for the man, his words for the deeds of love. Faulkner wrote, "I want to put the words into your hands and into your heart both," and Meta says that she knew he loved her "by looks, by touch, by the poems and the letters, only seldom by what he said to me."[26]

"Mr. Bowen" was both penis and pen name. In such letters, he asserted himself as an epistolary persona who was literally an instrument of self-expression, the living analog of the pen that created and conveyed him. In letters during the early 1940s, when Faulkner hoped to return to Hollywood, "Mr. Bowen" sometimes threatened to supplant the pen entirely and to silence writing. Wilde says: "The letters during this period of high expectancy were unabashedly erotic, the outpourings of a man too long denied carnal love. Bowen, asserting himself, was uncontrollable. At night, Bill found it difficult to sleep; Bowen was trying to take him over completely, and since Bowen couldn't write, though he did what he was designed to do competently enough, that would be unfortunate. 'I weigh 129 pounds and I want to put it all on you,' he said in one note, 'and as much in you as I can can can can must will will shall.'"[27] In time, Faulkner's imagination surpassed his physical capacity. "His letters left no doubt that he was still a passionate man," Wilde says, "but he was past the time of the blood's violent flood, the terrible hormonal ambush of the groin."[28] As that phrasing makes obvious his letters had a profound effect on their Receiver. She says of his first letter, "I was almost making tatters of Bill's letter, reading it, folding it, putting it away, opening it again. I was Bill's love, his dear, dear love. . . . Later, the letter placed reverently on tables, dresser, bedspread; regarded, smoothed over, hidden, retrieved, I committed every word of it to memory."[29] Such letters were a nearly physical experience for her, as were hers for him. "A Faulkner letter," she says, "made me shut myself off from everyone and allow images of our days together to cut like flung golden disks across my mind. . . . I would go to bed early, sometimes without food, and think on Bill happily, as a novitiate on her lord."[30] Late in their correspondence he wrote to her, "As soon as I touched that envelope, I knew who it was from. I dreamed about you that night and had to get up and change pajamas."[31]

When Faulkner returned to *Requiem* in 1949, he was writing to another "novitiate." Joan Williams was an aspiring writer, closer to Temple's own age than Meta Carpenter, and Faulkner early urged her to help him with his play. "After you read the enclosed section," he wrote her in March 1950, "maybe we can decide what is wrong with Temple."[32] Wilde remembers that "the idealization of me as a girl far too young for him was to last for a number of years and to appear in some of his letters to me. I never protested and my acceptance of his vision of me as a maiden nourished his fantasy."[33] The same epistolary fantasy is evoked in a 1949 letter to Joan, who was then a twenty-one-year-old college student. Her questions were the wrong ones to ask in letters, he said. "A woman must ask these of a man while they are lying in bed together . . . when they are lying at peace or at least quiet and maybe on the edge of sleep, so you'll have to wait, even to ask them. You may not find the answers even then; most dont. . . . I'd like to know if you ever do. Maybe you will tell me; that can be a good subject for the last letter you will need to write me."[34] The letter constructs a veiled erotic scene and includes a sexual proposal: both were repeated in the correspondence with Joan in several guises. In September 1950 Faulkner sent her a story idea about "a young woman, senior at school, a man of fifty, famous—could be artist, soldier, whatever seems best. . . . she likes him, feels drawn to an understanding, make it wisdom, of her, of people, man, a sympathy for her in particular; maybe he will of a sudden talk of love to her." When the man dies soon after, the girl will realize "that what he wanted was to walk in April again for a day, an hour" (SL, 307). He was drawing from two diverse sources. In a letter written early the same month, he had told Joan that she served the same function for him: "Something still comes out of [your] letters, the April wind out of the apple trees or the mountains."[35] Very likely, he also was comparing her to Renata in Hemingway's *Across the River and into the Trees* published that month, and himself to her lover, Colonel Cantwell.[36] In the novel Joan was by then helping him write, Temple compares herself to another of Hemingway's young women in love with an older soldier-writer, Maria in *For Whom the Bell Tolls* (RN, 133).

Epistolary courtships and master-student relationships in his own lettered fictions also are integral in the complex contexts of personal writing in which *Requiem* was written in 1949–1951. In September 1949, when he began writing to Joan, he was making final preparations for the publication of *Knight's Gambit*. In the title story of that collection, Gavin Stevens writes innocent love letters to his sixteen-year-old "betrothed," Melisandre Backus, and passionate ones written in German to his Russian mistress. Faulkner wrote no German, but the fictional situation recalls his addressing Meta as maiden-and-lover in letters written while she was married to the Austrian Wolfgang Rebner. The fragility of such lettered love affairs and the vulnerability of Sender and Receiver alike are portrayed when Gavin's letters are accidentally reversed. Neither the German nor the eroticism in the German letter is comprehensible to Melisandre: but when the "cloistered and nunlike maiden" (KG, 145) has the German translated, Gavin says, "whoever translated the German for her, translated the English too" (KG, 236). As if to emphasize the letterly nature of the story, and the assault on Melisandre represented by her reading the erotic letter, there pointedly is a copy of *Clarissa* in Gavin's family library.

By the time Faulkner resumed his love affair with Meta in Hollywood in February 1951, Joan had taken her place as "maiden" correspondent. He wrote to them simultaneously at this period, but apparently less erotically to Joan. In one letter to her, he had spoken of himself as Pygmalion, "creating not a cold and beautiful statue, in order to fall in love with it, but Pygmalion taking his love and creating a poet out of her—something like that. Will you risk it?"[37] Her work on his play was to encourage her in her own writing, but perhaps also to keep her writing letters to him and so provide him an outlet for his growing affection. He told her in March 1950, ". . . the play is yours too. If you refuse to accept it, I will throw it away too. I would not have thought of writing one if I hadn't known you" (SL, 300). To keep their epistolary relationship alive when she "repudiated" her claims on *Re-*

*quiem* (SL, 317), he encouraged her to write a novel of her own. According to Williams, he "envisioned it as a rush of letters, a quick exchange the way he conceived our relationship to have been."[38] As he outlined the plan in a letter in December 1951, her novel essentially would rewrite their affair in ways he would devise and direct. His epistolary persona there would be one of his own long-time favorites, the poet. "Rewrite that first letter you sent me, a young woman, girl, writing to a famous poet say, whom she called on against his will probably, and wrote to apologize: 'I didn't intend to bother you, interfere, I just wanted, hoped, you would tell me why life is, because you are wise and you know the answers.' You wrote that once, more or less; write it again, send it to me, I will answer it and outline your next letter. This story will be a series of letters" (SL, 323). The novel, when she wrote it, was *The Wintering*, and a number of her letters and his are transcribed there, altered for her own personal reasons and fictional ends. In his last letter to Amy Holland in that novel, the novelist, Jeff Almonder, tells her, *"I took you in only to shape you into what you wanted to be. But yours is the girl-woman face and figure I see when I close my eyes."*[39] Faulkner had written something very close to that in the Pygmalion letter. In 1954 the then fifty-six-year-old Faulkner would summon the same persona in a letter to Saxe Commins describing Jean Stein, the nineteen-year-old child-woman who, he said, "came to me in St Moritz almost exactly as Joan did in Oxford. But she has none of the emotional conventional confusion which poor Joan had. This one is so uninhibited that she frightens me a little. . . . She is charming, delightful, completely transparent, completely trustful. I will not hurt her for any price. She doesn't want anything of me—only to love me, be in love. . . . The other affair would have hurt of course, except for this" (LDB-II, 138).

From the changing contexts of Faulkner's life and art in the 1930s and 1940s, this tangle of real and fictional lovers and their letters produced Temple Drake's letters in *Requiem for a Nun*. And it naturally produced a changed Temple Drake, compounded of the Temple in *Sanctuary*, of course, but of Shakespeare's Goneril and Hemingway's Renata and Maria now, as well; and of Meta Carpenter and Joan Williams, and other women to whom Faulkner wrote intimately and who wrote to him—Else Jonsson, in Switzerland, and Ruth Ford, the actress to whom he also promised *Requiem*; and of the fictional women and imaginary relationships he had spun from feminine mystery and desire in the intervening twenty years since Horace Benbow became obsessed with Temple and his step-daughter, Little Belle, and wrote his frustrated desire into letters to his sister, Narcissa. Lena Grove defines one end of the spectrum; Rosa Coldfield, in her insistence on the *"root and urge . . . heired too from all the unsistered Eves since the Snake"* (AA, 144), the other. Joanna Burden is of this group, with Gail Hightower's wife, as are Laverne Shumann in *Pylon* and Charlotte Rittenmeyer in *The Wild Palms*. Masculine responses range, perhaps, from the Tall Convict's last words, "Women——t" (WP, 339), to Harry Wilbourne's, which Faulkner paraphrased in his letters to Joan: *"between grief and nothing I will take grief"* (WP, 324).[40] Gavin's obsession with Temple's past extends the theme of fascination with feminine desire from *Sanctuary,* and the historical prologues to the three acts of *Requiem* extend and expand its contexts. Still, the Temple Drake who tells Gavin and the Governor, "all that matters is that I wrote the letters," is most profoundly revealed, and concealed, by her letters, and it is of the most profound significance that no one except her lover reads them, including readers of the novel. Gowan contends at the beginning of the book that Temple was "kidnapped into a Memphis whorehouse . . . and loved it" (RN, 62–63), but Temple insists that she loved Red, "if love can be, mean anything, except the newness, the learning, the peace, the privacy: no shame: not even conscious that you are naked because you are just using the nakedness because that's a part of it" (RN, 132). This is a different Temple from the dangerously damaged child of *Sanctuary,* and to breach her letters of love would constitute a voyeuristic violation of that unashamed peace and privacy, analogous to the rape itself.[41]

Read in her "good letters" by Red (his name is homonymous with the past tense of the verb *to read*) Temple *is* and is *good.* Eight years later Pete succeeds so easily in his blackmail scheme because, through all of Gowan's self-serving forgiveness, Temple still clings to that epistolary self-as-word. Blackmail, as the word suggests, is a misappropriation of privacy in which the power of the letter is turned against Sender and Receiver and threatens to *blacken.* Temple protects her private image by sacrificing the public, "reformed" one that she calls "Mrs. Gowan Stevens": when Pete misreads the love in her letters to Red as lust, she reclaims them by offering herself to him "to produce the material for another set of them" (RN, 131). The consequences for Temple and her child and Nancy proceed from this crucial point, but they are impelled by tragic inevitability rather than innate evil or even the principle that Gavin propounds that human suffering is an inherent necessity. Temple's Temple Drake is no more evil than Caddy Compson, whose true self Faulkner likewise concealed in a fabric of masculine obsession, or Joanna Burden, who writes herself into untranscribed letters to Joe Christmas. "I'm trying to tell you about one

Temple Drake," Temple tells the Governor, "and our Uncle Gavin is showing you another one. So already you've got two different people begging for the same clemency; if everybody concerned keeps on splitting up into two people, you wont even know who to pardon, will you?" (RN, 135). More even than Cecelia Farmer's name scratched on the window of the Jefferson jail, Temple's letters from the prisoning confines of the Manuel Street brothel represent her own statement, *"Listen, stranger; this was myself: this was I"* (RN, 225).

Temple's appeal to her letters as the true transcriptions of her otherwise fragmented, contradictory, and inexpressible self is fully consistent with the subject matter of love and the inherent intimacy of epistolary writing, and it suggests a final, deep-running source for her love letters and for Faulkner's. Writing early in the twelfth century to the abbot of St. Gildas Abbey in Brittany, the abbess of the convent of the Paraclete found it equally difficult to determine whom to address, let alone how and in what person. The abbot was her lover, her husband, and the father of her child as well as her spiritual superior in orders. She was writing, moreover, after a separation of ten years, during which he had been castrated on orders from her uncle for seducing her and she confined to her nunnery. She addressed her letter in this fashion: "To her master, or rather her father, husband, or rather brother; his handmaid, or rather his daughter, wife, or rather sister; to Abelard, Heloise."[42] Whoever else Heloise was forced by circumstances to be, in her early letters she is a passionate lover. A gifted student, she had been brought to study with Abelard by her uncle, Fulbert, when she was seventeen and Abelard, then in his mid-thirties, was the justly famous master of Cloister Schools in Paris. Master and student immediately became lovers. When Fulbert found them together, Abelard sent Heloise to his sister in Brittany disguised as a nun, and there she bore him a child. To satisfy her uncle's honor they were secretly married in Paris, but Fulbert objecting to the secrecy, Abelard again sought sanctuary for Heloise in a nunnery, this time the convent at Argenteuil. After the castration, both took religious orders, she unwillingly. Although Heloise had renounced the world at nineteen, her letters to Abelard ten years later urge him to resume contact with her, if only in writing. Their letterly intercourse, she argues, will substitute for the sexuality no longer possible between them, and she begs him, "restore your presence to me in the way you can—by writing me some word of comfort."[43] Substitute, perhaps, but never satisfy. In answer to a letter from Abelard disguising his physical disability as spiritual commitment, Heloise portrays herself as a passionate woman, despairing of her confinement, and longing for sexual release.

In my case, the pleasures of lovers which we shared have been too sweet—they can never displease me, and can scarcely be banished from my thoughts. Wherever I turn they are always there before my eyes, bringing with them awakened longings and fantasies which will not even let me sleep. Even during the celebration of the Mass, when our prayers should be purer, lewd visions of those pleasures take such a hold upon my unhappy soul that my thoughts are on their wantonness instead of on prayers. I should be groaning over the sins I have committed, but I can only sigh for what I have lost. Everything we did and also the times and places are stamped on my heart along with your image, so that I live through it all again with you. Even in sleep I know no respite. Sometimes my thoughts are betrayed in a movement of my body, or they break out in an unguarded word. In my utter wretchedness, that cry from a suffering soul could well be mine: "Miserable creature that I am, who is there to rescue me out of the body doomed to this death?" Would that in truth I could go on: "The grace of God through Jesus Christ our Lord."[44]

Moved by the same anguished longing, she tells Abelard in a famous passage from her first letter, "The name of wife may seem more sacred or more binding, but sweeter for me will always be the word mistress, or, if you will permit me, that of concubine or whore."[45]

There are suggestive correspondences between this body of love letters and Faulkner's real and fictional letter canons. In his own correspondence, and in *Requiem for a Nun* where the master-student relationship is portrayed obliquely through Gavin and Temple, Faulkner was expressing the same passionate and anguished love depicted in the letters that gained immortality for Heloise and Abelard.[46] The power of their love over the Western imagination is suggested by the fact that for the next 650 years after Heloise's death in 1164 her bones and Abelard's were frequently exhumed, examined, and from 1800 to 1817 publicly displayed in Paris. In the eighteenth century Alexander Pope's poem *Eloïsa to Abelard* (1717) was popular enough to be translated into Italian, French, and German; and Rousseau's *La Nouvelle Héloïse* (1761) crossed the Channel translated into English almost immediately after its French publication. Modern instances include Moncrief's modern translation of the letters (1925), and Helen Waddell's novel *Peter Abelard* (1933).

By the time Faulkner invented Temple's letters in *Requiem*, he might have known the lovers from any of these. Certainly he knew them by reputation, and he could have encountered them directly in his great-grandfather's travel letters. In a letter from *Rapid Ramblings in Europe* dated Paris, August 13, 1883, W. C. Falkner reported on a visit to the tomb of Heloise and Abelard where, he said, "sentimental nonsense usually culminates and falls in the shape of tears on the grave of those unfortunate lovers. The names of Abelard and Heloise have furnished the theme of song for many an amateur poet and material for many a silly novel, most of which might justly be pronounced froth."[47] For Heloise, Colonel Falkner has great sympathy, for Abelard none. "He was a hypocrite, a villain, and a seducer," he wrote of the medieval priest. "At the mature age of forty, when men of virtue and integrity are supposed to be able to subdue and control their evil passions, he seduced Heloise, a beautiful maiden of eighteen, whom he had been employed to teach by her confiding uncle."[48] The Old Colonel could hardly have imagined then that eighty years later his own great-grandson would be involved in a master-student, lover-maiden relationship with two young women, one a protégée he was teaching to write, or that he would be transfiguring those personal relationships and their letterly antecedents in a novel of his own.

In 1925 Faulkner used Abelard, with Paris, in the short, ironic poem about frustrated love that became Poem XXXII of *A Green Bough*.[49] His earliest fictional Abelard, an ironic one, is the Rev. Gail Hightower, who exchanges secret love letters with his idealized wife-to-be at his seminary. "He did not believe that she could have lived there all her life and not be beautiful. He did not see the face itself for three years. By that time there had already been for two years a hollow tree in which they left notes for one another. If he believed about that at all, he believed that the idea had sprung spontaneously between them, regardless of whichever one thought of it, said it, first. But in reality he had got the idea not from her or from himself, but from a book" (LIA, 454). After his wife's death, Hightower is driven from church as a heretic. Their allusive letters echo and enrich Joanna's surreptitious correspondence with Joe. Like Heloise, the cloistered recluse Faulkner describes as a "priest" writes her sexual fantasies into letters, which, like Temple's, are not transcribed in the novel. Joe himself is called a "monk" (LIA, 140, 172), preaches a heretical sermon in a Negro church, and like Abelard is castrated for his forbidden relationship with a woman. "Now you'll let white women alone," Percy Grimm tells him, "even in hell" (LIA, 439).

Temple Drake is far more closely drawn to the pattern of Heloise's life than is Joanna, however: the intertextual relationship between *Requiem for a Nun* and the story of Heloise and Abelard is deeply rooted and extensive enough to have given the novel its title. Heloise and Temple both are students abducted to the ironic sanctuary of nunneries—one a convent literally, one in the Shakespearean sense of nunnery as brothel. Each is disguised as a member of her respective sister-hood, and each undergoes a sexual novitiate to which her passionate letters confess. Each set of letters depicts the letter writer to her lover in terms of erotic memories and fantasies, and each letter canon, in-sufficiently substituting for the woman herself, constitutes an artifact of her.[50] The seducers in each case are unmanned. The priest, Abe-lard, is castrated by order of Heloise's uncle, Fulbert; Popeye, the "black man" of *Sanctuary* (SR, 47), is impotent. In *Requiem* "our Uncle Gavin" imagines Popeye as a figure from a demonic *Arabian Nights* "to whom the ability even to read was vulgar and plebeian and, reclining on silk amid silken airs and scents, had eunuch slaves for that office, commanding death to the slave at the end of each reading, each eve-ning, that none else alive, even a eunuch slave, shall have shared in, partaken of, remembered, the poem's evocation" (RN, 126). Gavin's de-scription is adapted from the *Arabian Nights* story of the sultan who strangled his wives and of Scheherazade's saving herself by telling him stories, but the substitution of poetry for Schahriah's wives may owe something to Faulkner's 1925 essay "Verse Old and Nascent: A Pil-grimage," where he claimed to have substituted art for women in his own life, finding in poems a satisfactory emotional counterpart to sex-ual pursuit.[51] The description of Popeye as eunuch is borrowed from the original *Sanctuary*, where it occurs to Horace Benbow that Popeye "should have been a eunuch, serving his ends with a silken cord in a chamber lighted by a silver lamp of scented oil; a silent shadow high on the secret arras beyond which nightingales were singing" (SO, 25). From figurative castrato in the original to literal impotent in the re-vised *Sanctuary*, Popeye in *Requiem for a Nun* is again figuratively as well as literally the impotent sexual voyeur. His image there summons other unmanned lovers reminiscent of Abelard from the *Sanctuary* materials: bookish Horace himself, attracted to both Little Belle and Temple, and Lee Goodwin, accused of raping Temple with a corn cob, who is castrated and burned by the mob in Popeye's stead.

These parallels lead to the core of Temple's dilemma as wife and whore, victim and lover. In one letter to Heloise, Abelard resolves the paradox of the unmanned lover rhetorically by arguing from Scripture that her lust is the coarse outer garment of her loving heart as her body is of her soul. His illustration compares her to King Solomon's Ethiopian concubine in Song of Songs who says, "I am black but lovely, daughters of Jerusalem; therefore the king has loved me and brought me into his chamber."[52] Heloise had expressed in her first letter her wish to be Abelard's "concubine or whore," and he answers in this letter by turning her desire against her: in her nun's habit she is the Bride of Christ he calls her, outwardly "black" but inwardly "lovely," the sexually forbidden spiritual counterpart of a physical wife. In fact, Heloise knows herself to be the reverse of this—outwardly a nun but inwardly wanton—and it is precisely this recognition to which Temple Drake comes, first in the Manuel Street brothel and again when Pete threatens her with the letters and she discovers, as she says, that "I hadn't even reformed." With Temple, as with Heloise, the tension between the two aspects of self is what generates her letters of self-depiction. In this context, Abelard's analogy provides a symbolic frame of reference that helps to explain the function of Nancy Mannigoe. The "ex-dope-fiend nigger whore" (RN, 136) who urges Temple to "believe" (RN, 243) ironically combines the concubine and the nun in the way that Abelard means. And like Heloise, Temple is the reverse of that "reformed" image. The tension between Nancy and Temple is brought about by the return of the "good letters," and Nancy's death frees Temple to be the image of her written words, both lover and wife. At this core of intertextuality, it is broadly significant that Nancy's name, Mannigoe, once was Maingault according to Gavin and her heritage "runs Norman blood" (RN, 103). Gavin's own name and Gowan's suggest the same medieval era, and the setting of Temple's rape at the Old Frenchman Place recalls still another Frenchman, Abelard, as well as Gustave Flaubert. Heloise's name is the feminine of God's, Elohim, and Temple's is the name of His sanctuary. The last Receiver of Temple's letters is not Peter Abelard but simply Pete, a character Faulkner invented for the letterly plot of *Requiem for a Nun*.

*Requiem for a Nun* reminds us that Yoknapatawpha County is not only a literary world but also a lettered one, its backgrounds and history as mysteriously and intriguingly human in the accretive composition from novel to novel as the characters glimpsed in their broken letters who, by writing them, compose themselves in fragments of autobiographical fiction. The history of Yoknapatawpha as it is set forth in the prologues of *Requiem* reminds us, too, of the foundation of that world in letters, for Jefferson, we are told there, is named for Thomas Jefferson Pettigrew, a letter carrier. "I told that in a book called *Requiem for a Nun*," Faulkner said in 1958 at the University of Virginia, still expanding on fictional facts. "It was—the mail carrier in 1811 or '12 it was, who brought the mail into what was then an Indian trading post, had been a tenant on Mr. Jefferson's place, one of Mr. Jefferson's places here in Albermarle County. It's an involved, long story, but it explains how they named the town Jefferson."[53]

# VI. Personal Distances: The Public Man of Letters

". . . as Bill himself said in an unguarded moment, he is nothing but a writing man, and his ignorance on many subjects is so profound that it would shock you. I have been puzzled and perturbed the last few years at his habit of writing to the editors concerning subjects about which I know that he knows practically nothing."
—Phil Stone to Dave Womack, March 28, 1955

[ i ]

William Faulkner's public letters are of two kinds: those written for publication in newspapers and magazines, most of them in the late 1940s and the 1950s, and a second group written to individuals with the understanding that they might ultimately be published or to representatives of groups, such as the secretary of the American Academy of Arts and Letters or the president of the Glendora, Mississippi, Lions Club, with the understanding that they would be shared. In addition to these, several of Faulkner's public speeches and essays, including his introductions to his own books, are informed by epistolary strategies and conventions. In terms of its epistolarity, this body of public writing begins to span the carefully nurtured and sustained personal distances between the man and his work—between the Mississippi letter writer that Phil Stone described in 1955 as "nothing but a writing man" (LDB-II, 179) and the moral humanist lauded by the Swedish Academy five years before as a man who "mourns for and, as a writer, exaggerates a way of life which he himself, with his sense of justice and humanity, would never be able to stomach."[1] It constitutes a last and, in some respects, the most complete archive of the letter canon.

In subject, in theme, and in tone the public letters of the 1950s parallel and often complement the later canon of Faulkner's novels and stories. Here far more plainly than in his private correspondence, the crossings between letters and literature are pervasive and overt. The gradualist racial attitudes expressed in *Intruder in the Dust*, for example, are similar to positions Faulkner took in letters to regional and national newspapers and magazines, which in turn give a semblance of authorial authority to Gavin Stevens' rhetoric on human equality and justice in *Intruder*, *Requiem*, *The Town*, and *The Mansion*. It may be that the long-delayed notoriety following from the national and international awards Faulkner began receiving in the late 1940s released otherwise dormant aspects of his personality, as Phil Stone believed.[2] In letters about Faulkner in the 1950s, Stone spoke of the Falkner family's unweaning pride, and he suggested that the Nobel Laureate was suffering from "Nobelitis" (LDB-II, 220). It is possible, also, that after Stockholm Faulkner found a forum not available to him before where he could express himself as a citizen on issues he had dealt with in his fiction. A letter to Else Jonsson in June 1955 about his efforts in the integration struggle combines elements of Horace Benbow's despair with Gavin Stevens' strained idealism. "I am doing what I can," he wrote. "But human beings are terrible. One must believe well in man to endure him, wait out his folly and savagery and inhumanity" (SL, 382). Certainly, too, his reasons for writing publicly on such issues depended on his sense of the responsibilities of fame, and his specific responsibilities as a famous southern novelist.[3] It was in this capacity that he was sought out for his opinions, and in this that he most often wrote.

To whatever degree and however willingly Faulkner consciously became a spokesman for the South and the nation in his public letters and speeches in the 1950s, in his books he was inventing a fictional spokesman for many of the same issues, albeit a fumbling and impractical one, often frustrated, and in his active modes a near burlesque of his maker. No doubt the Gavin Stevens of the late novels and stories is part Faulkner, part Phil Stone: there were divisions enough in both men as well as between them to supply Stevens' self-frustrating brand of knight-errantry.[4] But the persona of Faulkner's public letters is equally—and here necessarily—an autobiographical fiction, although one of a different kind. In 1957 he would tell an audience at the University of Virginia that "if one begins to write about the injustice of society, then one has stopped being primarily a novelist and has become a polemicist or a propagandist."[5] In his essay "On Privacy" in 1955, he described his belief that "only a writer's works were in the public domain . . . his private life was his own" (ESPL, 66). His fame and the public letters it generated threatened both distinctions. Gavin Stevens is a fictional polemicist in novels that, as Faulkner also said at Virginia, are "about people, not about the injustice or inhumanity of people but of people, with their aspirations and their struggles and the bizarre, the comic, and the tragic conditions they get themselves into simply coping with themselves and one another and environment."[6] If Faulkner was not speaking directly through Stevens in his novels, he was equally polemical when he spoke for himself in public letters. The letters, like the novels, were in the public domain, but now the letter writer wrote in his own person, and his letters made him vulnerable to personal attack in ways that even the objectionable passages in his fiction did not. His fan mail, he told the Delta Council in 1952, reviled "my writing ability and my ideas both"; he was characterized as "a Mississippian who could debase and defile his native state and people" (ESPL, 126). Yet even when he wrote polemical letters and speeches, he still was writing in the name of the famous novelist—again necessarily. From the first, his fame and his fiction provided him a satisfactory *way* of addressing himself to the public as well as the opportunity—a form in which to express his ideas as well as a forum, and a voice in which to speak. The letters written for publication partake of and profit from epistolary conventions that permitted him to be personally present to his audiences but absent: they were at once the medium in which he met his public obligations as Nobel Laureate and the means by which he distanced his public from his private life. In Oxford he might sign himself "WILLIAM FAULKNER / Private Citizen" (ESPL, 208). The "William Faulkner" in the letters-to-the-editor pages of the *Memphis Commercial Appeal* and the *New York Times* and *Life* magazine was neither the private citizen nor quite the novelist, but rather an extraliterary public self compounded of them both, joint product of Oxford, Mississippi, and the fictional Yoknapatawpha County.

The distinction between the self and the written self inherent in all autobiographical writing is especially clear in nonfiction autobiography. "Bill's article, 'Mississippi,' in next month's Holiday explains the two Bills," Estelle Faulkner wrote Saxe Commins in March 1954. "He is so definitely dual I think—Perhaps artists must needs be" (LDB-II, 136). Public letters represent a similar duality of the man and the man-as-writing. In salutation, signature, and the form of the text, public and private letters appear much the same, but the public letter writer's intention to publish imposes restrictions on his letter to which private correspondence generally is not subject, even in its very formal modes. The public letter writer writes for a group rather than an individual, but in doing so he addresses himself to an intermediary. He writes "To the Editor," whose office it is to edit letters in conformity with law, public taste, and conventional usage. These involve restrictions on language and content, and even on length. Letters to the editor customarily are brief, and they seldom employ the kind of private shorthand codes that characterize personal letters between individuals. Nor is there need for intimate self-portrayal or extended length. Because public letters are less dialogic than personal correspondence, the Sender has less expectation of a reply and so less need to present himself in complementary relation to his Receiver. He does not extend his "hand" to his reader, who in any event "receives" his communication through the public medium of newspapers or magazines. Writer and reader are independently represented in the more fixed character of proponents of an idea rather than as parties to an ongoing correspondence. What *is* portrayed in public as in personal letters is the letter itself: the text, its subject, and its intended function. A Faulkner letter addressed to the editor of the *New York Times* begins typically: "This is about the Italian airliner which undershot the runway and crashed at Idlewild" (ESPL, 212). Often public letters address previous news stories: "I see by the papers that the G.O.C. Second Army has seen fit to discipline for cause a unit in his command" (ESPL, 199). When letters to the editor do respond to a prior letter, the previous letter writer inevitably is addressed in the third person: "Re Waugh on Hemingway in *Time*, Oct. 30" (ESPL, 210). Lacking the circular structure of epistolary discourse, they assume to themselves the immediacy of oral debate: "I have just read the letters of Mr Neill, Mr Martin and Mr Womack in your issue of March 27th, in reply to my letter in your issue of March 20th" (ESPL, 218). But even when prompted by previously published letters, letters to the editor are *to* the intermediary editor: "I have just read with interest the 'Letter to the Editor' of Mr Wolstenholme, of Hohenwald, Tenn., in your issue of Sunday, the 6th" (ESPL, 214).

Read *as letters*, and in terms of these modifications of the genre, Faulkner's public letters are as revealing of distinctions between William Faulkner the man and William Faulkner the writer as they are representative of his thought in the last decade of his life and his attitudes toward the social and political events that prompted him to write. A brief series of published and unpublished letters written to the *Memphis Commercial Appeal* in late 1955 illustrates the extreme detachment public letters permit. Faulkner wrote six letters to the *Commercial Appeal* that winter and spring on the subject of integration, and in September published a statement in the *New York Times* on the Emmett Till case. On December 4, 1955, John Falkner published a letter in the *Commercial Appeal* on the subject of the divided South, in which he argued that the NAACP was financed by communists, that communism was anti-Christian, and that white churches were threatened with dissolution by the Supreme Court decision on integration. He concluded with a paragraph that implicated his brother as a spokesman for division, but without naming him. "I have noticed this: Of those white men of the South who mount the platform to speak in favor of integration, I know a small few personally. Of those I do know, not a single one is a member or active communicant of any church."[7] The following day William Faulkner drafted a public reply for the *Commercial Appeal*, also without naming his brother.

Oxford, Miss.
Dec. 5, 1955

The Commercial Appeal:
Dear Sir:

I see in your correspondence of last Sunday that the threat of communism and atheism (agnosticism) are being used to defend status quo segregation. All lacking of the old Hitler formula is the threat of Semitism.

I dont remember ever seeing these three questions answered by the proponents of status quo segregation:

1. Christianity says: There are no distinctions among men since whosoever believeth in Me shall never die.
2. Morality says: Do unto others as you would have others do unto you.
3. The Constitution of the U.S. says: Before the law, there shall be no artificial inequality—creed race or money—among citizens of the United States.

If these questions were answered, maybe all of us would be on one side.

William Faulkner[8]

The letter was not published. Faulkner subsequently expanded it in a second draft that condemned the church's silence on integration, and that version was incorporated into the essay "On Fear: The Deep South in Labor: Mississippi" in *Harper's* in June 1956, where the detached rancor of the initial letter was fully distanced. For a time, however, the detachment of the Sender inherent in public correspondence, and the Sender's distance from the Receiver, had permitted John Falkner to imply in the pages of a Memphis newspaper that his brother was a communist, and William to contemplate condemning John as a Hitlerite fascist.

Such letters were public performances, in which the letter writer presented himself to an audience. They were the public modes of "protest and active self-defense" Faulkner had early attributed to all southern art, and many of them partake of the dramatic ceremony and spectacle he ascribed to the literature of his southern region, including his own work.[9] This is not to say that Faulkner was uncommitted to the stands he took publicly, but that he brought to public letters and essays the writing tactics and strategies of the professional man of letters as well as that persona. Never an animated, nor sometimes a very intelligible public speaker, he included in his public letters a significant range of dramatic performances and effects and something of the artistic integrity, as well as the subject matter, of his published books. A classified ad in the *Memphis Commercial Appeal* and *Oxford Eagle* in 1936 is a deliberate, formal gesture of repudiation: "I will not be responsible for any debt incurred or bills made, or notes or checks signed by Mrs. William Faulkner or Mrs. Estelle Oldham Faulkner."[10] When the *Eagle* declined to publish his letter to the editor about legalized beer in 1950, Faulkner had printed and distributed a satirical broadside countering the paid, printed statement signed by most of the town's clergy. It concludes, "Yours for a freer Oxford, where publicans can be law abiding publicans six days a week, and Ministers of God can be Ministers of God all seven days in the week, as the Founder of their Ministry commanded them to when He ordered them to keep out of temporal politics in His own words: 'Render unto Caesar the things that are Caesar's and to God the things that are God's'" (ESPL, 208). A week later he publicly objected to being listed among the proponents of legal beer in a letter where he said that his stand had been a calculated performance: "my effort in the recent election," he wrote, "was only secondarily concerned with beer. I was making a protest" (ESPL, 209). The unpublished drafts of letters to John Falkner self-consciously make a pretense of ignoring their audience; in the weeks following, they became the actual rehearsals for a national performance in which Faulkner addressed the South and the nation—the essay "On Fear." "This is a serious piece," he wrote Harold Ober when he sent him the essay in January 1956, "to help, I hope, my native country in a dilemma whose seriousness the rest of this country seems incapable not only of understanding but even of believing that to us it is serious" (SL, 392).

The very existence of such drafts, and of drafts of other public letters that were published in the 1950s, suggests their difference from most of Faulkner's private correspondence.[11] Blotner reports his once saying, "It's bad enough to have to write letters. . . . It's inexcusable to lose one that's already written. To have to rewrite one is intolerable" (SL, xv). Certainly even the letters he drafted and recopied are not art, but as with his European correspondence in 1925, which he knew would be shared in his family, many of his public letters are self-consciously literary in their language and style. In some, the performance outweighs and overwhelms the identity of the performer. He wrote to *Time* that he had not raised his own voice against critics of Hemingway's *Across the River and Into the Trees* because

> the man who wrote some of the pieces in *Men Without Women* and *The Sun Also Rises* and some of the African stuff (and some—most— of all the rest of it too for that matter) does not need defending, be-

cause the ones who throw spitballs didn't write the pieces in *Men Without Women* and *The Sun Also Rises* and the African pieces and the rest of it, and the ones who didn't write *Men Without Women* and *The Sun Also Rises* and the African pieces and the rest of it don't have anything to stand on while they throw the spitballs. (ESPL, 210–211)

Not all of his most literary public letters were on literary subjects. A letter to the *Commercial Appeal* about an Attala County murder trial in 1950 is equally conscious of dramatic effect. When three white men convicted of killing three black children were spared the death penalty, Faulkner wrote:

And those of us who were born in Mississippi and have lived all our lives in it, who have continued to live in it forty and fifty and sixty years at some cost and sacrifice simply because we love Mississippi and its ways and customs and soil and people; who because of that love have been ready and willing at all times to defend our ways and habits and customs from attack by the outlanders who we believed did not understand them, we had better be afraid too,— afraid that we have been wrong; that what we had loved and defended not only didn't want the defense and the love, but was not worthy of the one and indefensible to the other.

Which fear, at least, it is to be hoped that the two members of the jury who saved the murderer, will not share.

It is hoped that whatever reasons they may have had for saving him, will be enough so that they can sleep at night free of nightmares about the ten or fifteen or so years from now when the murderer will be paroled or pardoned or freed again, and will of course murder another child, who it is to be hoped—and with grief and despair one says it—will this time at least be of his own color. (ESPL, 204)

The long, somber sentences with their balanced repetitions, and the somber irony of the conclusion, are the work of the public man of letters. Again he would speak of his letter as a "protest" (ESPL, 205), and echoes would appear in similar letters and essays of protest, similarly crafted, in the decade to come.

Inevitably, such letters involved Faulkner in public debate with other letter writers. His stand on quality and equality in Mississippi schools in March 1955 generated letters to the editor from private citizens, a Mississippi State College dean, and a state representative. He answered them publicly in letters where he argued the logic of his gradualist position: he acknowledged that not only integration was at stake but also "the impasse of the emotional conflict over it" (ESPL, 219), but he insisted, "If we are to have two school systems, let the second one be for pupils ineligible not because of color but because they either can't or won't do the work of the first one" (ESPL, 220–221). At one point he borrowed the familiar, self-effacing persona of the "old veteran sixth-grader" to explain to Representative Womack his respect for education and his impatience with those who would "sit quiet and watch it held subordinate in importance to an emotional state concerning the color of human skin" (ESPL, 219). When his "A Letter to the North" appeared in March 1956, the *Life* editors described him in a headnote as "the South's Foremost Writer" and "the most famous portraitist of the American South, past and present."[12] The moderate position he advised in *Life* stimulated responses that he answered in a letter to the editor in April, explaining "the reason *behind* the letter, the reason behind the urgency for the widest possible circulation of it. . . . [which was] to save the South and the whole United States too from the blot of Miss Autherine Lucy's death" (ESPL, 224). He closed with the implication that "A Letter to the North" might be timeless, in the manner of his fiction: "the letter was not needed for that purpose. I hope it will never be. But if a similar situation bearing the seed of a similar tragedy should arise again, maybe the letter will help to serve" (ESPL, 224).

The formality of such letters is suited to their subject. The seriousness with which Faulkner took them is apparent in the care he gave to the epistolary strategies that give them the weight of personal authority. Like the companion piece Faulkner titled "A Letter to the Leaders in the Negro Race," "A Letter to the North" is a letter in the form of an essay, but if they are less *letterly* than his letters to the editor, they still are *lettered* in the manner of his lettered novels. He concluded "A Letter to the North" by saying, "Since I went on record as being opposed to compulsory racial inequality, I have received many letters. A few of them approved. But most of them were in opposition. And a few of these were from southern Negroes, the only difference being that they were polite and courteous instead of being threats and insults" (ESPL, 89). He quoted from and paraphrased one of these last to document his claim that the NAACP was not representative of southern Negroes and that its position on integration was a danger to peace in the South. In his essay "On Fear," published in *Harper's* in June, he documented his own position on Mississippi schools and the emotionalism of the opposition by quoting his published letter to the *Commercial Appeal* the previous year and paraphrasing his exchange of letters in the same pages with W. C. Neill, who had characterized him as "Weeping Willie Faulkner" (ESPL, 93). In a public letter written by Jefferson Davis in 1849, he found a precedent for his own warning that extremist southerners risked watching "our native land wrecked and ruined twice in less than a hundred years over the Negro question" (ESPL, 98): "The generation which avoids its responsibility on this subject," Jefferson had written, "sows the wind and leaves the whirlwind as a harvest to its children" (ESPL, 98).

"On Fear" combined the content of his address to the Southern Historical Association in November 1955 and the drafts of letters to his brother written in December and January. It also included a modification of language, used in that address, that he had drafted in a private letter to Neill the previous spring. There he wrote of his fear that "for the second time in a hundred years, we Southerners will have destroyed our native land just because of niggers" (SL, 391): the revision from "niggers" to "Negro question" signifies the letter writer–essayist's different conception of his two genres and their respective audiences. When his "A Letter to the Leaders in the Negro Race" was published in *Ebony* in September under the title "If I Were a Negro," there were further crossings. He opened by quoting from "A Letter to the North," and correcting misquotations attributed to him in an interview with Russell Howe of the *Reporter* in March (ESPL, 107).[13] As in the previous public essays, the letters inserted in the "Letter" authenticated his claims as a public spokesman and served as documentary evidence of his positions. As with his fictions, his own letters were source and outcome of his writing on these subjects—content and form for his public presentations of himself as "the South's Foremost Writer."

In addition to these lettered essays, Faulkner was solicited for public statements that were published over his name—on the Willie McGee and the Emmett Till cases, for example (ESPL, 211–212, 222–223). On the opposite periphera of the public canon are letters he addressed to a different kind of intermediary than a newspaper editor. He received and wrote letters to groups through their individual representatives and, occasionally, to individuals with the understanding that his letter might be published. In November 1950 he repaid a kindness by writing Swedish newsman Sven Ahman about the Nobel Prize. His initial decision not to go to Stockholm for the awards ceremony was unpopular in Sweden and with the U.S. State Department. By writing to Ahman, he could try to keep the Swedish Academy at a distance.

The following is a statement which is an explanation of my reply to the formal notification from the Secretary of the Swedish Academy of the Nobel award to my work, which the Secretary should have and perhaps should receive directly from me. I make it to you, since your predecessor, Mr. Jonsson, was my first personal contact with Sweden, and because it was your thoughtful kindness which first intimated to me from Sweden of the award, but with the further request on your kindness that you submit it first to the Academy Secretary and have his authorization to print it, if it should be public, any part of it, that is. (SL, 308–309)

When a University of Alabama student named David Kirk wrote him in March 1956 for his views on how to start an interracial dialogue among students and avert further violence, he answered with a generous letter of concern proposing that Kirk start by publishing their brief correspondence (SL, 394–396). With the help of Harvey Breit and the staff at Random House in late 1956 and 1957, he wrote letters that were mimeographed and signed by machine to selected American writers in President Eisenhower's People-to-People Program.[14] Even public letters of this kind were not to be written casually, however. When Breit asked Faulkner for a review of *The Old Man and the Sea* for his *New York Times Book Review* column, Faulkner sent him a hasty rehash of the letter he had written to *Time* two years before in defense of *Across the River and Into the Trees*. He opened with an oblique reference to an exchange of letters he had had with Hemingway in 1947, saying that he had forgotten its details but using that occasion to make the point that Hemingway did not need his or anyone's praise because "the sort of writers who need to band together willy nilly or perish, resemble the wolves who are wolves only in pack, and, singly, are just another dog." He paraphrased his letter about *Across the River* in a passage where he said that the Hemingway "who wrote the MEN WITHOUT WOMEN pieces and THE SUN ALSO RISES and A FAREWELL TO ARMS and FOR WHOM THE BELL TOLLS and most of the African stuff and most of all the rest of it, is not one of these, and needs no pack protection" (SL, 333). Breit sent this hastily written estimate to Hemingway, who responded, "He did not forget what the occasion was that I wrote him that. He remembers it very well. In one of his rummy moments (I hope) he had said, flatly, that I was a coward. . . . So he writes to you as though I was asking him a favour to protect me. Me, the dog."[15] Faulkner's subsequent review of *The Old Man and the Sea*, in *Shenandoah* in September, abandoned the terms of his previous letters and called the book "his best. Time may show it to be the best single piece of any of us, I mean his and my contemporaries. This time, he discovered God, a Creator" (ESPL, 193). But the damage done by the earlier letters could not be undone by this praise. Hemingway had not forgotten his objections to the "review" letter. He wrote Lillian Ross, "You ask if I know what he means. What he means is that he is spooked to die and he is moving in on the side of the strongest battalions. We will fight it out here and if there are no reserves it is too Faulking bad and they will find what is left of Dog company on that hill. Please do not quote me on any of the above as it is controversial."[16]

## [ ii ]

Faulkner's public writing about his own books is nearly as meager as his reviews of others' work. When Random House wanted an author's preface for the Modern Library combined edition of *The Sound and the Fury* and *As I Lay Dying* in 1946, Faulkner wrote Robert Haas, "I'm not a preface man, never read one and dont intend to, dont see why for them" (SL, 234). He told Robert Linscott, "I'm no good at this. To me, the book is its own prologue epilogue introduction preface argument and all. I doubt if any writing bloke can take seriously this or any other manifestation of the literary criticism trade" (SL, 236–237). When Linscott sent it to him, he found the introduction he had written for *The Sound and the Fury* "smug false sentimental windy shit" (SL, 235). He turned down proposals to have other writers do the preface to the double volume—among those proposed were Conrad Aiken, Hemingway, and Caroline Gordon—and Random House finally used instead the "Appendix: Compson" he had written for Cowley's *Portable Faulkner*. That piece, he had told Cowley, had been written "to give a sort of bloodless bibliophile's point of view" on the Compsons (SL, 206). The map, genealogy, and chronology he supplied for *Absalom, Absalom!* in 1936 were still more the matter of a "bloodless" appendix rather than authorial afterword.

When he did publish prefaces, however, he borrowed for them from the strategies of letters. In the 1932 introduction to *Sanctuary*, he divided himself into two personae, the village handyman—the carpenter–house painter who addresses the reader—and the writer he calls "Faulkner": "So I told Faulkner, 'You're damned. You'll have to work now and then for the rest of your life'" (ESPL, 177). He concluded that he had made a "fair job" of revising *Sanctuary*, "and I hope you will buy it and tell your friends and I hope they will buy it too" (ESPL, 178). In the foreword to *The Faulkner Reader* in 1954, the divided persona of the *Sanctuary* introduction gave way to that of the public man of letters. He introduced himself through his boyhood dreams of flying and his informal education in his family's library, mentioning Clarissa, as he had in "Knight's Gambit," before settling on Sienkiewicz to illustrate his point that writers write "to uplift men's hearts"

(ESPL, 180). This was the stuff of the Nobel Prize address, and of private letters to scholars, such as Warren Beck and Malcolm Cowley in the 1940s. In letters to Joan Williams he had explained his compulsion to write, as he did now in the foreword, and the division he told Joan he felt between "the work and the country man whom you know as Bill Faulkner" (SL, 348). That his work was a way of "saying No to Death" (ESPL, 181), he borrowed from Judith Sutpen's description of Charles Bon's letter in *Absalom, Absalom!*. As he had when he portrayed his physical vitality in love letters to Meta Carpenter and to Joan, he chose sexual terms to describe the force of feeling in his books that he said would give him immortality. He had written "while the blood and glands and flesh still remained strong and potent" (ESPL, 180). Engendered in "cold impersonal print," those passions were invulnerable, capable in their turn of "engendering still the old deathless excitement in hearts and glands whose owners and custodians are generations from even the air he breathed and anguished in; . . . capable and potent still" (ESPL, 182). By this figurative letter, William Faulkner the author was publicly delivering his words into the hands and hearts of readers of *The Faulkner Reader*.

Faulkner now began to write more freely to his "public" also: letters explaining his work that were only marginally private in that they contained sometimes intimate revelations to strangers. Estelle would note the duality of a real and a fictional self in the essay-story "Mississippi"; a private and a public self coexist in a similar way in these letters. The duality evident in the July 1941 letter to Professor Warren Beck, where Faulkner portrayed himself as both "an old 8th grade man" and reader of Shakespeare and Pater (SL, 142), is only slightly modified in two letters to academic correspondents a decade later. To Dayton Kohler, in January 1950, he spoke of himself interchangeably in the first and the third person. "Thank you for sending the piece from College English," he told Kohler. "I agree with it; I mean, re Faulkner's aim" (SL, 296). The awkwardness of written language, he said, is "a good workable excuse for Faulkner's writing style." In a postscript, he admitted to Kohler as he never had to Malcolm Cowley, "Am proud to have belonged to RAF even obscurely. But had no combat service nor wound" (SL, 297). Writing to Professor Henry F. Pommer in 1954 about a misprint in *Light in August,* he borrowed from the language of the book as he had that year from events in other fiction for "Mississippi." He wrote Pommer, "The curse of literacy, into which linotypers and proof-readers (editors too for that matter) are as a race such recent arrivers in America, is that the new brother quit there before he discovered that it is no cold dead quality imprisoned between the covers of a grammar but is rather the living catalyst of the whole long living record of man's imagination" (SL, 374). Elements of this phrasing are present in the passage from the novel that Pommer questioned, where the cursed race of man, race itself, and newly arrived interlopers in the South such as the Burdens are directly under scrutiny: Nathaniel Burden tells Joanna, "The curse of the black race is God's curse. But the curse of the white race is the black man who will be forever God's chosen own because He once cursed Him" (LIA, 240). Pommer thought that Faulkner had agreed without checking the text of the novel with his suggestion that "Him" should have been "Ham."[17] In fact, he appears to have adapted the language of his fiction and the admonitory tone of the passage to his private epistolary voice.

At this period, too, there built up around Faulkner a peripheral canon of private letters by detractors and admirers among his friends and associates that publicized him without his being aware of it. For example, Robert Coughlan's two-part *Life* magazine article and the book that followed from it were written with the substantial assistance of letters to Coughlan from Phil Stone. For four years before Faulkner's death, James Silver wrote letters to publishers and collectors trying unsuccessfully to arrange the publication of *A Wishing Tree* and then to make a record of the circumstances of its composition. Private though they were intended to be, each of these correspondences became public to a degree that embarrassed Faulkner and drew him into self-justifying correspondence of his own.

Stone's letters to Coughlan are part of a series of letters he wrote in the 1950s when Faulkner's sudden fame and Stone's business reversals and failing health combined to extend and broaden a division that had been between them since the mid-1930s.[18] They seriously disagreed on integration: in April 1955, when Faulkner publicly defended his stand on Mississippi schools against criticism in public letters written to the *Commercial Appeal* by Mr. Neill, Mr. Martin, and State Representative Womack, Stone wrote privately to Womack. "I have been puzzled and perturbed the last few years at his habit of writing to the editors concerning subjects about which I know that he knows practically nothing," he said (LDB-II, 179). "Of course you people are doing the best you can down there and any one of you knows more about this subject in ten minutes than Bill does or ever will know in a lifetime. So don't take him seriously." Typically, he asked not to be quoted: "Of course on account of our forty years' close friendship this letter is not for the press but simply for your private eye" (LDB-II, 180). In 1957 Stone told George Thatcher, owner of the Dixie Press in Gulfport, Mississippi, "Since he has taken the position he has in turning his back on his own people and his native land, I dont care to ask him anything" (LDB-II, 220). Many of Stone's letters about Faulkner were openly self-promoting, though often his claim to be a spokesman for Faulkner's work was brought into question by his pettish criticism. Clifton Fadiman found deep divisions in an unsolicited letter from Stone offering to meet him in New York for a talk about Faulkner's work. "The only part of your letter which is not clear to me," he wrote Stone, "is your estimate of Mr. Faulkner ('the best writer in contemporary American fiction') as contrasted with your three rather crushing judgments: (1) He has no style; (2) His novels are merely collections of episodes; (3) Most of his characters are puppets" (LDB-II, 192). In the Coughlan correspondence, Stone's willingness to write about Faulkner's politics and art extended beyond private sniping and personal self-promotion to publicizing the writer's private life.

*Life* had planned an article on Faulkner as early as 1948, when Malcolm Cowley first proposed doing for Faulkner the sort of essay he had done on Hemingway. Faulkner refused, and the project was canceled. It was revived briefly in May 1950, six months before the Nobel Prize announcement, when Carvel Collins considered it, but Collins withdrew when Stone wrote a semiofficial letter on Faulkner's behalf saying that the novelist still disapproved. In this instance, Stone refused his own help.

> Furthermore, from my own point of view, I simply do not feel that I can commercialize my friendship with Bill. After Emily, Philip and Araminta, I am fonder of Bill than I am of anybody in the world. In addition to that, if I did do such a thing I think it would be a very saddening shock to Bill, even more than he realizes, because I think that, of all the people in the world that he knows, he has a profound faith in my integrity and in my personal loyalty to him. If I should destroy this (although maybe I am now being vain) I don't know just how severe a shock it would be to him.
>
> So please let the Life Magazine article go. Certainly I shall have no part of it and shall take none of the money. (LDB-II, 56)

In the period of estrangement that followed the Nobel award, however, Stone broke his own self-imposed interdiction. When Robert Coughlan took up the project in late 1952, Stone willingly read the proofs and supplied lengthy personal commentaries. His information was not always accurate or up to date: he wrote Coughlan on September 30, ". . . you emphasize too much the fact that Bill occasionally, very occasionally, throws a drunk. . . . On the whole he drinks very little" (LDB-II, 84–85). That week Faulkner was so desperately ill with drink at Rowan Oak that Saxe Commins was called to help, and wrote his wife on the morning of October 8 that he was witnessing "a complete disintegration of a man" (LDB-II, 89). In November, Stone wrote Collins that he had read proof on Coughlan's article, and that "I told him that he could not use anything I gave him except my part in the production of the books" (LDB-II, 99); in fact, he had supplied Coughlan with information about Jill's school, Maud Falkner's religion, Faulkner's brothers, and Estelle's first marriage (LDB-II, 85–87). He even told him, "Bill and Estelle were married in the old Presbyterian Church at College Hill by the revered late Dr. W. D. Heddleston, and were not married in the Episcopal Church in Oxford. They ran off to get married like two children" (LDB-II, 87). He subsequently volunteered information about the birth and death of Faulkner's daughter Alabama for Coughlan's book, and he speculated that "another reason (strictly off the record) that Bill is not likely to come back here is that I think he is permanently getting rid of Estelle" (LDB-II, 143).

In effect, Stone went from insisting on Faulkner's privacy to insisting on his own anonymity as the source of painful public revelations about the novelist's private life. He wrote Coughlan October 1, 1953, when the first *Life* installment was published, "Your article, I think, has the town stewing. All of this I am telling you now is confidential and all I tell you about it in the future will be, but I look for a terrific feud in the Faulkner family because they surely can't blame those family photographs on me" (LDB-II, 120). On the same day, he wrote to the editor of *Life* correcting an error in the article about his own grandfather's name (LDB-II, 120). Stone's private and public letters publicized him as an intimate of the author. Whatever their impetus, they also publicized William Faulkner the man in ways that the author's own public epistolary persona was designed to conceal. Faulkner's reaction to the *Life* article, had he known what Stone was privately up to, is as much a condemnation of Stone as of the press. He wrote Phil "Moon" Mullen:

I tried for years to prevent it, refused always, asked them to let me alone. It's too bad the individual in this country has no protection from journalism, I suppose they call it. But apparently he hasn't. There seems to be in this the same spirit which permits strangers to drive into my yard and pick up books or pipes I left in the chair where I had been sitting, as souvenirs.

What a commentary. Sweden gave me the Nobel Prize. France gave me the Legion d'Honneur. All my native land did for me was to invade my privacy over my protest and my plea. No wonder people in the rest of the world dont like us, since we seem to have neither taste nor courtesy, and know and believe in nothing but money and it doesn't much matter how you get it.

Yours,

Bill

[P.S.] This time I wasn't even consulted, didn't even know it was being done, nor did my mother. She knew she was being photographed and specifically asked the photographer not to print the picture anywhere.

This seems to me to be a pretty sorry return for a man who has only tried to be an artist and bring what honor that implies to the land of his birth. (LDB-II, 122)

Earlier he had told Mullen, "I haven't seen the piece in LIFE yet, but if you had anything to do with it, I know it is alright and I hope you make a nickle out of it" (LDB-II, 121). In contrast to Mullen's openness about helping Coughlan, Stone had been secretive and proprietorial. In September 1952 he had warned Coughlan "in the strictest confidence . . . not to rely too much on Moon's ideas about Bill. . . . Since I know more about Bill than anybody in the world does, I realize how little Moon really knows probably much more clearly than you or any other outsider would suspect" (LDB-II, 87).

*The Wishing Tree* correspondence began in 1958. Faulkner had given a copy of the handmade book to Margaret Brown in 1928 when the child was dying, and a copy belonging to Phil Stone's son had been exhibited in 1948 with other Faulkner materials at Princeton. In 1958 Margaret's mother, Maud M. Brown, consulted with University of Mississippi history professor James Silver about publishing the book, then wrote Faulkner in July to ask his permission. When she received no answer, Silver wrote to *Life* in August on her behalf. *Life* editors inquired of Faulkner's agent, Harold Ober, and Faulkner wrote Ober in February 1959, "I was quite shocked when Mrs Brown wrote me that she even considered getting money from it. To tell the truth, I didn't believe her. When I told her the story (after the child's death) belonged to her, to do as she wanted with it, it never occurred to me that she would want to commercialise it, since it was, as I said, a gesture of pity and compassion from a neighbor to a neighbor's little child doomed to death without knowing it. If Mrs Brown needs money this badly, of course I will not stand in her way" (SL, 421). Mrs. Brown subsequently offered the book to Random House, again through Silver, and Bennett Cerf wrote Faulkner in November 1959 to ask about publishing it. This time Faulkner refused. When Cerf wrote Silver a week later, he inserted a transcription of Faulkner's letter in his own:

Dear Bennett:

This story was written as a gesture of pity and compassion for Mrs. Brown's little girl who was dying of cancer.

I would be shocked if Mrs. Brown herself wanted to commercialize it. But it belongs to her. I will not forbid her to sell it, but I myself would never authorize it being published, unless perhaps, the proceeds should go to save other children from cancer. (LDB-II, 266)

By inserting it into his own letter, Cerf had made Faulkner's private letter public, as did Silver when he subsequently shared it with Mrs. Brown, whose reaction was to share copies of her letters to Faulkner with Silver also. "I have no way of knowing just how Mr. Cerf presented this matter to Mr. Faulkner," she wrote Silver, "but, if he had known exactly my attitude, I think he would not have made his cruel remark about my 'commercializing' the story. That does not sound like Billy to me" (LDB-II, 272). By this time there were two William Faulkners in the correspondence—Mr. Faulkner and Billy. If it was Billy who had been Margaret Brown's friend, Cerf certified that it was William Faulkner the author with whom Silver and Mrs. Brown were dealing when he wrote Silver, after still another inquiry, "we have learned from William Faulkner himself that he is not anxious at all to have THE WISHING TREE published in any way, shape or form. Unless he himself brings the matter up again, we think we should drop all thought of it whatever" (LDB-II, 274).

Faulkner not only recognized such divisions in himself in the period of his public acclaim; in his public letters from the late 1940s on to the end of his life he nurtured them. In his early years he had written himself into being as an Artist through the personae of his carefully crafted private letters and the letterlike gift books he made to display his art in its various mediums. His books, as they came to publication, affirmed that identity, and throughout his career he drew on his letters and on letter writers for the materials of his fiction. Now the process had reversed itself, the creator of the fiction writing as a private citizen to newspaper and magazine editors in the fiction writer's name. If he was ignorant of the issues he wrote about now, as Phil Stone claimed, it had no more relation to the persona of the public letter writer than it had mattered, to that earlier writer of the European correspondence, that he was not yet then a proven artist. In his public letters, he laid claim to social and political expertise in the name of William Faulkner, author, in the same way that he had claimed the title of Artist in his private ones. He wrote it.

## [ iii ]

Surprisingly little of this public matter found its way into the late novels in the form of letters. Indeed, the crossings when they occurred were more often the reverse of early occasions, transmitted from the fiction into public letters. In the second of his lectures to Charles Mallison on the state of the South in *Intruder in the Dust*, for example, Gavin Stevens tells his nephew:

> I'm defending Lucas Beauchamp. I'm defending Sambo from the North and East and West—the outlanders who will fling him decades back not merely into injustice but into grief and agony and violence too by forcing on us laws based on the idea that man's injustice to man can be abolished overnight by police. Sambo will suffer it of course; there are not enough of him yet to do anything else. And he will endure it, absorb it and survive because he is Sambo and has that capacity; he will even beat us there because he has the capacity to endure and survive but he will be thrown back decades and what he survives to may not be worth having because by that time divided we may have lost America. (ID, 203–204)

In "A Letter to the North" eight years later, Faulkner addressed the same "Go slow now" program to "the NAACP and all the organizations who would compel immediate and unconditional integration" (ESPL, 87). To Faulkner then, as to Gavin earlier, laws insensitive to regional realities were at the root of racial violence: "the first implication, and—to the Southerner—even promise, of force and violence," he said in "A Letter to the North," "was the Supreme Court decision itself" (ESPL, 88). In the essay "On Fear" he phrased the Negro's capacity to endure and absorb and survive in terms of his vast progress against odds in the post–Civil War century:

> The white man knows that only ninety years ago not one percent of the Negro race could own a deed to land, let alone read that deed; yet in only ninety years, although his only contact with a county courthouse is the window through which he pays the taxes for which he has no representation, he can own his land and farm it with inferior stock and worn-out tools and gear—equipment which any white man would starve with—and raise children and feed and clothe them and send them to what schools are available and even now and then send them North where they can have equal scholastic opportunity, and end his life holding his head up because he

owes no man, with even enough over to pay for his coffin and funeral. (ESPL, 96)

Like Gavin, Faulkner saw racial integration in the South as an exclusively southern problem; like his character, he expressed that position publicly. And like him, he came to believe that America itself was at risk. In a press dispatch in 1955 regarding the Emmett Till case, he concluded, ". . . if we in America have reached that point in our desperate culture when we must murder children, no matter for what reason or what color, we don't deserve to survive, and probably won't" (ESPL, 223).[19]

Crossings of another kind in *A Fable* constitute a retrospective self-criticism of an early book in the letterly situations of a later one. It was a practice Faulkner had engaged in before, with very private writing, such as his gift books, and with novels. In 1949, a year after the publication of *Intruder*, he proposed to Robert Haas an addition for any subsequent edition of the novel: there Gavin Stevens uses an allusion to *Absalom, Absalom!* to corroborate his racial views, citing "the tag line of a book a novel of about twenty years ago by another Mississippian, a mild retiring little man over yonder at Oxford, in which a fictitious Canadian said to a fictitious self-lacerated Southerner in a dormitory room in a not too authentic Harvard: 'I who regard you will have also sprung from the loins of African kings.'"[20] With this passage appended, *Intruder* affirms the concluding judgment of Faulkner's earlier novel and in turn is certified by it. By contrast, *A Fable* looks back to, and by implication dismisses, Faulkner's earliest fictional persona, the World War I aviator.

Aviation and art are conjoined in Faulkner's fiction as early as the story "Carcassonne," where the Pegasus-like horse of the poet's soaring aspiration is described in terms that directly recall flight in open-cockpit planes: *"with eyes like blue electricity and a mane like tangled fire,"* the horse gallops in a deafening envelope of "soundless thunder" up "a piled silver hill of cumulae where no hoof echoed nor left print, toward the blue precipice never gained," becoming at last "a dying star upon the immensity of darkness and of silence" (CSWF, 895, 898, 895, 900). The aviator Bayard Sartoris, in *Flags*, rides a similarly winged horse, described in similar language, and in Poem XVIII of *A Green Bough* a child who aspires to fly watches the "silver shapes of aircarved cumulae" and sees in imagination "his own lonely shape on scudding walls / Where harp the ceaseless thunders of the sun" (GB, 40). In "The Lilacs" the aviator's "pointed eared machine" is a faun, another of Faulkner's earliest personae, and the flight is a dream reconstructed from memory at the moment of the aviator's death (GB, 8). In *Soldiers' Pay*, Cadet Lowe is a letter writer rather than a poet, but his writing is also tied to aviation. Four of Lowe's six love letters to Margaret Powers contain significant references to flying. He writes on April 5, "Home seems pretty good after you have been doing a pretty risky thing like lots of them cracked up at" (SP, 153). By April 14 he has "done a little flying but mostly dancing and running around" (SP, 187). Nine days later his imaginary flying experience sets him off from "fellows my age that did not serve specially flying which is an education in itself" (SP, 277), and two days after that he is working in a bank "talking to other people in the business that don't know anything about aviation" (SP, 280). Lowe's epistolary persona was Faulkner's own well into the 1940s, sometimes elaborately nurtured during the war in letters to Jimmy Faulkner, Malcolm Franklin, and Robert Haas, and to Malcolm Cowley after it. At Stockholm, in December 1950, he was publicly described as a Canadian Royal Air Force veteran who had "crashed twice, and returned home, not as a military hero but as a physically and psychically war-damaged youth with dubious prospects." [21] Perhaps because of his public identity, he abandoned the aviator in the 1950s, first in the letter to Professor Dayton Kohler where he admitted he had had no combat service or wound, and then in his foreword to *The Faulkner Reader*, written while he was working on *A Fable*. There he said that after the war he had turned from dreams of aviation to accept his destiny as artist. He had not thought of writing books when he began reading:

> The future didn't extend that far. This was 1915 and '16; I had seen an aeroplane and my mind was filled with names: Ball, and Immelman and Boelcke, and Guynemer and Bishop, and I was waiting, biding, until I would be old enough or free enough or anyway could get to France and become glorious and beribboned too.
>   Then that had passed. It was 1923 and I wrote a book and discovered that my doom, fate, was to keep on writing books: not for any exterior or ulterior purpose: just writing the books for the sake of writing the books . . . (ESPL, 180)

David Levine dreams of the same heroic airmen, then kills himself when his life fails to match the purity of that dream. By Levine's broken letter to his mother, transcribed on Tuesday morning of the truce, and his suicide on Thursday, Faulkner expunged the romantic persona in Lowe's and his own private letters from his fiction and his fictions of his life. [22]

Like that of Faulkner and Lowe, Levine's disillusion begins with the uniform he wears. Both characters and the author came of age too late to earn their wings before the Armistice; Levine has had to join the Royal Air Force instead of its predecessor service, the Royal Flying Corps, and he expresses the disdain all three felt for their cadet cap bands when he thinks that "those who had invented for him the lingerie pins and the official slacks in place of pink Bedfords and long boots and ordnance belt had closed the door even to the anteroom of heroes" (F, 88–89). In 1943, when Robert Haas' son died flying torpedo planes from carriers, and Jimmy Faulkner was about to be posted to carrier training, Faulkner had written Haas that he could imagine "the blood of your fathers and the blood of mine side by side at the same long table in Valhalla, talking of glory and heroes, draining the cup and banging the empty pewter on the long board to fill again, holding two places for us maybe, not because we were heroes or not heroes, but because we loved them" (SL, 175). In a letter about Haas' generosity to him, and his children's war service, he told Malcolm Franklin, "He's a Jew," and he said, "I just hope I dont run into some hundred percent American Legionnaire until I feel better" (SL, 175). In *A Fable* he specifically banished the Jewish David Levine from that heroic company—in language he had been using about flying in letters and literature since the early twenties.

> In Valhalla's un-national halls the un-national shades, Frenchman and German and Briton, conqueror and conquered alike—Immelman and Guynemer, Boelcke and Ball identical not in the vast freemasonry of death but in the closed select one of flying, would clash their bottomless mugs, but not for him. Their inheritors—Bishop and Mannock and Voss and McCudden and Fonck and Barker and Richthofen and Nungesser—would still cleave the earth-foundationed air, pacing their fleeing shadows on the scudding canyon-walls of cumulae, furloughed and immune, secure in immortality even while they still breathed, but it would not be his. Glory and valor would still exist of course as long as men lived to reap them. It would even be the same valor in fact, but the glory would be another glory. And that would be his: some second form of Elysium, a cut above dead infantry perhaps, but little more: who was not the first to think *What had I done for motherland's glory had motherland but matched me with her need*. (F, 89)

Disillusioned by the uniform, betrayed by the truce, and victimized by the treachery of having to fire unloaded ammunition at an unheeding adversary in a mock attack, Levine burns his aviator's Sitcom overall and shoots himself.

Cadet Lowe's letters had made a fiction of Faulkner's actual situation. When the novel was published in 1926, Lowe may have seemed a parody of the author: in fact he was in several respects an accurate self-portrait of the uncommissioned officer and spurned lover that Faulkner was in 1918. David Levine's letters in *A Fable* put that autobiographical fiction at a still greater distance by what amounts to an act of authorial self-erasure from the canon. Levine's broken letter to his mother is a fragment only partially transcribed: Levine signs, seals, and addresses it before he finishes writing it. In the fragment that he writes, he speaks of his potential to "be of some value in the squadron" (F, 102). In the postscript he *imagines* writing, the truce that mocks his will to heroic risk mocks the text of the letter on which it comments. "P.S. A delightful joke on you: they declared a recess at noon two days ago and if you had only known it, you would not have needed to worry at all from then until three o'clock this afternoon; you could have gone out to tea two afternoons with a clear conscience, which I hope you did, and even stayed for dinner too though I do hope you remembered what sherry always does to your complexion" (F, 102). A second letter he *plans* is never written: "the other one, the succinct and restrained and modestly heroic one to be found among his gear afterward by whoever went through it and decided what should be sent back to his mother" (F, 91). Literally, the premature cessation of the war—which had stimulated Faulkner's fictions of self in his letters and fictions—diminishes Levine's capacity to be what he dreams and even to write himself into being: "He could have gone to his hut too; there was a letter to his mother in it that he had not finished yet, except that now he could not finish it because the cessation of the guns yesterday had not only deleted all meaning from the words but effaced the very foundation of their purpose and aim" (F, 100). In a prepublication note on *A Fable*, Faulkner described Levine as a representative of the nihilistic third of man's conscience "who sees evil and refuses to accept it by destroying himself; who says 'Between nothing and evil, I will take nothing'; who in effect, to destroy evil, destroys the world too, i.e., the world which is his, himself."[23] Faulkner's ironic allusion to *The Wild Palms* in this piece affirms his dissociation from his last fictional aviator of the Great War. An Englishman and a Jew, Levine is here given sentiments opposite those that Harry Wilbourne expresses, which Faulkner so often quoted in his own letters to Meta Carpenter, Joan Williams, and others: *"between grief and nothing I will take grief"* (WP, 324).[24]

## [ iv ]

There is a variety of letters in the Snopes trilogy, public and private, whole and broken, written and unwritten, and Faulkner used them in ways that extend and play variations on the uses to which he had put letters previously. Especially this is so with the two Snopes books of the 1950s. The mode of *The Hamlet* is primarily the spoken word, of *The Town* and *The Mansion* speaking and writing.[25] As in *Sanctuary*, where Miss Reba's brothel has two back doors and no sign, physical objects in *The Hamlet* and *The Town* serve as sign and symbol of absent writing. Houston's shotgun-blasted body declares more clearly than the letter Mink wishes he could have written that *"this is what happens to the men who impound Mink Snopes's cattle"* (H, 218); Gavin's "corsage" from Manfred de Spain, composed of a rakehead and flowers wrapped in a used prophylactic, contains a message about Manfred and Eula that requires no text (T, 71). Unsigned public letters in the trilogy defame characters in the way that Faulkner himself was defamed in the 1950s in signed and unsigned letters for his moderate racial stand. Anonymous writing on Flem Snopes' sidewalk in *The Mansion* publicly names Linda *"Nigger Lover"* and "JEW COMMUNIST" (Man, 226, 228); to defend her from Flem, Gavin composes an imaginary anonymous letter to Herbert Hoover:

> *Herbert Hoover*
> *F B & I Depment*
> *Jackson Miss*
>    *If you will come up to Jefferson Miss and serch warant the bank and home of Flem Snopes you will fined a commonist party Card*
>                                *Patriotic Citizen* (Man, 243)

Signed public letters in the trilogy are still more powerful in that they exert the authority of a particular Sender over the Receiver. In *The Wild Palms* the tall convict is frustrated by a postcard from his lover that pictures a Birmingham hotel and reads, *"This is where were honny-monning at. Your friend (Mrs.) Vernon Waldrip"* (WP, 339). In *The Mansion* Mink's private letters at Parchman are inscrutable to him until read aloud and interpreted by the warden. He earns his freedom by thwarting an escape but is kept in prison by mock Valentines and Christmas cards from the murderer Stillwell, whose threats ironically are inscribed with the same power over Mink's life and death as the law he and Stillwell violated. In the context of law in *The Mansion*, even forgeries of private letters acquire material power from the threat of publication, and Flem uses them as instruments of manipulation with the same ease that he does notes of credit. Montgomery Ward Snopes is blackmailed into Parchman prison by an *Atelier Monty* envelope containing a pornographic photograph and certified authentic by a post office stamp. "It had been through the mail all right," he says, "even though I never mailed it and it hadn't been any further than through that damn cancelling machine inside the Jefferson post office" (Man, 69). Such letters in the trilogy extend the sense in which the self and the written word are one, and take that equation to extremes commensurate with other comic exaggerations and reversals in the Snopes chronicle. In *The Wild Palms* Harry speculates that "if Venus returned she would be a soiled man in a subway lavatory with a palm full of French post-cards" (WP, 136); Flem's blackmail works because the letter he forges in effect makes Montgomery Ward that man and then puts him in violation of postal law. At the end of *The Town*, children literally are made into letters when Byron Snopes mails Flem the dangerous half-Apache Snopes waifs, and Flem mails them back.

The most extreme letters in the trilogy, however, are those written by Gavin Stevens to Linda Kohl that impose a modicum of silence on the talky pages of the last Snopes book. Gavin's writing on the two-inch-by-three-inch pad of note sheets he gives Linda, and on the yellow legal sheets he subsequently employs, is one side of a half-spoken, half-written discourse in which the epistolary mode spans the barrier of Linda's deafness rather than distance in space or time. The letters are written in the presence of the beloved rather than alone, call forth and answer spoken rather than written responses, and dispense with such conventional letter forms as date, salutation, and signature. Unlike Faulkner's own letters written in the 1950s for publication, Gavin's notes to Linda are written in shorthand, without regard for grammatical rules, and enciphered in personal codes of his and Linda's mutual preconceptions and understandings. Each is a broken letter, a fragment of text almost fully dependent on its spoken rather than a written counterpart. Neither quite conversation, nor yet quite correspondence, they partake of and modify aspects of both. "I wrote rapidly," Gavin says in one self-referential comment on his text, "in three- or four-word bursts, gaggles, clumps, whatever you want to call them, so she could read as I wrote *Its all right dont Be afraid I Refuse to marry you 20 years too much Difference for it To work besides I Dont want to*" (Man, 238). Rather than coming together figuratively through their writing, the lovers come together literally to write letters in this scene at the middle of the book, but the outcome of their letters is the same: the writing substitutes for the body of the beloved. In the words of another of Gavin's notes, *"we are the 2 in all the world who can love each other without having to"* (Man, 239).

In his first novel, Faulkner had forced Cadet Julian Lowe into self-parodic prose by moving him physically away from Margaret Powers to San Francisco. His deafening Linda Snopes Kohl in his next-to-last book is the enabling impulse for letter writing by which the Sender distances himself figuratively from the Receiver he thereby idealizes. The letters are occasions for productive silence.[26] Unlike the silence of the truce in *A Fable*, which deprives David Levine's letters of their meaning and the foundation of their self-glorifying purpose and aim, the silence imposed on Linda by the war endows Gavin's written words with new meaning and brings him to private understandings beyond the easy generalities and reflex assumptions characteristic of his speech. Her deafness serves the symbolic function of changing her from the object of Gavin's quixotic courtship to the object of his aesthetic contemplation, and the letters necessitated by her deafness provide the necessary medium for Gavin to distance his love of her in spite of her physical presence.

Charles Mallison is right to describe Linda as "immured, inviolate in silence, invulnerable, serene. . . . no mere moment's child but the inviolate bride of silence, inviolable in maidenhead, fixed, forever safe from change and alteration" (Man, 203). But it is Gavin who sustains her inviolateness by his insistence on writing rather than making love to her, even in her presence and even when she offers herself in "the explicit word, speaking the hard brutal gutteral in the quacking duck's voice" (Man, 238). She writes him from Pascagoula, *"When you come we will* and then *If you come dont forget"* (Man, 246), but at the Pascagoula hotel they are Pyramus and Thisbe, tapping out messages from their separate rooms on the intervening wall. Figuratively, Gavin sees, they are like the immutable lovers on Keats' Grecian Urn, "All breathing human passion far above / That leaves a heart high-sorrowful and cloy'd," and by comparing Linda to the urn, Faulkner suggests that Gavin's fragmented letters are analogous to the "Ode"—celebrations of the "still unravish'd bride" written with new understanding of her and himself, free of sexual frustration and of bitterness. This represents no new understanding for Faulkner, who had compared writing *The Sound and the Fury* to a Platonic ecstasy he described in terms of the Old Roman and his Tyrrhenian vase.[27] He knew the difference, as he told Joan Williams, between the man and the writing, and knew the satisfactions of both, anguishing though they might be. This is a new understanding for most of Faulkner's characters, however, and Gavin's letters are the crucial medium of its expression. In *Flags in the Dust* Horace Benbow's sexual longing for Narcissa and his fear of it are expressed in his letters in the same lines from Keats cited by Charles, and Horace like Gavin writes letters to one woman while married to another man's former wife. But Horace's last letters to Narcissa only disguise a frustrated longing fulfilled incompletely in the writing of them. The letters that Charles first imagines as Gavin's sexual invitations out of "Jonson (or some of that old Donne or Herrick maybe or even just Suckling maybe. . . .)" (Man, 200), resolve themselves instead into affirmations of Platonic love as, gradually in the novel, the imperatives of the penis are supplanted by the pen, and the opportunities for lovemaking by moments of letter writing. *"We have had everything,"* Gavin writes on the day Linda leaves Jefferson, and he enforces his authority as author of that understanding by leaving no space on his page for a contradictory text.

> "No," she said.
> He wrote *Yes.*
> "No," she said.
> He printed *YES* this time in letters large enough to cover the rest of the face of the tablet. (Man, 425)

In this, the final scene of letter writing in the literary canon, we may find a metaphor for William Faulkner's own writing in the late 1940s and the 1950s. Like the immortal poet Faulkner imagined himself to be in the last poem of the gift book *Helen: A Courtship* Gavin asserts in his last letter the cold satisfactions of the written word and his own capacity, as letter writer, to *"have . . . everything"* through the medium of his letters. Faulkner was sixty-two when *The Mansion* was published in November 1969. In the last decade the nature, and perhaps the quality, of his own writing had changed with changed circumstances in the South and the nation and his sudden emergence as a public man of letters. Yet he continued to cover the pages of his own tablet with words. If the image of famous southern writer in his public letters was meant to conceal William Faulkner the man, it does not cancel the complex private images of the man writing that he had constructed in letters and fictions and continued to record to the end of his life. A postscript he wrote to a 1939 letter about *The Hamlet* is well suited as a postscript to both canons of his writing, and to this book: "I am the best in America, by God" (SL, 113).

# Notes

**Preface**

1. James Olney, "Autobiography and the Cultural Moment: A Thematic, Historical, and Bibliographical Introduction," in his *Autobiography*, 4.

**I. The Two Canons**

1. Joseph Blotner, *Faulkner: A Biography* (1984), 66–67.
2. Ibid., 66.
3. Carvel Collins points out that Faulkner's commission was in the Royal Air Force, which supplanted the name Royal Flying Corps before he joined (see Collins,"Biographical Background for Faulkner's *Helen*," HAC, 20). In his letters after the war, Faulkner used RAF to indicate his branch of the service, but the uniform he wore home from Toronto was all the more a disguise in that it was not even the one he was commissioned to wear. The same conflict becomes an issue for David Levine in *A Fable* (see Chapter VI, ii, herein).
4. See Margaret Yonce, " 'Shot Down Last Spring': The Wounded Aviators of Faulkner's Wasteland," *Mississippi Quarterly* 31 (Summer 1978): 359–368.
5. Blotner, *Faulkner* (1984), 83.
6. David Minter, *William Faulkner: His Life and Work*, 32, 33.
7. Blotner, *Faulkner* (1984), 437; see also SL, 125.
8. Malcolm Cowley, *The Faulkner-Cowley File*, 72.
9. Frederick L. Gwynn and Joseph L. Blotner, eds., *Faulkner in the University: Class Conferences at the University of Virginia, 1957–1958*, 68.
10. Warren Beck, *Faulkner: Essays*, 7, 10, 11.
11. Regarding Faulkner's knowledge of Pater and early admiration for him, see Collins, "Biographical Background," HAC, 92–93.
12. Beck, *Faulkner*, 49.
13. See, for example, Walter J. Ong, S. J., "The Writer's Audience Is Always a Fiction," *PMLA* 90 (January 1975): esp. 12, 17, 19.
14. See Cowley, *The Faulkner-Cowley File*, 8–102, 114–150.
15. James B. Meriwether and Michael Millgate, eds., *Lion in the Garden: Interviews with William Faulkner, 1926–1962*, 243.
16. A particularly valuable discussion of epistolary discourse, focused on epistolary novels, is Janet Gurkin Altman, *Epistolarity: Approaches to a Form;*

see esp. Chapters I, "Mediation"; II, "Of Confidence and Confidants"; III, "The Weight of the Reader"; and IV, "Epistolary Discourse."

17. Joseph Kestner, "The *Letters* of Jane Austen: The Writer as *Émetteur / Récepteur*," *Papers on Language and Literature* 14 (Summer 1978): 266.

18. Blotner, *Faulkner: A Biography* (1974), I, 467.

19. Blotner, *Faulkner* (1984), 170. The correspondence is transcribed with the poem in *Mississippi Quarterly* 27 (Summer 1974): 333–336. The carbon typescript of Faulkner's letter and the poem are in the Brodsky collection; see Louis Daniel Brodsky and Robert W. Hamblin, eds., *Faulkner: A Comprehensive Guide to the Brodsky Collection. Vol. I, The Biobibliography*, #54, #55; LDB-II, #55.

20. Blotner, *Faulkner* (1974), I, 481.

21. Ibid., 481, 483.

22. See Minter, *Life and Work*, 16, and Blotner, *Faulkner* (1984), 207.

23. The drawing in the first letter, September 6, 1925, is reproduced in Blotner, *Faulkner* (1974), I, 461. The second, in a September 10 letter to Mrs. McLean, is reproduced in Judith L. Sensibar, *The Origins of Faulkner's Art*, 217. The third, with the page on which it is drawn, is reproduced in Sensibar, *Origins*, 216. Sensibar analyzes this material in terms of Faulkner's attitudes toward women, sex, and art (213–214).

24. Compare Sensibar's discussion of the passage from the letter to Mrs. McLean as a "screen memory" in which the light and the dark figures represent Faulkner's two mothers, Maud Falkner and Mammy Caroline Barr. She traces this to Quentin's memory of the "dirty girl" Natalie in *The Sound and the Fury* and to the two aspects of Joanna Burden in *Light in August* (*Origins*, 52–53).

## II. Crossings

1. Meriwether and Millgate, *Lion in the Garden*, 11.

2. Joseph Blotner notes Faulkner's debt to the "Circe" chapter in *Ulysses* in *Faulkner* (1984), 144. For a discussion of the significance and function of the inserted letters in Joyce's novel, see Shari Benstock, "The Printed Letters in *Ulysses*," *James Joyce Quarterly* 19 (Summer 1982): 415–427.

3. Ruth Perry, *Women, Letters, and the Novel*, 83–84.

4. Some of the implications of the writer-reader phenomenon in the letter-novel are treated by Harold Toliver in *Animate Illusions: Explorations of Narrative Structure*; see esp. 138–165.

5. See Francis J. Bosha, *Faulkner's "Soldiers' Pay": A Bibliographic Study*, 292.

6. See Perry, *Women, Letters, and the Novel*, 95. Janet Gurkin Altman makes the point, in her chapter "The Dynamics of Epistolary Closure," that "epistolary narrative . . . adds to the usual dynamics of closure (resolution of conflict, restoration of order, marriage, death) a dynamics of its own. Because the letter is not merely the narrative medium but frequently acquires a symbolic value as well, the very continuation or cessation of the writing constitutes a message that is often appropriate closure material" (*Epistolarity*, 154).

7. Margaret Yonce writes that "Lowe's function in the novel as a whole presents something of a problem, and it is somewhat difficult to justify the

attention afforded him, even though he disappears after the first chapter except for his letters. . . . Perhaps the most useful function which Lowe serves is as Margaret's correspondent: his letters provide comic interludes and dates by which other events can be placed. Yet it must be admitted, Lowe is one of the least necessary figures in the novel and could have been omitted without damaging the structure irreparably" ("*Soldiers' Pay:* A Critical Study of Faulkner's First Novel," diss., University of South Carolina, 1970, 40–41). Elsewhere, Yonce argues convincingly that Faulkner began the novel with two separate short stories that he grafted together as he worked: one containing the Lowe-Gilligan material in chapter I, the other the Rector-Jones material. If, as she suggests, Faulkner's NOTES for the novel, which she publishes, antedate chapter I, he would have had in mind when he finished chapter I that Lowe would not rejoin the company: the second page of the NOTES includes six entries for "Letter from Lowe." Yonce does not investigate why Lowe is separated from the others ("The Composition of *Soldiers' Pay*," *Mississippi Quarterly* 33 [Summer 1980]:291–326).

8. Michael Millgate, "Starting Out in the Twenties: Reflections on *Soldiers' Pay*," *MOSAIC* 7 (Fall 1973): 14.

9. Michael Millgate, *The Achievement of William Faulkner*, 66. See also Millgate, "Starting Out in the Twenties," 2, 3–4; Minter, *Life and Work*, 53–54.

10. See Bosha, *Faulkner's "Soldiers' Pay*," 511–512.

11. Ibid., collations at 187:2, 278:3.

12. For a chronology of the novel, see Yonce, "Critical Study," 271ff.; Cleanth Brooks, *William Faulkner: Toward Yoknapatawpha and Beyond*, 366–370.

13. Carvel Collins, ed., *William Faulkner: Early Prose and Poetry*, 115.

14. James B. Meriwether, ed., "An Introduction for *The Sound and the Fury*," *Southern Review* 8 (October 1972):708.

15. Collins, "Biographical Background," HAC, 16.

16. Thomas Bonner, Jr., ed., Introduction, *William Faulkner: The William B. Wisdom Collection*, 4.

17. Quoted in Blotner, *Faulkner* (1984), 188.

18. Collins, "Biographical Background," HAC, 12.

19. Blotner, *Faulkner* (1974), I, 523–524.

20. The eight works are listed here in the order of their composition: *The Lilacs* (poems), described in Brodsky and Hamblin, *Brodsky Collection*, vol. I, #26; *The Marionettes* (play); *Vision in Spring* (poems), ed. Judith L. Sensibar; *Mississippi Poems*, ed. Joseph Blotner, in *Helen: A Courtship and Mississippi Poems; Mayday* (fiction), ed. Carvel Collins; *Helen: A Courtship* (poems), ed. Carvel Collins, in *Helen: A Courtship and Mississippi Poems; Royal Street: New Orleans* (sketches); and *The Wishing Tree* (story).

21. See "Mississippi Poems" in Brodsky and Hamblin, *Brodsky Collection*, vol. I, #45.

22. "'Hong Li' and *Royal Street*," in *A Faulkner Miscellany*, ed. James B. Meriwether, 143.

23. As I will show, there are other points of relationship between *Royal Street* and *The Marionettes*, especially involving the vignette "Hong Li." The child holding the candlestick in the *Royal Street* drawing, for example, may

have been meant to recall for Estelle Faulkner's description of her in the inscription to her infant daughter, Cho-Cho Franklin, in the copy of *The Marionettes* he gave her in 1920: there he called Cho-Cho "A TINY FLOWER OF THE FLAME, THE / ETERNAL GESTURE CHRYSTALLIZED." The illustration was described to me in a letter from Noel Polk, November 1984; see also his "'Hong Li' and *Royal Street*" and his "William Faulkner's 'Hong Li' on Royal Street," *Library Chronicle of the University of Texas* 13 (1980):27–30.

24. Collins, "Biographical Background," HAC, 9–110.

25. Ibid., 68.

26. T. S. Eliot, "*Ulysses*, Order, and Myth," *Dial* 75 (November 1923), repr. in *James Joyce: Two Decades of Criticism*, ed. Seon Givens, 200–201.

27. Although *Vision in Spring* dates from 1921, its relevance to the later books is suggested by Faulkner's having rebound it for Estelle, January 25, 1926, two days before he bound *Mayday* for Helen Baird.

28. *Royal Street: New Orleans*, transcribed by Leland H. Cox, Jr., in "Sinbad in New Orleans: Early Short Fiction by William Faulkner—An Annotated Edition," diss., University of South Carolina, 1977, 160, 157. As Cox shows, the vignettes in *Royal Street* differ slightly from the version published in the *Double Dealer*, January–February 1925.

29. Ibid., 152.

30. For a further discussion of this theme and "New Orleans," see James G. Watson, "New Orleans, *The Double Dealer*, and 'New Orleans,'" *American Literature* 56 (May 1984):214–226.

31. Blotner says that Estelle already had returned to Shanghai with her children for the self-imposed "probationary period" with Cornell Franklin when Faulkner finished the *Mosquitoes* typescript and returned to Oxford in mid-September (*Faulkner* [1984], 523–524). He does not mention *Royal Street*. Noel Polk speculates that Faulkner gave Estelle the book before she left ("Faulkner's 'Hong Li,'" 28). The October 29 date on the book belies this claim.

32. Quotations from "Hong Li" are from Polk, "'Hong Li' and *Royal Street*," 144.

33. In the second of the two reveries deriving from *Helen* V, Quentin thinks as he walks in the country with Julio's sister, "Madam, your daughter, if you please. No. Madam, for God's sake, your daughter" (SF, 164). Compare *Helen* V, "No: Madam, I love your daughter, I will say" (HAC, 116).

34. Meriwether, "An Introduction for *The Sound and the Fury*," 710.

35. James Meriwether, "An Introduction to *The Sound and the Fury*," in *A Faulkner Miscellany*, 158.

36. Noel Polk, Introduction, *The Marionettes*, xxviii.

37. See Judith L. Sensibar, ed., "Pierrot and the Marble Faun: Another Fragment," *Mississippi Quarterly* 32 (Summer 1979): 473–476.

38. Ibid., 475.

39. Judith L. Sensibar says, correctly I think, that "the important figure here is not the baby Cho-Cho, but 'the flame,' her mother. Faulkner celebrates not so much the child as the sex act itself, 'the eternal gesture,' of which Cho-Cho is the 'flower.' Juxtaposed to this act is another creative act: his play *The Marionettes*, a poor substitute" (*Origins*, 25). The relevant lines in the song

from *The Marionettes* read, in part: "Then we shall be one in the silence / . . . Till you are a white delicate flame, / Love! / A little slender flame, / Drawing my hotter flame like will-o-the-wisp in my garden" (20–21).

40. Quoted in Blotner, *Faulkner* (1984), 240.

41. A typescript of this unpublished poem is in the Leila Clark Wynn–Douglas C. Wynn Faulkner Collection at the John Davis Williams Library, Department of Archives and Special Collections, University of Mississippi.

42. See Watson, "New Orleans, *The Double Dealer*, and 'New Orleans.'"

43. Maurice Coindreau, "Preface to *The Sound and the Fury*," in *The Time of William Faulkner*, 49. See also Blotner, *Faulkner* (1984), 212.

44. See Collins, "Biographical Background," HAC, 75–76. Joseph Blotner says that he quickly changed his mind and substituted a less well known character for Quentin—Alec Holston, from *Requiem for a Nun* (*Faulkner* [1984], 520).

45. Blotner, *Faulkner* (1984), 213. Blotner says that "even allowing for exaggeration, something of this assertion must have come from elements within his psyche."

46. In this connection, see James G. Watson, "Literary Self-Criticism: Faulkner in Fiction on Fiction," *Southern Quarterly* 20 (Fall 1981):46–63.

47. Joseph Blotner dates the story from "the middle 1930s" on the basis of a letter from Faulkner to Morton Goldman, December 4, 1935 (SL, 93–94) (*Uncollected Stories of William Faulkner*, 710).

## III. Integrated Letters

1. The novel was *Flags in the Dust*. Boni and Liveright had published *Soldiers' Pay* in 1926 and *Mosquitoes* in 1927; the unfinished novels were *Elmer*, written in Paris in late 1925, and *Father Abraham*, written probably in 1926. In the following discussion I have used the 1973 edition of *Flags in the Dust*, edited by Douglas Day, because of the substantial amount of material it contains that was deleted before the publication of the book as *Sartoris*. Much of that has to do directly with letters and letter forms and conventions. For a summary and discussion of the several problems of Day's edition, see George F. Hayhoe, "William Faulkner's *Flags in the Dust*," *Mississippi Quarterly* 28 (Summer 1975): 370–386.

2. Gwynn and Blotner, *Faulkner in the University*, 285.

3. Meriwether and Millgate, *Lion in the Garden*, 255.

4. James B. Meriwether, "Faulkner and El Orens," *Faulkner Newsletter & Yoknapatawpha Review* 1 (April–June 1981):2.

5. In Blotner, *Faulkner* (1974), I, 560.

6. Meriwether, "An Introduction to *The Sound and the Fury*," 158–159. Commenting on Faulkner's "Introduction," Karl Zender writes that "art became for him an alternative to social existence rather than an extension or a reflection of it. . . . [His] sense of ecstatic union with the products of his imagination depended on a deliberate act of psychic withdrawal. Only when it seemed to him that 'a door had clapped silently and forever to' between him and all questions of acceptance by publishers or audiences was he able to say,

'Now I can write. Now I can just write'" ("Faulkner at Forty: The Artist at Home," *Southern Review* 17 [Spring 1981]:293).

7. Joseph Blotner, ed., "William Faulkner's Essay on the Composition of *Sartoris*," *Yale University Library Gazette* 47 (January 1973):122, 123.

8. Ibid., 124.

9. Gwynn and Blotner, *Faulkner in the University*, 90.

10. Blotner, "Essay on the Composition of *Sartoris*," 124.

11. Meriwether and Millgate, *Lion in the Garden*, 255.

12. On the significance of *Flags* to the evolution of Faulkner's art, and to his conception of the Yoknapatawpha stories that followed it, see Michael Millgate, "'A Cosmos of My Own': The Evolution of Yoknapatawpha," in *Fifty Years of Yoknapatawpha*, ed. Doreen Fowler and Ann J. Abadie, 23–43; idem, "William Faulkner: The Shape of a Career," *New Directions in Faulkner Studies*, ed. Doreen Fowler and Ann J. Abadie, 18–36.

13. Hugh Kenner, *A Homemade World: The American Modernist Writers*, 205–206.

14. Gwynn and Blotner, *Faulkner in the University*, 52.

15. Blotner, *Faulkner* (1974), 585.

16. The formal implications of the novel are discussed in James G. Watson, "'The Germ of My Apocrypha': *Sartoris* and the Search for Form," *MOSAIC* 7 (Fall 1973):15–33.

17. Ibid., 253, 255.

18. See Millgate, *The Achievement of William Faulkner*, 76–85.

19. In this regard, see John T. Matthews, *The Play of Faulkner's Language*, 52–54. Matthews points out that Narcissa reads books as a self-protective device. Letters are more intimate than novels, because more private, and so make more personal demands on the reader.

20. The stolen undergarment is a fetish, like Horace's vase. The symbolism of sexual conquest is carried into *Sanctuary*, where one of the town boys who had dated Temple Drake displays an undergarment he claims is hers (SR, 30).

21. Blotner, "Essay on the Composition of *Sartoris*," 123.

22. Stephen Dennis, "The Making of *Sartoris*: A Description and Discussion of the Manuscript and Composite Typescript of William Faulkner's Third Novel," diss., Cornell University, 1969, 117–118. Dennis notes that the block of manuscript pages numbered 52-a through 52-e represents "an exception to the consecutive numbering in most of the rest of the *Sartoris* manuscript."

23. Ibid., 120–121.

24. Blotner, "Essay on the Composition of *Sartoris*," 123.

25. Bruce F. Kawin, ed., *Faulkner's MGM Screen Plays*, 257–265. See also Blotner, *Faulkner* (1974), I, 648.

26. Meriwether, "An Introduction for *The Sound and the Fury*," 710, 709.

27. André Bleikasten, *The Most Splendid Failure: Faulkner's "The Sound and the Fury*," 50–51.

28. The times of events on Quentin's day are set forth in Edmond Volpe, *A Reader's Guide to William Faulkner*, 370–373.

29. Arguing from the point of view of manuscript revisions in *The Sound and the Fury*, Noel Polk reads this situation differently and finds that it pre-

sents problems of inconsistency. He assumes that there are but two letters, one to Mr. Compson and one to Shreve, both of which are stamped at the post office, and that Quentin gives Deacon a stamped letter to deliver, which he somehow subsequently mails himself. The inconsistency is resolved, however, if we understand that there are three letters, two of which Quentin refers to collectively as "Shreve's" (SF, 101) since Shreve ultimately will receive both. See Polk, *An Editorial Handbook for William Faulkner's "The Sound and the Fury,"* 133.

30. There are distinct parallels between the suicide note to Shreve that Quentin carries with him on June 2, 1910, in *The Sound and the Fury* and the love letter from Martha Clifford that Leopold Bloom secretly carries with him on June 16, 1904, in *Ulysses*. Among several others, the fascination with death symbolized by Quentin's letter is analogous to Bloom's masochistic attraction to Martha's threats to punish her "naughty boy" (James Joyce, *Ulysses*, 78). For a discussion of the letters in *Ulysses*, see Benstock, "The Printed Letters in *Ulysses*," 415–427; for the significance of Martha Clifford's letter, see Darcy O'Brien, *The Conscience of James Joyce*, esp. 116–121.

31. Appropriately, Jason uses "note" in reference to banking and money, Benjy not at all. Mrs. Compson uses the word to mean a letter.

32. The association of the dangerous writing of women with flowers recalls again Martha Clifford's letter containing a flower addressed to "Henry Flower" in *Ulysses*, and Bloom's paraphrases of it in which flowers substitute significantly for her words: "Language of flowers. They like it because no-one can hear. Or a poison bouquet to strike him down. Then, walking slowly forward, he read the letter again, murmuring here and there a word. Angry tulips with you darling manflower punish your cactus if you don't please poor forgetmenot how I long violets to dear roses when we soon anemone meet all naughty nightstalk wife Martha's perfume" (Joyce, *Ulysses*, 78).

33. See, for example, Nancy Miller, "'I's' in Drag: The Sex of Recollection," *Eighteenth Century* 22 (1981): 47–57.

34. Bleikasten, *The Most Splendid Failure*, 46.

35. Ibid., 52, 56.

36. Ibid., 52.

### IV. Letters at Hand

1. James B. Meriwether, "The Short Fiction of William Faulkner: A Bibliography," *Proof* 1 (1971): 315.

2. Millgate, *The Achievement of William Faulkner*, 11–12.

3. Sherwood Anderson, *Winesburg, Ohio*, 60, 94.

4. See Hans Skei, *William Faulkner: The Short Story Career*, 19, 87.

5. See ibid., 36–37.

6. James B. Meriwether, ed., "Faulkner's Correspondence with *Scribner's Magazine*," *Proof* 3 (1973): 256.

7. The recurrent figure of the tyrannical parent in Faulkner's fiction is identified and examined in detail by Noel Polk in two essays: see "'The Dungeon Was Mother Herself': William Faulkner: 1927–1931," in *New Directions in*

*Faulkner Studies,* ed. Doreen Fowler and Ann J. Abadie, 61–93, and "The Space between *Sanctuary,*" in *Intertextuality in Faulkner,* ed. Michel Gresset and Noel Polk, 16–35.

8. See Brooks, *Toward Yoknapatawpha and Beyond,* 152–165.

9. James B. Meriwether, ed., "Faulkner's Correspondence with the *Saturday Evening Post,*" *Mississippi Quarterly* 30 (Summer 1977): 470.

10. Ibid., 472.

11. Meriwether, "Faulkner's Correspondence with *Scribner's Magazine,*" 257.

12. Ibid., 258.

13. Skei, *The Short Story Career,* 38.

14. Skei points out that in one version of the story, tried late and rejected, the narrator was a photographic officer (ibid., 183).

15. See ibid., 114 n10, 36; Skei describes the story as a "sequel" to *Sartoris* (123).

16. Meriwether, "Faulkner's Correspondence with *Scribner's Magazine,*" 260.

17. On this complex of relationships, see Blotner, *Faulkner* (1984), 235–239; Noel Polk, Afterword, *Sanctuary: The Original Text,* 298.

18. Polk makes this point briefly in his Afterword (305).

19. See Polk's persuasive arguments on this subject in Afterword and "The Space between *Sanctuary.*"

20. See Max Putzel, *Genius of Place: William Faulkner's Triumphant Beginnings,* 256.

21. See Polk, "The Space between *Sanctuary,*" 32–33.

22. For other such connections between *Sanctuary* and Faulkner's life, see Judith Bryant Wittenberg, *Faulkner: The Transfiguration of Biography,* 89–102; Minter, *Life and Work,* 107–112, 123–126. Wittenberg calls the book Faulkner's "Bleak Epithalamion" (89–102).

23. Blotner, *Faulkner* (1984), 239–240.

24. Ibid., 240.

25. Ibid.

26. Ibid.

27. See Thomas L. McHaney, "*Sanctuary* and Frazier's Slain Kings," *Mississippi Quarterly* 24 (Summer 1971): 223–245; Margaret Yonce, "'His True Penelope Was Flaubert': *Madame Bovary* and *Sanctuary,*" *Mississippi Quarterly* 29 (Summer 1976): 439–442; André Bleikasten, "'Cet affreux goût d'encre': Emma Bovary's Ghost in *Sanctuary,*" in *Intertextuality in Faulkner,* ed. Michel Gresset and Noel Polk, 36–56. Bleikasten notes that "Flaubert's heroine is brought in by the most bookish, most romantic, most Bovary-like character in the novel"—Horace Benbow (41).

28. Gustave Flaubert, *Madame Bovary,* ed. and trans. Paul de Man, 146–147.

29. Bleikasten, "Emma Bovary's Ghost in *Sanctuary,*" 48.

30. See James G. Watson, "Faulkner: The House of Fiction," in *Fifty Years of Yoknapatawpha,* ed. Doreen Fowler and Ann J. Abadie, 134–158.

31. Gwynn and Blotner, *Faulkner in the University,* 49–50.

32. See, for example, Polk, Afterword, 296–297.

33. Henry James, *The Novels and Tales of Henry James,* III, xvi.

34. See Regina K. Fadiman, *Faulkner's "Light in August": A Description and Interpretation of the Revisions*, 89.

35. See Polk, "'The Dungeon Was Mother Herself.'"

36. Fadiman, *Faulkner's "Light in August,"* 71.

37. Blotner, *Faulkner* (1974), I, 829.

38. See David Krause, "Reading Bon's Letter and Faulkner's *Absalom, Absalom!*," *PMLA* 99 (March 1984): 225–241. Krause argues that the letter creates "in and through each of its several readers a series of sustained meditations on the problems of reading. These self-conscious commentaries on reading can perhaps help us to (re-)read not only the letter itself but also the Faulknerian text that generates—and is generated by—the letter" (225).

39. Ibid., 230. Krause explains that Compson's attempt to read the letter as personal correspondence fails because he sustains a "deterministic worldview" in which there is no room for love. See also Olga Scherer, "A Polyphonic Insert: Charles's Letter to Judith," in *Intertextuality in Faulkner*, ed. Michel Gresset and Noel Polk, 173. Scherer points out that Mr. Compson borrows ideas and phrases from Bon's letter that he reshapes to his own preconceptions to explain it.

40. For Judith's reading of the letter, see Elisabeth Muhlenfeld, "'We have waited long enough': Judith Sutpen and Charles Bon," *Southern Review* 14 (Winter 1978): 66–80.

41. See James G. Watson, "Faulkner: Short Story Structures and Reflexive Forms," *MOSAIC* 11 (Summer 1978): 127–137. Faulkner sold "Wash" to *Harper's* in November 1933. It was published in February 1934 and collected in *Doctor Martino and Other Stories* in April.

42. David Krause makes several of the same points about Shreve's letters, again from the point of view of reading and the ways in which the novel "imagines its own reading" (see "Reading Shreve's Letters and Faulkner's *Absalom, Absalom!*," *Studies in American Fiction* 2 [Autumn 1983]: 153–169).

43. Krause argues that Mr. Compson imposes his own view of history on Judith in his account of her appeal to Grandmother Compson ("Reading Bon's Letter," 233). Scherer suggests that both sound like Bon ("A Polyphonic Insert," 170, 173). Because of the sequence of the letter's handling, however, it is more reasonable to suppose that Judith borrows from Bon, that Mr. Compson borrows from Bon and Judith, and that Quentin and Shreve borrow from and modify all three.

44. Krause finds that the lawyer's letter "calls attention to the distances—spatial, temporal, social, psychological—between the sites of writing and reading" ("Reading Shreve's Letters," 160). However, the phrasing of the final sentence, in a letter designed as this one is to bridge just such distances, suggests contiguity more than separation.

45. Jacques Lacan, "Seminar on 'The Purloined Letter,'" *Yale French Studies* 48 (1972): 72. "The Purloined Letter" itself is only indirectly relevant to *Absalom, Absalom!*, but Poe's interest for Faulkner was deep. See, for example, Richard P. Adams' discussion of *Absalom, Absalom!* and "The Fall of the House of Usher" in "The Apprenticeship of William Faulkner," *Tulane Studies in En-*

*glish* 12 (1962):113–156. Estelle Schoenberg points out "Faulkner's significant use in *Absalom, Absalom!* of two words on which Poe virtually held the patent—*ratiocination* and *nevermore*" (see *Old Tales and Talking: Quentin Compson in William Faulkner's "Absalom, Absalom!" and Related Works*, 118 n4). Both words are used in *Absalom, Absalom!* in letter contexts (AA, 258, 373).

46. Lacan, "Seminar," 59 n29, 56, 58, 57.

47. Krause overlooks the evocative power of letters when he argues, in the first case, that Quentin's vision results from "extrasensory perceptions." The description of Shreve and Quentin belies his statement, in the second case, that it is the outside narrator who narrates the scene in Carolina ("Reading Bon's Letter," 234, 237).

48. See John T. Irwin, *Doubling and Incest / Repetition and Revenge.* The psychological patterns of spatial and temporal doubling that Irwin identifies and explicates are particularly relevant to letters and private writing.

49. See Michael Millgate, "'The Firmament of Man's History': Faulkner's Treatment of the Past," *Mississippi Quarterly* 25 Suppl (Spring 1972):25–35. Millgate goes so far as to say of the book that it "is not so much about Sutpen as about what the narrators, and especially Quentin, make of the Sutpen legend—or even what the Sutpen legend makes of Quentin" (27).

50. There is no certain way of knowing what "textbook" Quentin's letter covers to form the repeatedly described palimpsest, but the allusion to Poe at this climactic juncture at the end of the novel makes possible the speculation that it is "The Raven," and that Quentin is reading his own future in that poem through his father's letter.

## V. Broken Letters

1. Altman, *Epistolarity*, 119.

2. Altman points out that each letter "retains its own unity while remaining a unit within a larger configuration" (ibid., 167).

3. See ibid., 92.

4. For an examination of this anomaly, see Irwin, *Doubling and Incest*; Thadious Davis, *Faulkner's Negro: Art and the Southern Context*; Eric J. Sundquist, *Faulkner: The House Divided.* Sundquist says, "The slave father whose 'son' was not his son and particularly the slave son who had, therefore, no father at all stand in the most painful roles in this reciprocal tragedy" (125).

5. See Matthews, *The Play of Faulkner's Language.* Matthews argues that the twins attempt to hide old Carothers' crimes, and hide from them, by their miswritten shorthand records (265).

6. See Schoenberg, *Old Tales and Talking*; Millgate, "'A Cosmos of My Own.'" Schoenberg points out that Ike McCaslin grew out of Quentin Compson (18–19). Millgate remarks that several stories "on the fringes of *Go Down, Moses . . . must also have been Quentin Compson narratives*" (29). Matthews makes the point that "the moment of awkward, fierce, and tender intimacy between the cousins might remind us of Quentin and Shreve's narrative

flight, and Isaac uses his conversation for similar purposes" (*The Play of Faulkner's Language*, 260).

7. Skei, *The Short Story Career*. Skei points to the extensive revisions Faulkner did for the 1938 publication of *The Unvanquished* as a mark of his interest in the book, and says that four years earlier "what he actually sacrificed was work he should have been doing on *Absalom, Absalom!*" (90–93, 84).

8. See Bleikasten, *The Most Splendid Failure*. Bleikasten says the novel "grows out of and refers back to an empty center, a center which one might paradoxically call eccentric . . . insofar as it represents at once the novel's origin and its *telos*, its generating principle and the ever-receding object of its quest" (51).

9. The term is Joseph Reed's; see *Faulkner's Narrative*, 50.

10. See, for example, Toliver, *Animate Illusions*. According to Toliver, each letter "has its own calculated art, even a letter of apparent pell-mell confession. . . . The intensity of the letter's dramatic transaction, whether it is an act of beseeching, advice-giving, commanding, praise-rendering, confession, or reconciliation, is cooled considerably by the act of writing what is after all a member of the document family. Letters flow from and are often delivered to private sanctuaries; but they are also semi-public postures" (148).

11. See Jean Leymarie, *The Spirit of the Letter in Painting*, trans. James Emmons.

12. See, for example, Miller, "'I's' in Drag," 47–57. Miller uses the unhappy term "female impersonation" to account for "the masculine appropriation of the feminine" in epistolary works, such as *The Letters of a Portuguese Nun* (48). Faulkner, however, shows little reluctance to "impersonate" his female characters and great skill when he does so.

13. The phrase is Shoshana Felman's, and she concludes that reading the unreadable in *The Turn of the Screw*, which is her text, can be accomplished only through "a radical modification of the meaning of 'reading' itself. To read on the basis of the unreadable would be . . . to ask not *what* does the unreadable mean, but *how* does the unreadable mean? Not what is the meaning of the letters, but in what way do letters *escape* meaning? In what way do the letters *signify via*, precisely, their own *insignificance*?" In *The Turn of the Screw*, Felman finds it is precisely because indecipherable letters "*fail* to narrate, to construct a coherent, transparent story, that there is a story at all: there is a story *because* there is an unreadable, an unconscious. Narrative, paradoxically, becomes possible to the precise extent that a story becomes *impossible*— that a story, precisely, '*won't tell.*' Narrative is thus engendered by the displacement of a 'won't tell' which, being transmitted through letters, forwards itself as *writing effect*" ("Turning the Screw of Interpretation," in *Literature and Psychoanalysis: The Question of Reading: Otherwise*, ed. Shoshana Felman, 142, 143).

14. Gwynn and Blotner, *Faulkner in the University*, 96.

15. Panthea Reid Broughton, "An Interview with Meta Carpenter Wilde," *Southern Review* 18 (October 1982): 801.

16. Ibid., 776–778.

17. Meta Carpenter Wilde and Orin Borsten, *A Loving Gentleman: The Love Story of William Faulkner and Meta Carpenter*, 89.

18. Joan Williams, "Twenty Will Not Come Again," *Atlantic Monthly* 245 (May 1980):63.

19. Joseph Blotner, in a letter to JGW, October 26, 1984.

20. James Silver, *Running Scared: Silver in Mississippi*, 38.

21. Ibid., 38–39.

22. Wilde and Borsten, *A Loving Gentleman*, 97.

23. Broughton, "Interview," 787.

24. Wilde and Borsten, *A Loving Gentleman*, 76.

25. Ibid., 63. Faulkner used the names "Mr. Bowen" and "Mrs. Bowen" throughout his correspondence with Meta: Meta says he still was addressing her in that way in letters written well after her marriage to Wolfgang Rebner in 1937. In an ironic reversal by which life imitated art, Joan Williams would marry in 1954 a man named Ezra Bowen, and become literally a Mrs. Bowen. Faulkner wrote to her in that name, but his extant letters show no indication of the sexual connotations he attached to it in letters to Meta.

26. Ibid., 166, 248.

27. Ibid., 264.

28. Ibid., 330.

29. Ibid., 96.

30. Ibid., 117.

31. Ibid., 330.

32. Blotner, *Faulkner* (1974), II, 1313.

33. Wilde and Borsten, *A Loving Gentleman*, 78. See also Minter, *Life and Work*, 162–163.

34. Blotner, *Faulkner* (1974), II, 1299.

35. Ibid., 1328.

36. Faulkner knew the novel well enough to have written a letter to the editor of *Time*, published October 30, 1950, in support of Evelyn Waugh's review of *Across the River and into the Trees*. See ESPL, 210–211.

37. Blotner, *Faulkner* (1974), II, 1303.

38. An interview with Judith Bryant Wittenberg; in Wittenberg, "Joan Williams: The Rebellious Heart" (manuscript).

39. Joan Williams, *The Wintering*, 329.

40. See Faulkner to Joan Williams, in Blotner, *Faulkner* (1974), II, 1431.

41. See Perry, *Women, Letters, and the Novel*. Perry says that "reading the letters written and intended for other eyes is the most reprehensible invasion of privacy and consciousness in epistolary fiction. There are overtones of sexual invasion—mind-rape—in the intercepting or 'violating' of another's words. This equivalence is suggestive for the audience as well since they are reading letters not intended for public consumption" (130–131).

42. "Letter I. Heloise to Abelard," in *The Letters of Abelard and Heloise*, trans. Betty Radice, 109. For information about Heloise and Abelard and their letters, see Radice's "Introduction," and Peggy Kamuf, *Fictions of Feminine Desire: Disclosures of Heloise*.

43. "Letter I. Heloise to Abelard," *Letters*, 117.

44. "Letter III. Heloise to Abelard," *Letters*, 133.

45. "Letter I. Heloise to Abelard," *Letters*, 113.

46. In his chapter on *The Town*, Cleanth Brooks places Faulkner in the tradition of courtly love, which he traces to the story of Tristan and Iseult as it is described in Denis de Rougemont's *Love in the Western World* (see *William Faulkner: The Yoknapatawpha Country*, 192–218). In Rougemont's description of the evolving conception of love, however, Heloise and Abelard are the central figures. Their story shaped Gottfried's version of *Tristan*, where the marriage of Tristan and Iseult is consummated for the first time (see *Love in the Western World*, trans. Montgomery Belgion, 74–75, 131–136). Prior to his work on *Requiem*, Faulkner could have known Rougemont's book in French or in its first English edition, issued in 1940.

47. William C. Falkner, *Rapid Ramblings in Europe*, 417. I am indebted to Donald Duclos for pointing out to me the reference to Abelard and Heloise in *Rapid Ramblings* and for providing me with his copy of the book.

48. Ibid.

49. For this dating of the poem, see James B. Meriwether, *The Literary Career of William Faulkner*, 24, #106; 90, #22; and fig. 4.

50. Peggy Kamuf calls such epistolary traces in Heloise's letters "the residue of a woman's excessive desire" (*Fictions of Feminine Desire*, xiv).

51. Collins, *Early Prose and Poetry*, 115.

52. "Letter IV. Abelard to Heloise," *Letters*, 138.

53. Gwynn and Blotner, *Faulkner in the University*, 266.

## VI. Personal Distances: The Public Man of Letters

1. Gustaf Hellström, "Presentation Address," in *Nobel Prize Library: William Faulkner, Eugene O'Neill, John Steinbeck*, 4.

2. In addition to his Nobel Prize, Faulkner was elected to the American Academy of Arts and Letters in 1948 and won the academy's Howells Medal for Fiction in 1950; he received the National Book Award for Fiction in 1951 and 1955, the Legion of Honor in 1951, the Pulitzer Prize in 1955, the Silver Medal of the Greek Academy in 1957, and the Gold Medal for Fiction from the National Institute of Arts and Letters in 1962.

3. Joseph Blotner says that "he did not shirk what he felt to be the responsibilities that came with . . . fame, and so he raised his voice, upon a surprisingly varied number of rostrums, both for his craft and for his country" (Introduction, SL, xiii). James B. Meriwether finds that the public letters "reflect the increased sense of his responsibility as a public figure which Faulkner showed after he won the Nobel Prize for Literature in 1950" (Editor's Preface, ESPL, viii).

4. See Blotner, *Faulkner* (1984), 493, 504.

5. Gwynn and Blotner, *Faulkner in the University*, 177.

6. Ibid.

7. Quoted in Eileen Gregory, "Faulkner's Typescripts of *The Town*," in *A Faulkner Miscellany*, ed. James B. Meriwether, 136.

8. Ibid.

9. Meriwether, "An Introduction to *The Sound and the Fury*," 157.

10. Blotner, *Faulkner* (1974), II, 938.

11. The several drafts are transcribed in Gregory, "Faulkner's Typescripts of *The Town*," 127–138.

12. *Life*, May 5, 1956, 51.

13. The Howe interview is in Meriwether and Millgate, *Lion in the Garden*, 257–264.

14. Various of these are transcribed in the following: Blotner, *Faulkner* (1984), 626–630; Blotner, *Selected Letters of William Faulkner*, 403–404; and Brodsky and Hamblin, *Brodsky Collection*, vol. II, *The Letters*, 196–201, 205.

15. Carlos Baker, ed., *Selected Letters of Ernest Hemingway: 1917–1961*, 768–769.

16. Ibid., 807.

17. Henry F. Pommer, *"Light in August:* A Letter by Faulkner," *English Language Notes* 4 (September 1966):47–48.

18. On Stone's relationship with Faulkner, see Susan Snell, "Phil Stone of Yoknapatawpha," diss., University of North Carolina, 1978; Blotner, *Faulkner* (1974) and (1984); and Robert W. Hamblin, Introduction, *Brodsky Collection*, vol. II, *The Letters*, xviii–xxiv.

19. For a range of views on Stevens' and Faulkner's positions in this regard, see Brooks, *The Yoknapatawpha Country*, 420–424; Millgate, *The Achievement of William Faulkner*, 215–216; Charles D. Peavy, *Go Slow Now: Faulkner and the Race Question*, 46–50. See also Charlotte Renner, "Talking and Writing in Faulkner's Snopes Trilogy," *Southern Literary Journal* 15 (Fall 1982):73. Renner notes that Faulkner's anxiety about the future of the South spills from the Snopes Trilogy "into his last letters, speeches, and public pronouncements."

20. Patrick Samway, S. J., ed., "New Materials for Faulkner's *Intruder in the Dust*," in *A Faulkner Miscellany*, ed. James B. Meriwether, 111.

21. Hellström, "Presentation Address," 4. Hellström's source for this partial misinformation may have been the same as Malcolm Cowley's in 1945–1946—Stanley J. Kunitz and Howard Haycraft's 1942 book *Twentieth Century Authors* (see Cowley, *The Faulkner-Cowley File*, 71–72).

22. See Keen Butterworth, *A Critical and Textual Study of Faulkner's "A Fable."* Butterworth notes that Lowe is "a forerunner of Levine; but Lowe is a comic creation. Levine is tragic" (44). The conjunction of aviators' letters suggests a more personal distancing than Butterworth implies, however.

23. James B. Meriwether, ed., "A Note on *A Fable*," in *A Faulkner Miscellany*, 163.

24. See also Wilde and Borsten, *A Loving Gentleman*, 318; Faulkner to Joan Williams, in Blotner, *Faulkner* (1974), II, 1431; Faulkner to Marjorie Lyons, in Blotner, *Selected Letters of William Faulkner*, 301. Doreen Fowler and Campbell McCool have traced these sentiments in Faulkner's fiction from a 1934 letter of condolence he wrote to Mr. and Mrs. James Warsaw Bell, Jr., about the loss of

their first child ("On Suffering: A Letter from William Faulkner," *American Literature* 57 [December 1985]:650–652).

25. See Renner, "Talking and Writing in Faulkner's Snopes Trilogy," 61–73.

26. The most acute discussion of silence in Faulkner's late work, including *The Mansion*, is Karl Zender, "Faulkner and the Power of Sound," *PMLA* 99 (January 1984):89–108.

27. Meriwether, "An Introduction to *The Sound and the Fury*," 160.

# Works Cited

Adams, Richard P. "The Apprenticeship of William Faulkner." *Tulane Studies in English* 12 (1962): 113–156.

Altman, Janet Gurkin. *Epistolarity: Approaches to a Form.* Columbus: Ohio State University Press, 1982.

Anderson, Sherwood. *Winesburg, Ohio.* 1919; reprint New York: Viking, 1960.

Baker, Carlos. *Selected Letters of Ernest Hemingway: 1917–1961.* New York: Scribner's, 1981.

Beck, Warren. *Faulkner: Essays.* Madison: University of Wisconsin Press, 1976.

Benstock, Shari. "The Printed Letters in *Ulysses.*" *James Joyce Quarterly* 19 (Summer 1982): 415–427.

Bleikasten, André. "'Cet affreux goût d'encre': Emma Bovary's Ghost in *Sanctuary.*" In *Intertextuality in Faulkner,* ed. Michel Gresset and Noel Polk, 36–56. Jackson: University Press of Mississippi, 1985.

———. *The Most Splendid Failure: Faulkner's "The Sound and the Fury."* Bloomington: Indiana University Press, 1976.

Blotner, Joseph. *Faulkner: A Biography.* 2 vols. New York: Random House, 1974.

———. *Faulkner: A Biography.* New York: Random House, 1984.

———, ed. *Selected Letters of William Faulkner.* New York: Random House, 1977.

———. "William Faulkner's Essay on the Composition of *Sartoris.*" *Yale University Library Gazette* 47 (January 1973): 121–124.

Bonner, Thomas, Jr., ed. *William Faulkner: The William B. Wisdom Collection.* New Orleans: Tulane University Libraries, 1980.

Bosha, Francis J. *Faulkner's "Soldiers' Pay": A Bibliographical Study.* Troy, N.Y.: Whitson Publishing Co., 1982.

Brodsky, Louis Daniel, and Robert W. Hamblin, eds. *Faulkner: A Comprehensive Guide to the Brodsky Collection.* Vol. I, *The Biobibliography.* Jackson: University Press of Mississippi, 1981.

———, eds. *Faulkner: A Comprehensive Guide to the Brodsky Collection.* Vol. II, *The Letters.* Jackson: University Press of Mississippi, 1984.

Brooks, Cleanth. *William Faulkner: The Yoknapatawpha Country.* New Haven: Yale University Press, 1963.

———. *William Faulkner: Toward Yoknapatawpha and Beyond.* New Haven: Yale University Press, 1978.

Broughton, Panthea Reid. "An Interview with Meta Carpenter Wilde." *Southern Review* 18 (October 1982):776–801.

Butterworth, Keen. *A Critical and Textual Study of Faulkner's "A Fable."* Ann Arbor, Mich.: UMI Research Press, 1983.

Coindreau, Maurice. "Preface to *The Sound and the Fury.*" In *The Time of William Faulkner,* by Maurice Coindreau, 41–50. Columbia: University of South Carolina Press, 1971.

Collins, Carvel, ed. *William Faulkner: Early Prose and Poetry.* Boston: Little, Brown, 1962.

———, ed. *William Faulkner: New Orleans Sketches.* New York: Random House, 1958.

———, and Joseph Blotner, eds. "Biographical Background for Faulkner's *Helen.*" In *Helen: A Courtship and Mississippi Poems,* by William Faulkner. Oxford, Miss., and New Orleans: Yoknapatawpha Press and Tulane University Press, 1981.

Cowley, Malcolm. *The Faulkner-Cowley File: Letters and Memories, 1944–1962.* New York: Viking, 1966.

Cox, Leland H., Jr. "Sinbad in New Orleans: Early Short Fiction by William Faulkner—An Annotated Edition." Dissertation, University of South Carolina, 1977.

Davis, Thadious. *Faulkner's Negro: Art and the Southern Context.* Baton Rouge: Louisiana State University Press, 1983.

Dennis, Stephen. "The Making of *Sartoris:* A Description and Discussion of the Manuscript and Composite Typescript of William Faulkner's Third Novel." Dissertation, Cornell University, 1969.

Eliot, T. S. "*Ulysses,* Order, and Myth." *Dial* 75 (November 1923). Reprinted in *James Joyce: Two Decades of Criticism,* ed. Seon Givens, 198–202. New York: Vanguard Press, 1963.

Fadiman, Regina K. *Faulkner's "Light in August": A Description and Interpretation of the Revisions.* Charlottesville: University Press of Virginia, 1975.

Falkner, William C. *Rapid Ramblings in Europe.* Philadelphia: J. B. Lippincott, 1884.

Faulkner, William. *Absalom, Absalom!.* New York: Random House, 1936.

———. *As I Lay Dying.* New York: Random House, 1930.

———. *Collected Stories of William Faulkner.* New York: Random House, 1950.

———. "Elmer." Ed. Diane L. Cox. *Mississippi Quarterly* 36 (Summer 1983): 343–448.

———. *A Fable.* New York: Random House, 1954.

———. *Flags in the Dust.* New York: Random House, 1973.

———. *Go Down, Moses.* New York: Random House, 1942.

———. *A Green Bough.* In *The Marble Faun and A Green Bough.* New York: Random House, 1960.

———. *The Hamlet.* New York: Random House, 1940.

———. *Helen: A Courtship.* In *Helen: A Courtship and Mississippi Poems.* Ed. Carvel Collins. Oxford, Miss., and New Orleans: Yoknapatawpha Press and Tulane University Press, 1981.

———. *Intruder in the Dust.* 1948; reprint New York: Vintage, 1972.

————. *Knight's Gambit*. New York: Random House, 1949.

————. *Light in August*. New York: Random House, 1932.

————. *The Lilacs*, 1920. Handmade book, described in Louis Daniel Brodsky and Robert W. Hamblin, eds. *Faulkner: A Comprehensive Guide to the Brodsky Collection*. Vol. I, *The Biobibliography*, 26–27. Jackson: University Press of Mississippi, 1981.

————. *The Mansion*. 1959; reprint New York: Random House, 1964.

————. *The Marionettes*. Charlottesville: Bibliographical Society of the University of Virginia and the University Press of Virginia, 1977.

————. *Mayday*. Ed. Carvel Collins. Notre Dame: University of Notre Dame Press, 1978.

————. *Mississippi Poems*. In *Helen: A Courtship and Mississippi Poems*. Ed. Joseph Blotner. Oxford, Miss., and New Orleans: Yoknapatawpha Press and Tulane University Press, 1981.

————. *Mosquitoes*. New York: Liveright, 1927.

————. "New Orleans." Typescript, Leila Clark Wynn–Douglas C. Wynn Faulkner Collection, John Davis Williams Library, Department of Archives and Special Collections, University of Mississippi.

————. *New Orleans Sketches*. Ed. Carvel Collins. New York: Random House, 1958.

————. *Requiem for a Nun*. 1951; reprint New York: Vintage, 1975.

————. *Royal Street: New Orleans*. Handmade book, Academic Center Library, University of Texas at Austin. Reprinted in Leland H. Cox., Jr., "Sinbad in New Orleans: Early Short Fiction of William Faulkner—An Annotated Edition," 161–165, Dissertation, University of South Carolina, 1977. The final vignette reprinted in Noel Polk, "'Hong Li' and *Royal Street:* The New Orleans Sketches in Manuscript." In *A Faulkner Miscellany*, ed. James B. Meriwether, 143–144. Jackson: University Press of Mississippi, 1974.

————. *Sanctuary*. 1931; reprint New York: Vintage, 1958.

————. *Sanctuary: The Original Text*. Ed. Noel Polk. New York: Random House, 1981.

————. *Soldiers' Pay*. New York: Liveright, 1926.

————. *The Sound and the Fury*. 1929; reprint New York: Random House, 1966.

————. *The Town*. 1957; reprint New York: Random House, 1964.

————. *Uncollected Stories of William Faulkner*. Ed. Joseph Blotner. New York: Random House, 1979.

————. *The Unvanquished*. 1938; reprint New York: Vintage, 1966.

————. *Vision in Spring*. Ed. Judith L. Sensibar. Austin: University of Texas Press, 1984.

————. *War Birds*. In *Faulkner's MGM Screen Plays*, ed. Bruce F. Kawin, 275–420. Knoxville: University of Tennessee Press, 1982.

————. *The Wild Palms*. 1939; reprint New York: Vintage, 1966.

————. *The Wishing Tree*. New York: Random House, 1964.

Felman, Shoshana. "Turning the Screw of Interpretation." In *Literature and Psychoanalysis: The Question of Reading: Otherwise*, ed. Shoshana Felman, 94–207. Baltimore: Johns Hopkins University Press, 1982.

Flaubert, Gustave. *Madame Bovary*. Ed. and trans. Paul de Man. New York: Norton, 1965.

Fowler, Doreen, and Campbell McCool. "On Suffering: A Letter from William Faulkner." *American Literature* 57 (December 1985):650–652.

Gregory, Eileen. "Faulkner's Typescripts of *The Town*." In *A Faulkner Miscellany*, ed. James B. Meriwether, 113–138. Jackson: University Press of Mississippi, 1974.

Gresset, Michel, and Noel Polk, eds. *Intertextuality in Faulkner*. Jackson: University Press of Mississippi, 1985.

Gwynn, Frederick L., and Joseph L. Blotner, eds. *Faulkner in the University: Class Conferences at the University of Virginia, 1957–1958*. Charlottesville: University of Virginia Press, 1959.

Hayhoe, George F. "William Faulkner's *Flags in the Dust*." *Mississippi Quarterly* 28 (Summer 1975):370–386.

Hellström, Gustaf. "Presentation Address." In *Nobel Prize Library: William Faulkner, Eugene O'Neill, John Steinbeck*, 3–6. New York: Alexis Gregory, and Del Mar, Calif.: CRM Publishing, 1971.

Irwin, John T. *Doubling and Incest / Repetition and Revenge*. Baltimore: Johns Hopkins University Press, 1975.

James, Henry. *The Novels and Tales of Henry James*. 26 vols. New York: Scribner's, 1907–1917.

Joyce, James. *Ulysses*. 1922; reprint New York: Random House, 1961.

Kamuf, Peggy. *Fictions of Feminine Desire: Disclosures of Heloise*. Lincoln: University of Nebraska Press, 1982.

Kawin, Bruce F., ed. *Faulkner's MGM Screen Plays*. Knoxville: University of Tennessee Press, 1982.

Kenner, Hugh. *A Homemade World: The American Modernist Writers*. New York: William Morrow, 1975.

Kestner, Joseph. "The *Letters* of Jane Austen: The Writer as *Émetteur / Récepteur*." *Papers on Language and Literature* 14 (Summer 1978):249–269.

Krause, David. "Reading Bon's Letter and Faulkner's *Absalom, Absalom!*." *PMLA* 99 (March 1984):225–241.

———. "Reading Shreve's Letters and Faulkner's *Absalom, Absalom!*." *Studies in American Fiction* 2 (Autumn 1983):153–169.

Lacan, Jacques. "Seminar on 'The Purloined Letter.'" *Yale French Studies* 48 (1972):38–72.

*The Letters of Abelard and Heloise*. Trans. Betty Radice. New York: Penguin, 1974.

Leymarie, Jean. *The Spirit of the Letter in Painting*. Trans. James Eamons. New York: Hallmark Cards, 1961.

McHaney, Thomas L. "*Sanctuary* and Frazier's Slain Kings." *Mississippi Quarterly* 24 (Summer 1971):223–245.

Matthews, John T. *The Play of Faulkner's Language*. Ithaca: Cornell University Press, 1982.

Meriwether, James B., ed. *Essays, Speeches and Public Letters by William Faulkner*. New York: Random House, 1965.

————. "Faulkner and El Orens." *Faulkner Newsletter & Yoknapatawpha Review* 1 (April–June 1981):2.

————, ed. "Faulkner's Correspondence with *Scribner's Magazine.*" *Proof* 3 (1973):253–282.

————, ed. "Faulkner's Correspondence with the *Saturday Evening Post.*" *Mississippi Quarterly* 30 (Summer 1977):461–475.

————, ed. "Faulkner's 'Ode to the Louver.'" *Mississippi Quarterly* 37 (Summer 1974):333–335.

————, ed. "An Introduction for *The Sound and the Fury.*" *Southern Review* 8 (October 1972):705–710.

————, ed. "An Introduction to *The Sound and the Fury.*" In *A Faulkner Miscellany*, ed. James B. Meriwether, 156–161. Jackson: University Press of Mississippi, 1974.

————. *The Literary Career of William Faulkner.* Columbia: University of South Carolina Press, 1971.

————, ed. "A Note on *A Fable.*" In *A Faulkner Miscellany*, ed. James B. Meriwether, 163–164. Jackson: University Press of Mississippi, 1974.

————. "The Short Fiction of William Faulkner: A Bibliography." *Proof* 1 (1971): 293–329.

Meriwether, James B., and Michael Millgate, eds. *Lion in the Garden: Interviews with William Faulkner, 1926–1962.* New York: Random House, 1968.

Miller, Nancy. "'I's' in Drag: The Sex of Recollection." *Eighteenth Century* 22 (1981):47–57.

Millgate, Michael. *The Achievement of William Faulkner.* New York: Random House, 1966.

————. "'A Cosmos of My Own': The Evolution of Yoknapatawpha County." In *Fifty Years of Yoknapatawpha*, ed. Doreen Fowler and Ann J. Abadie, 23–43. Jackson: University Press of Mississippi, 1980.

————. "'The Firmament of Man's History': Faulkner's Treatment of the Past." *Mississippi Quarterly* 25 Supp. (Spring 1972):25–35.

————. "Starting Out in the Twenties: Reflections on *Soldiers' Pay.*" *MOSAIC* 7 (Fall 1973):1–14.

————. "William Faulkner: The Shape of a Career." In *New Directions in Faulkner Studies*, ed. Doreen Fowler and Ann J. Abadie, 18–36. Jackson: University Press of Mississippi, 1984.

Minter, David. *William Faulkner: His Life and Work.* Baltimore: Johns Hopkins University Press, 1980.

Muhlenfeld, Elisabeth. "'We have waited long enough': Judith Sutpen and Charles Bon." *Southern Review* 14 (Winter 1978):66–80.

O'Brien, Darcy. *The Conscience of James Joyce.* Princeton: Princeton University Press, 1968.

Olney, James. "Autobiography and the Cultural Moment: A Thematic, Historical, and Bibliographical Introduction." In *Autobiography: Essays Theoretical and Critical*, ed. James Olney, 3–27. Princeton: Princeton University Press, 1980.

Ong, Walter J., S.J. "The Writer's Audience Is Always a Fiction." *PMLA* 90 (January 1975):9–21.

Peavy, Charles D. *Go Slow Now: Faulkner and the Race Question*. Eugene: University of Oregon Press, 1971.

Perry, Ruth. *Women, Letters, and the Novel*. New York: AMS Press, 1980.

Polk, Noel. Afterword. In *Sanctuary: The Original Text*, 293–309. New York: Random House, 1981.

————. "'The Dungeon Was Mother Herself': William Faulkner, 1927–1931." In *New Directions in Faulkner Studies*, ed. Doreen Fowler and Ann J. Abadie, 61–93. Jackson: University Press of Mississippi, 1984.

————. *An Editorial Handbook for Faulkner's "The Sound and the Fury."* New York: Garland, 1985.

————, ed. "'Hong Li' and *Royal Street:* The New Orleans Sketches in Manuscript." In *A Faulkner Miscellany*, ed. James B. Meriwether, 143–144. Jackson: University Press of Mississippi, 1974.

————. Introduction. In *The Marionettes*, ix–xxii. Charlottesville: Bibliographical Society of the University of Virginia and the University Press of Virginia, 1977.

————. "The Space between *Sanctuary*." In *Intertextuality in Faulkner*, ed. Michel Gresset and Noel Polk, 16–35. Jackson: University Press of Mississippi, 1983.

————. "William Faulkner's 'Hong Li' on Royal Street." *Library Chronicle of the University of Texas* 13 (1980):27–30.

Pommer, Henry F. "*Light in August:* A Letter by Faulkner." *English Language Notes* 4 (September 1966):47–48.

Putzel, Max. *Genius of Place: William Faulkner's Triumphant Beginnings*. Baton Rouge: Louisiana State University Press, 1985.

Radice, Betty. Introduction. In *The Letters of Abelard and Heloise*, trans. Betty Radice, 9–55. New York: Penguin, 1974.

Reed, Joseph. *Faulkner's Narrative*. New Haven: Yale University Press, 1973.

Renner, Charlotte. "Talking and Writing in Faulkner's Snopes Trilogy." *Southern Literary Journal* 15 (Fall 1982):61–73.

Rougemont, Denis de. *Love in the Western World*. Trans. Montgomery Belgion. Rev. and augmented ed. New York: Pantheon, 1956.

Samway, Patrick, S.J., ed. "New Materials for Faulkner's *Intruder in the Dust*." In *A Faulkner Miscellany*, ed. James B. Meriwether, 107–112. Jackson: University Press of Mississippi, 1974.

Scherer, Olga. "A Polyphonic Insert: Charles's Letter to Judith." In *Intertextuality in Faulkner*, ed. Michel Gresset and Noel Polk, 168–177. Jackson: University Press of Mississippi, 1985.

Schoenberg, Estella. *Old Tales and Talking: Quentin Compson in William Faulkner's "Absalom, Absalom!" and Related Works*. Jackson: University Press of Mississippi, 1977.

Sensibar, Judith L. *The Origins of Faulkner's Art*. Austin: University of Texas Press, 1984.

————, ed. "Pierrot and the Marble Faun: Another Fragment." *Mississippi Quarterly* 32 (Summer 1979):473–476.

Silver, James. *Running Scared: Silver in Mississippi*. Jackson: University Press of Mississippi, 1984.

Skei, Hans. *William Faulkner: The Short Story Career*. New York: Columbia University Press, 1981.

Snell, Susan. "Phil Stone of Yoknapatawpha." Dissertation, University of North Carolina, 1978.

Sundquist, Eric J. *Faulkner: The House Divided*. Baltimore: Johns Hopkins University Press, 1983.

Toliver, Harold. *Animate Illusions: Explorations of Narrative Structure*. Lincoln: University of Nebraska Press, 1974.

Volpe, Edmond. *A Reader's Guide to William Faulkner*. New York: Noonday Press, 1964.

Watson, James G. "Faulkner: Short Story Structures and Reflexive Forms." *MOSAIC* 11 (Summer 1978):127–137.

———. "Faulkner: The House of Fiction." In *Fifty Years of Yoknapatawpha*, ed. Doreen Fowler and Ann J. Abadie, 134–158. Jackson: University Press of Mississippi, 1980.

———. "'The Germ of My Apocrypha': *Sartoris* and the Search for Form." *MOSAIC* 7 (Fall 1973):15–33.

———. "Literary Self-Criticism: Faulkner in Fiction on Fiction." *Southern Quarterly* 20 (Fall 1981):46–63.

———. "New Orleans, *The Double Dealer*, and 'New Orleans.'" *American Literature* 56 (May 1984):214–226.

Wilde, Meta Carpenter, and Orin Borsten. *A Loving Gentleman: The Love Story of William Faulkner and Meta Carpenter*. New York: Harcourt, Brace, Jovanovich, 1976.

Williams, Joan. "Twenty Will Not Come Again." *Atlantic Monthly* 245 (May 1980):58–65.

———. *The Wintering*. New York: Harcourt, Brace, Jovanovich, 1966.

Wittenberg, Judith Bryant. *Faulkner: The Transfiguration of Biography*. Lincoln: University of Nebraska Press, 1979.

———. "Joan Williams: The Rebellious Heart." Manuscript.

Yonce, Margaret. "The Composition of *Soldiers' Pay*." *Mississippi Quarterly* 33 (Summer 1980):291–326.

———. "'His True Penelope Was Flaubert': *Madame Bovary* and *Sanctuary*." *Mississippi Quarterly* 29 (Summer 1976):439–442.

———. "'Shot Down Last Spring': The Wounded Aviators of Faulkner's Wasteland." *Mississippi Quarterly* 31 (Summer 1978):359–368.

———. "*Soldiers' Pay*: A Critical Study of Faulkner's First Novel." Dissertation, University of South Carolina, 1970.

Zender, Karl. "Faulkner and the Power of Sound." *PMLA* 99 (January 1984):89–108.

———. "Faulkner at Forty: The Artist at Home." *Southern Review* 17 (Spring 1981):288–302.

# Index